PENNSYLVANIA COLLEGE OF TECHNOLOGY LIBRARY

5 0608 01149350 8

MORE Science Adventures with Children's Literature

D1372031

Recent Titles in
Through Children's Literature

of Technology
One College Avenue
Williamsport, PA 17701-5799

MORE Science Adventures with Children's Literature

Reading Comprehension and Inquiry-Based Science

Anthony D. Fredericks

Illustrated by Rebecca N. Purvis

Through Children's Literature

Teacher Ideas Press
An imprint of Libraries Unlimited
Westport, Connecticut • London

Madigan Library
Pennsylvania College
of Technology

One College Avenue
Williamsport, PA 17701-5799

NOV 15 2010

Library of Congress Cataloging-in-Publication Data

Fredericks, Anthony D.
  More science adventures with children's literature : reading comprehension and inquiry-based science /
Anthony D. Fredericks ; illustrated by Rebecca N. Purvis.
    p. cm. -- (Through children's literature)
  Includes bibliographical references and index.
  ISBN 978-1-59158-619-7 (alk. paper)
  1. Science--Study and teaching (Elementary) 2. Education, Elementary--Activity programs. 3. Children's
literature in science education. 4. Reading comprehension. 5. Inquiry-based learning. I. Title.
  LB1585.F6858 2008
  372.3'5--dc22   2007042466

British Library Cataloguing in Publication Data is available.

Copyright © 2008 by Anthony D. Fredericks

All rights reserved. No part of this book may be reproduced
in any form or by any electronic or mechanical means, including
information storage and retrieval systems, without permission in
writing from the publisher, except by a reviewer, who may quote brief
passages in a review. Reproducible pages may be copied for classroom
and educational programs only.

Library of Congress Catalog Card Number: 2007042466
ISBN: 978-1-59158-619-7

First published in 2008

Libraries Unlimited/Teacher Ideas Press, 88 Post Road West, Westport, CT 06881
A Member of the Greenwood Publishing Group, Inc.
www.lu.com / www.teacherideaspress.com

Printed in the United States of America

The paper used in this book complies with the
Permanent Paper Standard issued by the National
Information Standards Organization (Z39.4.8–1984).

10 9 8 7 6 5 4 3 2 1

Contents

Part III: Extending the Possibilities: Readers Theatre

Preface

Science can and should be one of the most exciting subjects of the elementary curriculum! A major focus for the creation of this book was that children are naturally curious about the world around them ("Why is the sky blue?", "Why do geese fly south?", "Where do babies come from?"), and that the investigation of that world can be made a stimulating and meaningful part of their lives. This is particularly true when those questions are integrated with comprehension instruction—in short, a blending of reading and science instruction that supports and enhances students' knowledge of the world.

I think it important at this point that you understand how this book came to be and what propelled me as I prepared the manuscript. Basically, I was driven by three mutually exclusive, yet highly related concepts. First, in my conversations with educators around the country, work with fellow teachers, observations of elementary classrooms, and some detailed interviews, I knew that reading comprehension was spotlighted by teachers as the single most important aspect of the elementary curriculum. The emphasis on reading instruction (and the attendant emphasis on the reading/language arts standards) underscores reading comprehension as a vital and significant part of each teacher's curricular focus. Helping students learn to read and helping students learn to read with understanding are high on any teacher's list of priorities.

Second, my research and interviews also revealed that teachers are increasingly committed to helping students achieve a measure of success throughout the science curriculum. Obviously, science achieves its greatest import when it becomes a vehicle for children to learn and appreciate its utility throughout their lives and the world in which they live. Essentially, science is a way of asking questions (much as scientists do when conducting experiments) and pursuing answers to those self-initiated queries (also known as "inquiry-based science"). That emphasis is a significant element in any successful science program.

Third, I earnestly believe that children's literature offers an incredible "bridge" between the two subjects of READING and SCIENCE. That bridge is a way for teachers to help children see the natural connections that exist in an inquiry-based curriculum. Even more important is that children can now use their reading abilities (e.g., comprehension) to make sense of their world (e.g., science) and develop personally rewarding learning opportunities. What an incredible combo!

I also believe that reading and science are processes of thinking and doing. In fact, if we can guide our students in the practices and procedures of thinking about text *and* using text, then we can also assist them in learning about the practices and procedures of comprehending text, specifically in the area of science. In other words, if we are committed to helping youngsters achieve a measure of success in all their reading experiences, we should be equally committed to helping students learn and use strategies that will assist them in a subject such as science.

This book is designed for anyone wishing to actively engage children in all the dynamics of reading comprehension and science instruction. It is my hope that you will discover in these pages all the vibrancy, creativity, magic, and wonder of a hands-on, minds-on science program. To that end, I encourage you to consider this book a resource that helps your students participate actively in the wide-ranging dimensions of both reading and science. I also hope that this book will stimulate and encourage your students' active participation in meaningful classroom experiences, learning, growing, and discovering throughout the entire elementary curriculum.

We are about to begin a most incredible journey. Hop on board!

Tony Fredericks

Acknowledgments

This book would not have been possible without the support, contributions, and creativity of many individuals.

I am especially indebted to my dynamic, engaging, and wonderful research assistant on this project, Nicole Markel. Nicole was responsible for combing the shelves of countless elementary school libraries and a host of public libraries for the best in children's science literature. She doggedly tracked down hundreds of titles; investigated a plethora of lists, compilations, and recommendations; and interviewed librarians from a wide range of institutions to secure the finest examples of science resources for any classroom or school library. Her assistance, energy, and enthusiasm for this project are liberally sprinkled across the pages in this book—a project that could not have been completed without her constant dedication, creative zeal, and rapt attention to deadlines. Nicole is one of those rare teachers whose passion, excitement, and commitment make a difference not only in the lives of each her students, but also in the success of every science activity and classroom project. I am forever grateful for her embrace of, and contributions to, this book!

Once again, my daughter Rebecca has lent her considerable artistic talents and vast creative interpretations to yet another of my books. Her magnificent ability to design a dynamic array of illustrations while maintaining a household, holding down a job, and raising a very active daughter is truly exceptional. Her investment in this project and her artistic insights helped make this project more dynamic than it ever would have been otherwise. She is an artist of exceptional talents, and my pride in and love for her know no limits.

I am also indebted to the hundreds of teachers and scores of school librarians I met across the country on my school visits, conference presentations, and in-service workshops, each of whom willingly shared resources, tips, and ideas as I researched this book. Their insights about the effective teaching of elementary science and their "right on" suggestions for a literature-rich science curriculum are most appreciated and forever valued. Their creativity and imagination are reflected in so many ways throughout this book.

And last, but certainly not least, my dog Sienna deserves special recognition for listening to the mumblings and musings of this author during our early morning walks. So too, did she find a convenient place in my office that assured an occasional stroking and accompanying doggy bone. She was both companion and counsel throughout the entire creative process, and her favorite corner is forever reserved.

Part I

Science, Reading, and Children's Literature

CHAPTER 1

Teaching Elementary Science

Science is fun! Science is an exploration of and an investigation into the unknown. Science is learning more about what we don't know . . . filling in gaps in our knowledge base, changing old ideas, modifying concepts, and discovering that we don't necessarily have all the answers just because we know a bunch of facts. In some ways, science is a testament to our own innate ignorance —an ignorance born of a desire to know more about ourselves and our world, not one signifying a complete lack of knowledge.

For children, science can and should become a dynamic and interactive discipline. It should allow children to examine new ideas, play around with concepts and precepts, and discover that there is no such thing as a body of finite knowledge. What does this mean for teachers? It means that students must be given a multitude of opportunities to probe, poke, and peek into the mysteries of their world—whether that world is their own backyards or a country far away.

Science should also give children a host of opportunities to think, instead of just memorize. Indeed, science is a venture and an *adventure* of the mind—constantly learning and relearning new data and new ideas. Providing youngsters with opportunities to pose questions about their world, question basic assumptions, or actively seek solutions to various mysteries places a value on the power of the human mind—particularly the minds of children. More popularly known as *inquiry-based science,* it places students at the center of their own instruction. Let's take a look at some of its underlying principles.

PRINCIPLES OF INQUIRY-BASED SCIENCE INSTRUCTION

Students need many opportunities to make sense out of their world as well as lay a foundation from which future discoveries can emanate. The following guidelines should be considered as *markers* from which kids can grow in science:

1. Students need to be provided with a basic body of knowledge that will form the foundation for future discoveries. Yet meaningful science programs must move beyond just facts. In short, an accumulation of facts is no more science than a collection of bricks is a house. Thinking (i.e., comprehension) about those facts, and ultimately understanding those facts, is one of the primary goals of any science program.

2. Students must take some responsibility for their own learning. Students need opportunities to make their own choices or select learning opportunities based on their goals and interests. Students who are given those choices begin to assume greater control over their personal learning and are more willing to pursue learning for its own sake. In short, science is *learned* more than it is *taught.*

3. For science instruction to be effective, children need to be stimulated in diverse ways. The elementary curriculum is enhanced when students have multiple and varied learning opportunities. Students need to know that science is more about divergent ways of thinking than it is about memorizing "absolutes."

4. Students need to use science information in practical and personal ways. Possessing the skills of science is one thing; being able to use those skills in a meaningful and personal context is quite another. Elementary science instruction should be geared toward offering youngsters a myriad of opportunities to use their knowledge in "real-life" learning ventures.

5. Children need to be engaged in intellectually stimulating encounters with their world. Inquiry-based science provides children with a host of opportunities to question and think about their world (as does good literature). Students must be provided with critical thinking opportunities and challenging situations that allow them to set their own learning goals and satisfy them through self-discovery.

The principles above support the notion that science education, to be productive, requires a partnership between teachers and students, the joy of learning, and youngsters' developing curiosity about their environment. This is science instruction at its finest—that is, instruction that shifts its focus from the teacher as a repository of information (traditional view) to the student as a generator —and pursuer—of self-initiated questions (current view).

CONSTRUCTIVISM AND SCIENCE INSTRUCTION

Inquiry-based science instruction is founded on the constructivist model of education. Constructivism is not new—its theoretical underpinnings have been around for more than 70 years. However, it is a significant shift in teaching priorities. The traditional form of teaching relies on educators giving or delivering instruction to students. You may recognize this as a teacher lecturing students and students dutifully recording information or "attacking" skills sheets or endless workbook pages. In short, an expert tells novices what they need to know.

Psychologists have helped us look at the teaching–learning partnership in a new way. Through intensive research, we have learned that learning is not simply the accumulation of knowledge (which is passive), but rather how we make sense of knowledge. This is *constructivism*. Constructivism recognizes that knowledge is created in the mind of the learner. Teachers help students relate new content to the knowledge they already know. In addition, students have opportunities to process and apply that knowledge in meaningful situations (sometimes called "hands-on, minds-on" learning).

Educators who embrace a constructivist philosophy of teaching promote learning, especially the learning of science concepts and principles, through a multitude of actions and behaviors. These may include several of the following:

- linking background knowledge with textual knowledge

- asking lots of open-ended questions

- lots of hands-on learning opportunities

- relating concepts to the "real world" of students' lives

- assisting children in pursuing answers to their self-initiated queries

- posing questions at higher levels of cognition (application, analysis, synthesis)

- using collaborative activities (student/student; student/teacher)

- engaging students in metacognitive thinking

- providing individual learning opportunities more than whole-class presentations

- promoting self-initiated investigations and discoveries

The most important consideration in any discussion of constructivism is that students need to know that knowledge is never a product; rather, it is a process. How we learn is intrinsically more important than what we learn. For science, this is a critical factor in the success children have within this subject as well as the success they can have as active, thinking, and participating members of society.

NATIONAL SCIENCE EDUCATION STANDARDS

In response to a growing concern about the state of science education in the United States, hundreds of people, including teachers, school administrators, parents, curriculum coordinators, college faculty, scientists, engineers, and government officials, cooperated in developing an outline of what students need to know, understand, and be able to do to be scientifically literate.

The *National Science Education Standards* that resulted from this intensive examination of science education focus on a blending of "science as process" and "science as inquiry." This inquiry-based approach to science education helps students actively develop their understanding of science by combining scientific knowledge with reasoning and thinking skills. *MORE Science*

Adventures with Children's Literature underscores these standards by engaging students in meaningful, comprehension-based experiences that invite them to construct their own knowledge.

> The standards are based on the premise that science is an active process and that learning science is something that students do, not something that is done to them.

Not only do the standards provide an outline (as opposed to a curriculum) for the development of science instruction; they also bring coordination, consistency, and coherence to the improvement of science education. All of the lessons, strategies, and activities in *MORE Science Adventures with Children's Literature* have been coordinated with these standards. Each featured children's book includes a listing of relevant standards so that you will be able to easily integrate the accompanying activities into the regular classroom science program irrespective of the science series, program, or curriculum used in your school.

The lessons and strategies in this book emphasize students' role as active learners. The wide variety of learning opportunities emphasize specific science content objectives for students in grades 1–6. (NOTE: The *National Science Content Standards* are divided into three broad categories: Grades K–4, Grades 5–8, and Grades 9–12). The content standards for Grades K–4 and Grades 5–8 are presented on pages 7 and 8.

In reviewing the standards, it's evident that many of their elements are embodied in the philosophy and design of a literature-based approach to science education (see Chapter 2). The chart on page 9 illustrates how each of the featured children's books in *MORE Science Adventures with Children's Literature* endorses and supports the Science Content Standards.

Content Standards

STANDARD A (Science as Inquiry)
All students should develop:

- Abilities necessary to do scientific inquiry (K–4, 5–8)
- Understanding about scientific inquiry (K–4, 5–8)

STANDARD B (Physical Science)
All students should develop an understanding of

- Properties of objects and materials (K–4)
- Position and motion of objects (K–4)
- Light, heat, electricity, and magnetism (K–4)
- Properties and changes in properties of matter (5–8)
- Motions and forces (5–8)
- Transfer of energy (5–8)

STANDARD C (Life Science)
All students should develop understanding of

- The characteristics of organisms (K–4)
- Life cycles of organisms (K–4)
- Organisms and environments (K–4)
- Structure and function in living systems (5–8)
- Reproduction and heredity (5–8)
- Regulation and behavior (5–8)
- Populations and ecosystems (5–8)
- Diversity and adaptations of organisms (5–8)

STANDARD D (Earth and Space Science)
All students should develop an understanding of

- Properties of earth materials (K–4)
- Objects in the sky (K–4)
- Changes in earth and sky (K–4)
- Structure of the Earth system (5–8)

- Earth's history (5–8)

- Earth in the solar system (5–8)

STANDARD E (Science and Technology)

All students should develop

- Abilities of technological design (K–4, 5–8)

- Understanding about science and technology (K–4, 5–8)

- Abilities to distinguish between natural objects and objects made by humans (K–4)

STANDARD F (Science in Personal and Social Perspectives)

All students should develop understanding of

- Personal health (K–4, 5–8)

- Characteristics and changes in population (K–4)

- Types of resources (K–4)

- Changes in environments (K–4)

- Science and technology in local challenges (K–4)

- Populations, resources, and environments (5–8)

- Natural hazards (5–8)

- Risks and benefits (5–8)

- Science and technology in society (5–8)

STANDARD G (History and Nature of Science)

All students should develop understanding of

- Science as a human endeavor (K–4, 5–8)

- Nature of science (5–8)

- History of science (5–8)

National Science Education Standards (NRC, 1996)

Books ↓ Standards →	A	B	C	D	E	F	G
1. *The Dinosaurs of Waterhouse Hawkins*	✓			✓			✓
2. *Actual Size*	✓		✓				
3. *Under One Rock*	✓		✓			✓	✓
4. *Hurricanes*		✓		✓	✓	✓	
5. *Rocks in His Head*	✓			✓			✓
6. *Song of the Water Boatman*			✓				
7. *Parts*	✓		✓			✓	✓
8. *W Is for Wind*	✓	✓		✓	✓		
9. *Antarctic Journal*	✓			✓	✓		✓
10. *The Tarantula Scientist*	✓		✓				✓
11. *Outside and Inside Mummies*	✓		✓		✓		✓
12. *Over in the Jungle*			✓				
13. *The Flower Hunter*	✓		✓				✓
14. *The Tsunami Quilt*	✓	✓		✓		✓	
15. *A Mother's Journey*			✓	✓			
16. *Earthshake*				✓		✓	
17. *Eyes and Ears*			✓		✓	✓	
18. *The Sea, the Storm, and the Mangrove Tangle*			✓				
19. *Science Verse*	✓	✓	✓	✓	✓		✓
20. *Near One Cattail*	✓		✓			✓	✓
21. *Leaf Man*	✓		✓				
22. *Reaching for the Moon*		✓		✓	✓		✓
23. *Nature in the Neighborhood*	✓		✓			✓	
24. *Following the Coast*	✓		✓			✓	
25. *Hidden Worlds*	✓		✓		✓		✓
26. *The Star People*		✓		✓			✓
27. *Guts*			✓			✓	
28. *Forces of Nature*	✓	✓		✓	✓	✓	✓
29. *Red Eyes or Blue Feathers*			✓				
30. *G Is for Galaxy*		✓		✓	✓		✓
31. *Flotsam*	✓	✓	✓		✓		✓
32. *Plantzilla*			✓				
33. *Diary of a Worm*			✓				
34. *Around One Cactus*	✓		✓			✓	✓
35. *What Do You Do with a Tail Like This?*	✓		✓				

CHAPTER 2

Science and Children's Literature

Trying to teach science in an overactive and overburdened curriculum may seem daunting to many teachers, yet my own classroom experiences, as well as those of several colleagues, suggest that it need not be so. I have discovered that when good children's literature is integrated fully into the science curriculum, children have learning opportunities that extend far beyond the pages of the text and enhance their attitudes and aptitudes—not just in science, but across the curriculum.

The integration of literature into the science curriculum is timely in that there is a wealth of new and exciting children's books now being published that enhance science in intriguing and interesting ways. A variety of trade books add immeasurably to the entire science program. Also, the integration of children's literature into the science program is supported by recent curricular changes in many states, which have implemented guidelines underscoring a strong relationship between literature and science teaching. Even more interesting is that many textbook publishers are now rushing to include literature selections as part of the lessons in their new text series. Although there is increasing interest in and emphasis on making the "literature connection" in science, teachers often do not take advantage of these supplemental materials. Instead, they rely on the textbook as their primary source of information.

This book is based on the idea that incorporating trade books into the elementary science program provides students with extended learning opportunities going far beyond the facts and figures of textbook science. New worlds of discovery and exploration open up for students through the magic of literature, worlds that expand the curriculum and enlarge students' appreciation of their environment and their place in it.

THE LITERATURE-BASED APPROACH TO SCIENCE INSTRUCTION

Many science programs are designed to *give* children lots of information, have them *memorize* the data, and then ask them to *recall* the information on various assessment instruments. As discussed previously, that may be a significant reason for students' less-than-enthusiastic response to science, because that type of instruction does not allow for the active involvement of students in their own learning, nor does it allow children opportunities to think creatively about what they are learning.

My own experiences as a teacher have taught me that when students, no matter what their abilities or interests, are provided with opportunities to manipulate information in productive ways, learning becomes much more meaningful. I refer to this as a *process approach to learning,* which provides students with an abundance of projects, activities, and instructional designs that allow them to make decisions and solve problems. Through this approach students get a sense that learning is much more than the commission of facts to memory. Rather, it is what children do with that knowledge that determines its impact on their attitudes and aptitudes.

A process approach to science is one in which children *do* something with the concepts and generalizations they learn. It implies that students can manipulate, decide, solve, predict, and structure the knowledge of science in ways that are meaningful to them. When teachers and librarians provide opportunities for students to actively process information, then learning becomes more child centered and less text based. This results in a science program that is expansive, integrated, and dynamic.

A literature-based approach to science is a combination of activities, children's literature, "hands-on, minds-on" projects, and materials used to expand a science concept or idea. Literature-based science teaching and learning is multidisciplinary and multidimensional—it has no boundaries and no limits. In essence, a literature-based approach to science offers students a realistic arena within which they can learn and investigate science concepts for extended periods of time. It is a process approach to learning of the highest magnitude.

This approach to science instruction is built on the idea that learning can be integrative and multifaceted. A literature-based approach to science education provides children with a host of opportunities to become actively involved in the dynamics of their own learning. In so doing, they will be able to draw positive relationships between what "happens" in the classroom and what is happening outside the classroom. Literature-based teaching promotes science education as a sustaining and relevant venture.

The inclusion of children's literature within the science curriculum should be a natural and normal part of students' experiences with science. Doing so provides youngsters with valuable opportunities to extend and expand their knowledge of the world around them as well as to develop a rich appreciation for the science concepts, values, and generalizations contained within good literature. By infusing books and literature into your science program, you are helping students understand that science is much more than a dry accumulation of facts and dates. You are helping your students explore and investigate their immediate and far-flung world in an arena that knows no limits.

The use of literature within science is based on several precepts:

1. Literature provides an ever-expanding array of information in a welcome and familiar format to students.

2. Literature extends the science curriculum beyond any textbook constraints.

3. Literature relates to children's lives in diverse and divergent ways.

4. Literature, both fiction and nonfiction, helps children understand science as a universal quest for information and knowledge.

5. Literature assists children in developing positive attitudes about themselves, people in their immediate environment, and peoples from around the world.

6. Literature provides vicarious *and* first-hand experiences with all science disciplines.

7. Literature provides students with new information and knowledge unobtainable in any other format.

8. Literature stimulates creative thinking and problem-solving abilities in a variety of contexts.

9. Literature opens up the world and draws students in to make self-initiated discoveries.

10. Literature is fun!

When quality literature is made a significant part of the science program, children can become involved in activities and gain experiences that they may not be exposed to in a text-based program. In fact, literature-based instruction allows you to extend, expand, and take advantage of students' natural curiosity about how the world works. It also provides you with many opportunities to combine the multiple intelligences of your students with the resources, information, and principles of your entire science curriculum. In short, literature-based teaching celebrates varied learning opportunities that provide students with a meaningful and balanced approach to science learning. Above all, literature-based instruction supports and emphasizes the many relationships that exist among science inquiry, a process approach to learning, and the exercise of constructivist teaching (and learning) in a positive and supportive environment.

ADVANTAGES OF LITERATURE-BASED INSTRUCTION

Literature-based instruction in science offers a plethora of advantages for both educators and students. The following list synthesizes some of those benefits.

- It emphasizes and celebrates an individual's multiple intelligences in a supportive and creative learning environment.

- It focuses on the *processes* rather than the *products* of science.

- It reduces and/or eliminates the artificial barriers that often exist between curricular areas and provides an integrative approach to learning.

- It promotes a child-centered science curriculum—one in which children are encouraged to make their own decisions and assume a measure of responsibility for learning.

- It stimulates self-directed discovery and investigation both in and out of the classroom.

- It assists youngsters in developing relationships between science ideas and concepts, thus enhancing appreciation and comprehension.

- It stimulates the creation of important science concepts through firsthand experiences and self-initiated discoveries.

- More time is available for instructional purposes. Science instruction does not have to be crammed into limited, artificial time periods, but can be extended across the curriculum and throughout the day.

- The connections that can and do exist between science and other subjects, topics, and themes can be logically and naturally developed. Teachers and librarians can demonstrate relationships and assist students in comprehending those relationships.

- Science can be promoted as a continuous activity—one not restricted by textbook designs, time barriers, or even the four walls of the classroom. Educators can help students extend science learning into many aspects of their personal lives.

- Teachers and librarians are free to help students look at a science problem, situation, or topic from a variety of viewpoints, rather than the "right way" frequently demonstrated in a teacher's manual or curriculum guide.

- There is more emphasis on *teaching* students and less on telling students.

- Teachers and librarians can promote problem solving, creative thinking, and critical thinking processes within all dimensions of a topic.

Literature-based instruction facilitates the teaching of science as much as the learning of science. The entire science curriculum is broadened, strengthened, and made more attentive to the development of individual science competencies. The "marriage" of literature and science facilitates instruction and helps students view science as a process of discovery and exploration, rather than one of memorization and regurgitation.

We know that the use of quality trade books is generating some remarkable changes in the ways that science is taught and students are learning. Literature-based instruction not only offers students unique opportunities to process and practice "hands-on, minds-on" science, it also provides teachers with integrative strategies and activities that enhance and promote science concepts in all curricular areas. In addition, students are assisted in drawing realistic parallels between classroom events and circumstances outside the classroom. In short, literature-based instruction can aid students in understanding the relevance of science to their everyday lives— certainly a major goal of any science curriculum.

Children's literature provides multiple learning opportunities for children (and multiple reading comprehension connections), both in and outside the classroom . Literature is electric—it opens doors; it promotes possibilities. In short, literature is a vehicle that can drive youngsters to new ventures and discoveries. It also becomes a way of underscoring reading as a way of learning about and making sense of the world.

This approach to science instruction is built on the idea that learning can be integrative and multifaceted. A literature-based approach to science education provides children with a host of opportunities to become actively involved in the dynamics of their own learning. In so doing, they will be able to draw positive relationships between what "happens" in the classroom and what is happening outside the classroom. Literature-based teaching promotes science education as a sustaining and relevant venture.

The inclusion of children's literature in the science curriculum should be a natural and normal part of students' experiences with science. It provides youngsters with valuable opportunities to extend and expand their knowledge of the world around as well as to develop a rich appreciation for the science concepts, values, and generalizations contained in good literature. Literature also places a value on comprehension as something more than a reading-related element; rather, it is a valued component of any and all subjects—especially science.

CHAPTER 3

Collaboration: Making Magic in Science

What both elementary teachers and school librarians have long known intuitively, which has been validated with a significant body of research, is that the literature shared in both classroom and library has wide-ranging and long-lasting implications for the educational development of children. More important, however, is the unassailable fact that when teachers and librarians join together to promote literature collaboratively, they are opening incredible windows that expand the influence of literature and extend the learning opportunities for youngsters as never before.

In preparation for writing this book, I talked with school librarians and teachers throughout the United States. I discovered that the "collaboration factor" had a significant influence on the success of science programs—especially those in which children's literature played a major role. A substantial level of collaboration between the classroom teacher and the school librarian was essential for literature to be made a successful element and a dynamic feature of any science curriculum. The partnership between teacher and librarian is, and continues to be, the crucial element in the success children enjoy within and throughout any academic endeavor.

As you might imagine, this partnership does not happen overnight. It involves a mutual sharing of ideas, possibilities, and projects. When teachers and librarians band together, the curricular effect of literature in the science curriculum can be expanded exponentially. It involves trust and coordination, but the overall result is more than worth the effort.

BENEFITS

In my discussions with elementary school librarians and classroom teachers, I discovered the following benefits of this collaboration:

- Instructional projects can be designed, developed, and taught over an extended period of time (days, weeks, months).

- Students can be exposed to a greater range of resources—both print and nonprint.

- Science standards can be promoted in a coordinated and systematic fashion.

- A constructivist philosophy of teaching and learning is promoted throughout the science curriculum.

- Teaching (and learning) can be individualized—the specific educational needs of selected students can be addressed and supported.

- More time is available for instructional purposes. In schools or districts where science is not emphasized, a partnership between teacher and librarian can expand instructional possibilities.

- Science is promoted as a continuous activity, rather than being an isolated subject taught on an intermittent basis.

- There is a greater emphasis on science as *problem solving* and *critical thinking* instead of the "traditional" view of it as simply the memorization of facts and figures.

- Science instruction becomes a mandate of the school rather than an instructional "add-on" to the curriculum.

- The "real lives" of students outside the school can be linked with science instruction taking place within the school.

- Cooperative teaching and cooperative learning can be promoted simultaneously.

FORGING THE PARTNERSHIP

When teachers and librarians work together, great things happen. When they do it as an essential ingredient of the science curriculum, then fantastic things happen—short term as well as long term. Following is a discussion of the ways in which teachers and librarians can develop partnerships that are mutually supportive, educationally sound, and dynamically oriented toward a literature-based approach to science instruction. The first subsection lists strategies for librarians to reach out to classroom teachers. The second is an assembly of techniques for classroom teachers to partner with their school librarian to effect a viable science program.

Consider these suggestions for your own school or educational setting. Share them with friends and colleagues, discuss them at in-service meetings or off-site conferences, post them in the faculty room, incorporate them into the school newsletter or other communiqués, and bring them up in your various conversations with colleagues. The more these ideas become a part of the conversation in school, the more they can become part of the process of an exciting science program.

Librarian ➜ Classroom Teacher

Here are some suggestions for how school librarians or media specialists can reach out to classroom teachers at the start of and throughout the school year:

- Before the new school year begins, obtain the addresses of new staff members from the school principal. Send all new faculty members a welcoming note introducing yourself and your staff. Provide them with a brief description of your programs and services.

- Offer an orientation for new staff members. Show them where various materials are located, explain the procedures for checking them out, and answer any questions they have.

- Present each new teacher with a book for his or her classroom bookshelf. Place a sticker in front to indicate who provided the book.

- Make a concentrated effort to visit each staff member in his or her classroom during the opening weeks of school. Make sure teachers have what they need in the way of materials, AV equipment, or other resources.

- Establish a system whereby teachers can inform you (via e-mail) about the need for various books or resources in the library. Reach out and ask for suggestions on a regular and systematic basis.

- Each month, ask teachers about forthcoming topics or units of study. Ask them about materials or literature that you might be able to provide for designing long-term science projects.

- Make yourself available as much as possible by planning cooperatively for special events and library instruction, assisting with research projects, and helping students locate appropriate reading materials.

- Make yourself visible by participating on special committees outside the library (e.g., the science curriculum committee).

- Keep track of what is being taught (or not being taught) in the science curriculum. Put together a relevant collection of materials and resources for specific components of the science program and promote those components to teachers on a regular basis.

- Lobby your administration on behalf of teachers for much-needed print and nonprint materials.

- Send teachers a monthly e-mail list of new science materials and resources.

- Display new materials and resources during faculty meetings.

- Know the science curriculum and pay attention to special topics being studied so that you will be prepared to recommend resources that will enhance the teaching of those topics.

- Provide teachers with a variety of teaching tools beyond the print collection, such as appropriate Web sites, videos, software, and the latest in technology.

- Solicit and entertain ideas from teachers relative to library services and materials.

- Plan for collaborative units to be taught together

- Offer to team teach units with teachers

- Offer to help in formative and summative assessments of student work.

Classroom Teacher ➜ Librarian

Here are some suggestions for how classroom teachers can reach out to school librarians or media specialists throughout the school year:

- Use the library regularly. This may seem simplistic, but many school librarians say that the library is often underused by teachers. Nothing makes a librarian happier than having teachers (especially new teachers) utilizing the resources and services of the library on a regular basis throughout the school year.

- Encourage the school librarian to be your teaching partner by planning cooperatively for instruction in library and reference skills (as they relate to the science curriculum) and working together to make those sessions successful for your students.

- Don't be afraid to make suggestions to the librarian about specific materials, both print and nonprint.

- Notify the librarian well ahead of time about forthcoming topics or upcoming units of study in your science program. Invite the librarian to partner with you in assembling relevant material.

- Make it a regular practice to stop by the library to search for new materials, books, and other teaching resources.

- Provide your school librarian with a list of topics and assignments you will be tackling throughout the year. Invite the librarian to make suggestions regarding available resources.

- Work closely with the librarian to develop joint projects in which selected literature is introduced in the library and followed up with specific instructional activities in the classroom.

- Inform the librarian if there are insufficient materials or books on a forthcoming topic. Inquire about the possibility of obtaining those materials in time for the unit to be taught or for a later school year.

- Stop by the library informally and take the time to chat and talk about suggested instructional plans and ideas for forthcoming units.

- Provide your librarian with a list of upcoming topics and ask for ideas on available literature.

- Make sure you are informed of any new materials obtained by the library.

This book is designed to help you create a dynamic and exciting science program through the use of children's literature. It is also designed to expand and extend the school library's services and cement the influence of quality literature in any academic endeavor. Its success will depend on how eagerly literature is embraced as a teaching tool and how actively teachers and librarians work toward that goal.

The projects, activities, and comprehension strategies offered in this book are designed to open up worlds of discovery for youngsters irrespective of grade level or program design. They are also offered as a way for teachers and librarians to effect a cooperative relationship that enjoins them in a mutually beneficial and academically successful endeavor. The bonds of communication between teachers and librarians will ultimately determine the success of these ventures.

It is my sincere hope that you will discover a plethora of possibilities to expand and extend the *science + children's literature* equation into all aspects of your instructional program. By working collaboratively you are helping to "cement" a bond that will extend far beyond the walls of the school—a bond that can promote a lifelong love of reading, a deeper appreciation of science, and an enduring appreciation for interrelated and coordinated learning ventures.

CHAPTER 4

Teaching Comprehension: Principles and Practices

Science instruction is much more than a collection of well-designed experiments extracted from a teacher's manual. Science, at its best, is a way of helping students look at the world—to ask questions and seek the answers to self-initiated queries. It is figuring out what we don't know and then engaging in activities that help us discover (on our own) how things work, or operate, or function.

Reading is very much like science simply because reading—in its purest state—is how we look for answers formed inside our own heads. Like science, reading involves an active engagement with a subject or topic. It is not something done to us, but rather something that we control, manipulate, and investigate.

TRANSACTIONAL APPROACH TO READING INSTRUCTION

Most elementary teachers subscribe to the notion that reading involves an active and energetic relationship between the reader and the text. That is, the reader–text relationship is reciprocal and involves the characteristics of the reader as well as the nature of the material. This philosophy of reading, often referred to as a *transactional approach* to reading, has particular applications for teachers building effective student-based reading programs. As you might expect, it can also serve as a foundation for the construction, implementation, and effectiveness of a balanced science program.

A transactional approach to reading suggests that we all have our own unique backgrounds that we bring to any reading material. As a result, we will all have our own unique and personal interpretations of that material, which may or may not be similar to the interpretations of others reading the same text. Reading a piece of literature opens up interpretive possibilities for youngsters and provides opportunities for extending that literature in personal and subjective ways.

The transactional approach to reading instruction is significant because it places emphasis on three critical and interrelated stages in the reading process—before reading, during reading, and after reading. Together, these stages (or instructional opportunities) are essential in the comprehension and appreciation of all types of reading materials. The following table illustrates each of these divisions along with the responsibilities of teachers in any instructional setting. This list, while not comprehensive, suggests possibilities for the textual materials you use in your reading and/or science program. You may wish to consider possibilities in each of the three major areas as options for the design of literature experiences.

CONTEXT	TEACHER RESPONSIBILITIES
Before Reading	Encourage students to activate background knowledge. Help students establish purposes for reading. Encourage students to generate questions. Invite students to make predictions about text. Encourage students to construct semantic webs. Stimulate prediction making. Encourage journal entries. Present skills.
During Reading	Model metacognitive and cognitive processes. Invite students to verify or reformulate predictions. Encourage students to integrate new data with prior knowledge. Help students think about what they are reading. Invite students to summarize text. Observe readers' behaviors. Encourage additional questions. Incorporate strategies.
After Reading	Encourage retellings. Encourage students to reflect on what was read. Invite students to evaluate predictions and purposes. Promote closure between pre-reading and post-reading. Develop questions that guide reading. Encourage students to respond to text through a variety of holistic endeavors. Assist students in linking background knowledge with textual knowledge. Encourage students to seek additional information. Reflect on strategies.

Adapted from *Guided Reading in Grades 3–6* (Fredericks, 2001)

TEACHING READING COMPREHENSION

The success of reading comprehension instruction is highly dependent on the opportunities provided to students for actively engaging in the dynamics of text. What follows is a structure that has been used successfully in thousands of classrooms across the country. Although this format provides you with a working outline, it is important to note that there is a great deal of flexibility inherent within this design. That is, you are encouraged to modify or alter this plan in line with the structure of your own classroom program.

It should be emphasized that this sequence of processes and procedures is designed to help students become competent and independent readers. As such, it is a model that can be easily changed as the needs and abilities of class members change.

1. **Setting the Stage**—This element involves all the pre-lesson activities a teacher needs to do prior to actual instruction.

2. **Before-Reading Strategies and Activities**—This stage includes those instructional activities that are done before students begin to read or listen to a book.

3. **During-Reading Strategies and Activities**—These are done while students are reading a book independently or listening to a read-aloud.

4. **After-Reading Strategies and Activities**—These activities and strategies are done upon completion of a selected book.

5. **Literature Extensions**—These are book-related activities that encourage students to use the information in a book in dynamic and creative ways.

In the chart on page 26 there are several suggestions for any single stage. This does not mean that *all* those activities should be done for every reading lesson. For example, for most lessons you will not want to conduct a "Before," a "During," *AND* an "After" reading strategy. Rather, you will want to select an appropriate strategy for any one of those three stages in keeping with the theme, tone, style, and "message" of a selected book.

Component	Strategies and Activities
Setting the Stage	• Select an appropriate book. • Make sure each student has an individual copy. • Familiarize yourself with the text. • Consider and select appropriate strategies. • Think through reasons for grouping students. • Ask introductory questions. • Demonstrate excitement about the text.
Before Reading	• Introduce the book. • Read and discuss the title. • Do a "walk" through the book. • Activate background knowledge. • Conduct activities that create interest. • Introduce and discuss an appropriate "Before" reading strategy. • Stimulate question asking.
During Reading	• Allow each child to read independently at his or her own pace. • Introduce an appropriate "During" reading strategy. • Assist students (as necessary) with problem solving. • Confirm good reader strategies. • Ask appropriate questions.
After Reading	• Conduct a group reading conference. • Review reading strategies. • Introduce an appropriate "After" reading strategy. • Encourage retellings. • Encourage re-readings. • Assess individual progress. • Pose open-ended questions.
Literature Extensions	• Provide activities for responding to text. • Promote written responses. • Include cross-curricular activities. • Read related literature. • Provide integrated language arts projects. • Invite further research and/or reading.

Adapted from *Guided Reading in Grades 3–6* (Fredericks, 2001)

THE SIX PRINCIPLES OF COMPREHENSION

Reading is a constructive process—that is, readers build meaning and understanding by interacting with text (Pearson et al., 1992). This implies that there is an interaction between the reader's prior knowledge and the "knowledge" in text. Building meaning is done through the use of strategies that assist readers in solving problems at all stages of the reading process. Mastery of specific strategies is essential in helping students become successful readers.

A plethora of research (Harvey and Goudvis, 2000; Pearson et al., 1992; Pressley, 2000; Cooper and Kiger, 2003; Fredericks, 2006) identifies six critical reading principles necessary for comprehension development:

1. Tapping into background knowledge (schema)

2. Mental imagery (visualizing)

3. Predicting and inferring

4. Questioning

5. Identifying important ideas

6. Synthesizing and summarizing

The first principle (tapping into background knowledge) and the last (synthesizing and summarizing) should be part of every literacy encounter (at the beginning and at the end). A reading strategy that emphasizes one of the other four principles should be selected for a literacy lesson depending on the needs of students and the nature of the text used. Using this multiplicity of comprehension strategies in any single lesson helps underscore the need for accomplished "comprehenders" to use several strategies in combination.

Tapping into Background Knowledge (Schema)

Background knowledge is what we already know about a topic or concepts. We use (or tap into) our background knowledge to make sense of new ideas or information. Thus it stands to reason that the more background knowledge we have about a forthcoming topic, the better we will be able to understand (and remember) it.

For students, the essential concept to keep in mind is that what they already know affects what they will learn from text. That is to say, their prior knowledge interacts with text to create meaning. Or, to put it another way, more background knowledge = more understanding. Background knowledge is often called schemata, the mental frameworks we have for organizing and understanding information. Our ability to tap into our schemata (known as schema theory) determines how we process new data.

What is most critical is the need to make a connection between what students know and what they *can* know. This is the very foundation of comprehension. To achieve this, you will sometimes need to overcome inadequate prior knowledge through focused introduction to basic concepts. At other times, you will need to correct erroneous prior knowledge before students participate in a literacy experience.

Mental Imagery

Mental imagery is the creation of pictures in a reader's mind prior to, during, or after reading. Once images are created (and colored by the reader's experiences), they become a permanent part of long-term memory. Thus, creating images during any literacy activity will result in learning and comprehension.

However, it is important to know that imagery is a sequentially learned skill. For students who do not have this skill, simply telling them to create pictures in their minds is not sufficient. This may be due in large measure to the increasing amount of visual information (TV, movies, etc.) to which students are subjected during the course of a day. Many of those images have been artificially created by other people to convey a message (e.g., advertising). Yet the most powerful, meaningful, and lasting images are those we create in our own minds.

Assisting children in creating mental images facilitates listening and reading comprehension and also offers numerous speaking opportunities. An additional benefit is that students begin to use thinking skills in concert with listening skills. In turn, they learn to focus on the processes of comprehension rather than on just the products.

Predicting and Inferring

Predicting is the process of extrapolating information based on a minimum of information already known. It is also a process of making "educated guesses" about future events—whether those events may happen one minute from now or several years from now. Predicting is highly dependent on the depth and breadth of one's background knowledge. The more concrete experiences one has had, the more able he or she is to make predictions. Making predictions is one of the most powerful pre-reading and reading abilities children can learn. That's because predicting is a "mental investment" in a future event—one the learner now wants to discover.

For predicting and inferring to be successful, there must be a certain level of background knowledge. Since both of these strategies are "educated guesses," the "educated" part is a measure of the depth and breadth of prior knowledge. Without adequate background knowledge, predictions and inferences are quite difficult to make (for students as well as for adults). It is important, therefore, that you are aware of or provide for the necessary prior knowledge that will form the foundation for future predictions and inferences.

Children also need to know that predictions and inferences are temporary. They are based on the best available knowledge at the time. As more knowledge is obtained, predictions and inferences are modified. In this way, competent readers monitor and adjust their reading as they "blend" their prior knowledge with new knowledge encountered in text. This is an active response—one that engages an individual in the dynamics of comprehension. It can best be taught through lots of modeling and lots of "think-alouds" by the teacher as he or she reads.

Questioning

Self-questioning is an important reading comprehension strategy for all students. Although considerable attention is given to teacher questions over the years, it is equally important that students be offered viable and authentic opportunities to generate their own questions about text as they read. In fact, the opportunity for students to ask questions of themselves (metacognition) is one of the most significant processes we can teach.

Although questions are widely used and serve many functions, teachers frequently overrely on factual questions. There is a convincing body of research (Fredericks and Cheesebrough, 1993; Fredericks et al., 1997) suggesting that as much as 80 percent of all the questions asked of students during the course of a day are of the literal or recall variety. This seems to suggest that little creative or divergent thinking (hallmarks of comprehension) may be taking place.

One of the most significant and important statements I've encountered in more than three decades of teaching is the following:

> *Students tend to read and think based on the types of questions they anticipate receiving from a teacher.*

This means that if students are constantly bombarded with questions that require only low levels of cognitive involvement (literal or recall questions, for example), they will tend to think accordingly. Conversely, children who are asked questions based on higher levels of cognition will tend to think more creatively and divergently. In other words, if we want our students to engage in higher levels of problem solving and creative thought, we need to ask questions that promote a multiplicity of responses.

Identifying Important Details

One of the significant strategies all readers use is to identify important information in text. This strategy is not learned quickly or easily. It is part of a developmental process that is highly dependent on the amount and quality of reading material to which a child is exposed. In other words, children's schema for important ideas is developed through sustained and constant exposure to books and read-aloud sessions. More experience with good literature equates to more familiarity with the components of a good story.

While the principles discussed previously in this chapter have their greatest application in narrative text, they are also important for expository text. On the other hand, identifying important details, although appropriate for narrative text, will have its greatest application in nonfiction materials. It is much more than identifying isolated bits of factual information. Rather, it is how those facts and concepts "blend" together to form coherent ideas or complete concepts.

Many students have a tendency to focus on a few isolated facts as they listen to a story or read a book. It is a constant challenge for teachers to assist students in connecting factual information to form complete concepts. To do that effectively means helping them (over extended periods of time) select the most important elements of a nonfiction book. This can be facilitated and enhanced through systematic and sustained teacher modeling.

Synthesizing and Summarizing (Retelling)

Synthesizing is the process of combining elements to form a new whole. It is a way for children to engage in creative and original thinking. Combining story elements from two or more sources to form a new idea or interpretation is a valuable and important reading comprehension ability. It is a way for students to combine new information (in the text, for example) with old information (schema theory). Synthesizing is appropriate for both expository as well as narrative text. In many ways, synthesizing is a personal reaction to key elements in text.

Summarizing is the process of assembling major ideas in a text into a single statement or idea. It is how readers sift through important and unimportant data to arrive at the major point in a piece of text. While many people summarize at or near the end of a piece of text, it is often a strategy that can be effectively employed throughout text—particularly in longer books or stories. When we ask students to conceptualize the main idea of a story, we are providing them with a means to create a summary—one couched in their own words, terminology, and interpretation of text.

Synthesizing and summarizing (retelling) should be part of every literacy encounter. It underscores several critical learning processes:

- Making decisions about important details

- Fostering good listening skills

- Enhancing appreciation of story sequence

- Stimulating personal monitoring of individual levels of comprehension

- Bringing important ideas to a level of consciousness or awareness

- Helping students think about what they hear

- Underscoring the value of cooperative sharing

SUMMARY OF THE SIX PRINCIPLES

The six essential comprehension principles are summarized in the following chart.

Principle	Description/Explanation
Tapping into Background Knowledge	Background knowledge forms the foundation and the structure for all reading experiences. What readers know affects what they can learn.
Mental Imagery	Good readers create "mind pictures" as they read. Visualizing the characters, elements, or events of a story is critical to overall comprehension.
Predicting and Inferring	Good readers are able to combine background knowledge and text knowledge as they read. This helps them make "educated guesses" about the content of text throughout the reading process. These "educated guesses" take place in advance of reading as well as during the act of reading.
Questioning	Readers continually ask themselves questions throughout the text. This is done to check or confirm an understanding of the book or story. Metacognitive questions are ways in which readers self-assess their understanding as well as stay engaged with the dynamics of a story.

Principle	Description/Explanation
Identifying Important Details	Good readers are able to separate important from unimportant information in text. They can identify critical details and separate them from extraneous material.
Synthesizing and Summarizing	Good readers are able to pull together all that they have read into an inclusive statement. Their comprehension is based on their ability to synthesize and summarize setting, characters, plot, theme, and point of view into a single statement.

Adapted from *Guided Reading in Grades 3–6* (Fredericks, 2001)

These comprehension principles are appropriate for all students. Indeed, all readers use them throughout the reading process. More important, however, is that they are also "thinking" principles—that is to say, they can be taught and promoted through both verbal and written text. In short, they are not dependent on reading ability, but rather on every student's interaction with text.

Coordinating these principles with our model of reading instruction is illustrated in the following chart. Each of the six comprehension principles has greatest instructional value and application at select stages of reading.

	Before Reading	**During Reading**	**After Reading**
Tapping into Background Knowledge	X	X	
Mental Imagery	X	X	
Predicting and Inferring	X	X	
Questioning	X	X	X
Identifying Important Details		X	X
Synthesizing and Summarizing		X	X

CHAPTER 5

Reading Comprehension Strategies That Work

Good science teaching (and learning) rests on the notion that children's literature can and should be woven throughout the science curriculum. It seems likely, then, that teachers will want to use that literature in ways that stimulate comprehension development and conceptual understandings in a host of contexts. The following techniques and strategies are both exciting and dynamic, not only for specific books and reading selections, but also in terms of the overall impact on your science program.

These strategies are all supported by the latest research in the field of reading instruction. They have been used in elementary classrooms just like yours. In addition, they have received the "stamp of approval" from classroom teachers across the country as well as from students in a wide range of classroom environments. In short, these strategies work! When they are combined with the best in children's literature, you will see a noticeable improvement in students' understanding and appreciation of the role of literature within and throughout the entire science program

Understandably, these ideas should not be used only with a single book or group of books. Instead, the intent is to offer you a selection from which you can choose and begin to build meaningful and lasting experiences with all sorts of literature—with small groups, large groups, or an entire class. This is not intended to be an exhaustive list, but rather a collection of the most successful comprehension strategies used by teachers just like you. Here, you can begin to create dynamic lesson plans that assist your students in becoming competent and energetic readers.

THE STRATEGIES

Possible Sentences

"Possible Sentences" (Moore and Moore, 1986) is an exciting reading strategy that assists students in (1) learning new vocabulary, (2) generating appropriate story predictions, (3) developing individual (or group) purposes for reading, and (4) stimulating their intellectual curiosity about a book or story. It is appropriate for all types of expository material and revolves around a five-part lesson plan:

1. List 12 to 15 essential critical vocabulary words from the book. These words are preselected by you and may be presented to students on sheets of paper or on the chalkboard.

2. Students are invited to select at least two words from the list and construct a sentence —one they think might be in the book. Students can record their sentences on the chalkboard.

3. Ask students to read the book to check the accuracy of the sentences they generated.

4. Each of the sentences is evaluated in terms of the information presented in the book. Sentences may be eliminated, revised, changed, altered, or modified in light of the information gleaned from the book. At times, students will need to re-read portions of the book to confirm or alter their original predictions.

5. After the original sentences have been evaluated, students are encouraged to generate additional sentences using the selected vocabulary. As new sentences are generated, they are checked against the original story for accuracy.

"Possible Sentences" allows students to integrate important vocabulary and their predictive abilities in a worthwhile activity. This strategy assists students in developing connections between prior knowledge and textual knowledge while incorporating a variety of languaging skills. Although "Possible Sentences" was originally designed to help students focus on expository materials, I have found it to be equally successful with selected narrative books. In addition, you are provided with some important pre-lesson assessment information that can be addressed later in the reading process.

NOTE: See *Hurricanes* and *A Mother's Journey* for lessons that use this strategy.

What If

Many of the questions we typically ask our students are of the literal or factual variety. An enormous body of research suggests that students (at any grade level) need to be exposed to a greater proportion of higher-level questions, divergent questions, and creative-thinking questions. By doing so, we are ensuring that our students will be able to approach any reading task with a creative spirit—thus ensuring a dynamic interpretation of text.

I have found that one of the most effective strategies for promoting an active engagement with text is called "What iffing." In this strategy, you take some of the questions that you would normally ask students at the conclusion of a reading passage and add the two words "What if" to the front of each question. For example, instead of asking "Where did Brian (in *Hatchet*) live for 54 days?" an appropriate "What if" question would be: "What if Brian had crashed in the desert?"

It is important to note that there are no right or wrong answers in "What iffing." Rather, students are given opportunities to "play" with interpretations and the possibilities that might exist within or beyond a story. Students' divergent thinking is stimulated and enhanced in a wide variety of reading materials.

You will notice that "What if" questions encourage and stimulate the generation of multiple queries and responses. Its advantage lies in the fact that all students are encouraged to participate and all responses can be entertained and discussed.

NOTE: See *Parts* and *Diary of a Worm* for lessons that use this strategy.

Concept Cards

"Concept Cards" allow students to tap into their background knowledge about the topic of a book, share that information with classmates, and make predictions about the content of a piece of literature. At the same time, students can manipulate their vocabulary and share ideas related to word study and comprehension of text. Although this strategy works particularly well with nonfiction materials, it can also be used with narrative text.

1. Before students read a book, select 20 to 25 words from throughout the book. It is preferable to have words from the front, middle, and back. Include words you know students are familiar with, words essential to comprehension of text, and a few unknown words.

2. Print each set of words on index cards and distribute them to a small group of students (e.g., a guided reading group).

3. Invite students to assemble the cards into categories of their own choosing. (NOTE: Do not tell them a specific number of categories or the number of "word cards" that should be in each grouping.) Encourage students to place words in categories according to their own knowledge of those words or their predictions of how those words might be used in the forthcoming text.

4. Invite students to share their various categories and grouping and provide a rationale for the placement of word cards within specific groups.

5. Invite students to read the book, looking for the words on the index cards. After reading, encourage students to rearrange cards or manipulate words into new categories or groupings based on the information gleaned from the text.

6. Afterwards, invite students to discuss reasons for any rearrangements and compare their placements with those they did in the pre-reading stage.

NOTE: See *Under One Rock* and *Forces of Nature* for lessons that use this strategy.

MM & M (Metacognitive Modeling and Monitoring)

MM & M provides readers with an opportunity to "see" inside the mind of a reader as he or she goes through the reading process. In essence, the teacher serves as a model of efficient reading, demonstrating for students the thought processes and mental activities used while reading. When struggling readers are made aware of the strategies readers use (inside their heads), they can emulate those strategies. MM & M gives students insight into the mind and demonstrates processes that can go on inside their heads as they read.

In this strategy you choose a reading selection and begin to "think out loud," verbalizing what is going on inside your head as you read. Since students cannot observe the thinking process firsthand, the verbalization allows them to get a sense of good thinking as practiced by an accomplished reader. Because you serve as the most significant role model for students in all their literacy endeavors, your "talking while reading" gives them some firsthand experiences with reading as a thinking process, which they can begin to incorporate into their schema.

Initially, you will want to select a piece of textual material that is short and contains some obvious points of difficulty (vocabulary, sequence of events, ambiguities, etc.). Read this passage aloud to the class, stopping at selected points and verbalizing the thought processes you are using to work through any difficulties. This verbalization is essential because it provides a viable model for students to "copy." Here are examples of the five steps:

Make Predictions (Demonstrate the importance of forming hypotheses.)

"From this title, I predict that this story will be about the discovery of electricity."

"In the next chapter, I think we'll find out how the planets got their names."

"I think this next part will describe the different kinds of precipitation."

Describe your mental images (Show how mental pictures are formed in your head as you read.)

"I can see a picture of a rain forest just before nightfall."

"I'm getting a picture in my mind of a scientist looking into a microscope."

"The picture I have in my mind is of a group of boy scouts walking through the woods."

Share an analogy (Show how the information in the text may be related to something in one's background knowledge.)

"This is like the time I had to take my dog to the animal hospital in the middle of the night."

"This is similar to the time I took a trip across the country on a train."

"This seems to be like the night we saw a meteor shower in our backyard."

Verbalize a confusing point (Show how you keep track of your level of comprehension as you read.)

"I'm not sure what is happening here."

"This is turning out a little differently than I expected."

"I guess I was correct in my original prediction."

Demonstrate "fix-up" strategies (Let students see how you repair any comprehension problems.)

"I think I need to re-read this part of the story."

"Maybe this word is explained later in the story."

"Now that part about the hurricane makes sense to me."

These five steps can and should be modeled for students using several different kinds of reading material. As you read and model, allow students opportunities to interject their thoughts about what may be going on in their heads as they listen to the selection. Your goal, obviously, will be to have students internalize these processes and be able to do them on their own with all kinds of reading material.

NOTE: See *Outside and Inside Mummies* for a lesson that uses this strategy.

Answer First!

"Answer First!" is a questioning strategy that encourages and stimulates thinking at higher levels of comprehension. It allows you to direct students to more sophisticated levels of comprehension through the careful and judicious sequencing of questioning skills. This strategy has proven to be quite successful with all types of readers and is a particularly worthwhile addition to the work of any guided reading group. In fact, it can be used as either an individual activity or a small group activity with equal results.

In "Answer First!," students are invited to read a selected book or text. In advance of the reading you have designed a series of answers, which are duplicated on sheets of paper. The task of students, upon completion of the book, is to formulate questions based on the material read that could be posed so as to generate the answers on an "Answer First!" sheet.

The answers (to the questions students will generate after reading the story) are previously determined, begin at the literal level of cognition, and progressively move students to higher levels of cognition (comprehension, application, analysis, synthesis, evaluation) in a systematic way. This is the major advantage of this strategy—students can begin to read and interpret various forms of reading material at increased levels of understanding. Many teachers have successfully used "Answer First!" with both fiction and nonfiction materials and across a wide range of student abilities. The result is often students who are able to generate their own questions at higher levels of cognition.

NOTE: See *Actual Size* and *Eyes and Ears* for lessons that use this strategy.

Reflective Sharing Technique

The "Reflective Sharing Technique" demonstrates the interrelationships that naturally exist between the language arts and science. This strategy also stimulates children to use language as a basis for learning across the curriculum. This technique encourages students to share and discuss ideas that are important to them, while at the same time reacting in positive ways to each other.

1. Divide the class into small groups of four students each (this number is critical). Choose a book or story appropriate to the ability level of the students. Select the general subject area of the story and record it on the chalkboard.

2. Invite individual students in each group to brainstorm for approximately three to five minutes for as many ideas, concepts, or items as possible that could be included in that subject area (see below). These items are recorded on individual sheets of paper. Brainstorming should stimulate a free flow of ideas, irrespective of their quality. The emphasis should be on generating a quantity of ideas and a wide range of responses.

3. Ask students to each select one of the brainstormed ideas from his or her list. Invite each student to write about his or her selected item for about five minutes (this time limit can be adjusted according to the age or ability level of students).

4. Sharing what each person has composed is the most important part of this activity.

   a. Students are assigned specific tasks (it is very important to have a group of four for the sharing process). In the group, members take specific roles:

      1) Person 1 reads what he or she wrote.

      2) Person 2 summarizes what Person 1 read.

      3) Person 3 tells what he or she liked about what Person 1 read.

      4) Person 4 tells something else he or she would like to know about the subject upon which Person 1 wrote.

   NOTE: This completes Round 1.

   b. After one round of sharing, the process is repeated until four rounds are completed and everyone has taken on all four roles (see the following chart).

ROLE	Round 1	Round 2	Round 3	Round 4
Reads what he or she wrote	Person 1	Person 2	Person 3	Person 4
Summarizes reader's story	Person 2	Person 3	Person 4	Person 1
Tells what he or she liked	Person 3	Person 4	Person 1	Person 2
Tells something else he or she wants to know	Person 4	Person 1	Person 2	Person 3

5. Point out to students the wealth of information they already have about the subject of the book or story even before they begin to read it. You may wish to invite students to discuss how their experience melded with ideas in the book.

6. At this point invite students to read the book independently.

NOTE: With some students you may wish to conduct the "Reflective Sharing Technique" as an oral activity. A designated student is selected to talk about special interests. The rest of the group members take on the roles of summarizer, positive reactor, and those asking about other things they would like to know.

NOTE: See *W Is for Wind* for a lesson that uses this strategy.

Question Master

Providing students with opportunities to initiate their own questions throughout the reading process can be a valuable goal of reading instruction. The chart on page 40 provides you with a list of questions accomplished and mature readers tend to ask themselves. Following is a modeling procedure you may wish to follow:

1. Select a piece of children's literature.

2. Ask yourself (out loud) some of the "Before Reading" questions and provide answers for yourself (again, out loud).

3. Read the book aloud to the class.

4. Periodically throughout the reading, continue to ask yourself questions (this time from the "During Reading" list).

5. Complete the oral reading and ask yourself a sampling of questions from the "After Reading" section.

6. After several readings, ask a student to come forward and model similar processes for the class.

7. Invite other group members to demonstrate the steps outlined above.

8. Encourage students to select several questions from each of the three sections and respond to them in writing in their journals. After the reading of a piece of literature, use their questions and responses as discussion points in individual conferences.

Self-Initiated Reading Queries

Before Reading	• Is this similar to anything I have read before? • Why am I reading this? • Why would this information be important for me to know? • Do I have any questions about the text before I read it? If so, what are they?
During Reading	• Am I understanding what I'm reading? • What can I do if I don't understand this information? • Why am I learning this? • Are these characters or events similar to others I have read about? • How does this information differ from other things that I know? • Why is this difficult or easy for me to understand? • Is this interesting or enjoyable? Why or why not? • Do I have any questions about this text that have not been answered so far? • What new information am I learning? • What information do I still need to learn?
After Reading	• Can I write a brief summary of the story? • What did I learn in this story? • Where can I go to learn some additional information on this topic? • Did I confirm (or do I need to modify) my initial purpose for reading this text? • Is there anything else interesting I'd like to find out about this topic? • Do I have some unanswered questions from this text?

NOTE: See *Reaching for the Moon* for a lesson that uses this strategy.

Chapter Slam

"Chapter Slam" is an activity designed to elicit students' background knowledge. Based on an inquiry model of reading, it offers you data on what students already know about a topic, while helping students establish a purpose for exploring the body of knowledge to be presented.

1. Invite students to list everything they can think of that might pertain to a designated topic. Students may wish to generate ideas on their own or brainstorm as a group for all the background knowledge they have on a particular topic. A master list is maintained by the group.

2. Students group the items in their list into categories. It may be necessary for you to model the categorizing behavior for students.

3. Students assign a name to each group of items and arrange them as though they were a table of contents for a book. This should be done as a group activity until students have sufficient practice in assigning titles to their respective categories.

4. Each student is invited to write a "book" about the upcoming topic using the categories as chapter titles. Students are encouraged to write as much about each topic as they can, summarizing what each section is about. If students get stuck, they are allowed to make up what they don't know. The "books" are kept on file. They can be edited as students read the actual piece of literature or be rewritten at the conclusion of the individual reading.

NOTE: See *Over in the Jungle* and *Guts* for lessons that use this strategy.

Semantic Webbing

One method used as a framework for making linkages between prior knowledge and knowledge encountered in text is "Semantic Webbing," which is a graphic display of students' words, ideas, and images in concert with textual words, ideas, and images. A semantic web helps students comprehend text by activating their background knowledge, organizing new concepts, and discovering the relationships between the two. A semantic web includes the following steps:

1. A word or phrase central to the story is selected and written on the chalkboard.

2. Students are encouraged to think of as many words as they can that relate to the central word. These can be recorded on separate sheets or on the chalkboard.

3. Students are asked to identify categories that encompass one or more of the recorded words.

4. Category titles are written on the board. Students then share words from their individual lists or the master list appropriate for each category. Words are written under each category title.

5. Students should be encouraged to discuss and defend their word placements. Predictions about story content can also be made.

6. After the story has been read, new words or categories can be added to the web. Other words or categories can be modified or changed depending on the information gleaned from the story.

NOTE: See *Earthshake* and *What Do You Do with a Tail Like This?* for lessons that uses this strategy.

Anticipation Guides

Anticipation Guides alert students to some of the major concepts in textual material before it is read. They give students an opportunity to share ideas and opinions as well as activate their prior knowledge about a topic before they read about it. This is also a helpful technique for eliciting students' misconceptions about a subject. Students become actively involved in the dynamics of reading a specified selection because they have an opportunity to talk about the topic before reading about it.

1. Read the story or selection and attempt to select the major concepts, ideas, or facts in the text.

2. Create five to ten statements (not questions) that reflect common misconceptions about the subject, are ambiguous, or are indicative of students' prior knowledge. Statements can be written on the chalkboard or photocopied and distributed.

3. Give students plenty of opportunities to agree or disagree with each statement. Whole group or paired discussions would be appropriate. After discussions, let each student record a positive or negative response to each statement. Initiate discussions focusing on reasons for individual responses.

4. Invite students to read the text, keeping in mind the statements and their individual or group reactions to those statements.

5. After reading the selection, engage the students in a discussion of how the textual information may have changed their opinions. Provide them with an opportunity to record (once again) their reactions to each statement based on what they read in the text. It is not important for a consensus to be reached, or that the students agree with everything the author states. Rather, it is more important for students to engage in an active dialogue that allows them to react to the relationships between prior knowledge and current knowledge.

NOTE: See *The Dinosaurs of Waterhouse Hawkins* and *Nature in the Neighborhood* for lessons that use this strategy.

Story Frames

A "Story Frame" (Fowler, 1982) is a basic outline of a story that is designed to help the reader or writer organize his or her thoughts about a story. A "frame" consists of a series of extended blanks linked together by transition words or phrases. Students are provided with blanks to complete and are given considerable latitude in selecting appropriate words or phrases. Following is a story frame that could help students focus on the information in a nonfiction book.

Information Frame

This story was written to teach us about _____.

One important fact I learned was _____.

Another fact I learned was _____.

A third important fact I learned was _____.

If I were to remember one important thing from this story, it would be

_____

_____ because _____.

Completed "Story Frames" can serve as discussion starters for the components of good stories as well as an outline for students who need a support structure for the creation of their own stories. Obviously, the intent is not to have all students arrive at an identical story, but rather to provide them with the freedom they need to create stories within appropriate grammatical contexts.

NOTE: See *The Flower Hunter* for a lesson that uses this strategy.

Directed Reading-Thinking Activity (DRTA)

The DRTA (Stauffer, 1969) is a comprehension strategy that stimulates students' critical thinking about text. It is designed to allow students to make predictions, think about those predictions, and verify or modify the predictions with text, as well as stimulate a personal involvement with many different kinds of reading material.

DRTAs are guided by three essential questions, which are inserted throughout the reading and discussion of a book:

- "What do you think will happen next?" (Using prior knowledge to form hypotheses.)

- "Why do you think so?" (Justifying predictions; explaining one's reasoning.)

- "How can you prove it?" (Evaluating predictions; gathering additional data.)

Vacca and Vacca (1989) outline a series of general steps for the DRTA:

1. Begin with the title of the book or with a quick survey of the title, subheads, illustrations, and so forth. Ask students, "What do you think this story (or book) will be about?" Encourage students to make predictions and to elaborate on the reasons for making selected predictions ("Why do you think so?").

2. Have students read to a predetermined logical stopping point in the text (this should be located by the teacher before students read). This point can be a major shift in the action of the story, the introduction of a new character, or the resolution of a story conflict.

3. Repeat the questions from step 1. Some of the predictions will be refined, some will be eliminated, and some new ones will be formulated. Ask students, "How do you know?" to encourage clarification or verification. Redirect questions to several students (if working in a group situation).

4. Continue the reading to another logical stopping point. Continue to ask questions similar to those above.

5. Continue through to the end of the text. Make sure the focus is on large units of text rather than small sections, which tend to upset the flow of the narrative and disrupt adequate comprehension. As students move through the text, be sure to encourage thoughtful contemplation of the text, reflective discussion, and individual purposes for reading.

> **NOTE:** See *The Sea, the Storm and the Mangrove Tangle* for a lesson that uses this strategy.

Story Map

This "organizer" helps students determine the essential elements of a well-crafted story. Not only can students focus on important details (e.g., setting, characters, problem, etc.), but more important, they begin to see how these "parts" of a story are woven together into a coherent whole. Equally significant is that most well-written stories present some sort of problem for the main character or characters to solve. Students can begin to understand this oft-used writing technique by analyzing the elements of a story.

Provide individual copies of a story map to the members of a reading group. (An alternative plan would be to offer one sheet to the entire group; one student is the designated scribe, while all group members contribute ideas.) Students are encouraged to complete the form either while reading the story or (more appropriately) upon completion of the story. Be sure to provide sufficient opportunities for students to share and discuss their respective interpretations of a story. It is not essential that students all arrive at the same conclusions, but rather that they have adequate opportunities to talk about their perceptions and conclusions.

> **NOTE:** See *Rocks in His Head* for a lesson that uses this strategy.

Student Motivated Active Reading Technique (S.M.A.R.T)

S.M.A.R.T. is a comprehension strategy providing students with opportunities to become personally involved in reading—both expository and narrative. Self-initiated questions and concept development underscore the utility of S.M.A.R.T. throughout a wide range of reading situations and abilities.

S.M.A.R.T, which is appropriate for individuals as well as small and large groups, can be organized as follows:

1. A book, story, or reading selection is chosen for discussion.

2. The title of the book is recorded on the chalkboard and the students are encouraged to ask questions about the title or the contents of the selection. All questions are recorded.

3. The students make predictions about the content of the selection. They decide on the questions they feel to be most appropriate for exploration.

4. Any illustrations found in the book or story are examined and additional questions are proposed. The initial prediction(s) is modified or altered according to information shared on the illustrations.

5. Students read the selection (either aloud or silently), looking for answers to the recorded questions. New questions may be generated for discussion as well. As answers are found in the text, students talk about them and attempt to arrive at mutually satisfying responses.

6. The procedure continues throughout the remainder of the selection, (1) seeking answers to previously generated questions and (2) continuing to ask additional questions. Upon completion of the book, all recorded questions and answers provided in the selection are discussed. Students decide on all appropriate answers. Questions that were not answered from the text are also shared. Students are encouraged to refer back to the book to answer any lingering questions.

NOTE: See *Following the Coast* for a lesson that uses this strategy.

Asking Divergent Questions

Selected use of the following questions can help students appreciate the diversity of observations and responses they can make to literature. The intent is not to have students all arrive at "right answers," but rather to help them look at the diversity of thinking that can take place within a piece of literature.

You may wish to post several of these questions on a chalkboard or duplicate and distribute them to all students. Take a few moments to discuss some of these questions prior to having students read a book. Work with students to identify four to six questions that they may wish to "be on the lookout for" during the course of their reading. As appropriate, invite students to stop at one or two predetermined points in the book. Take time at these junctures to talk about possible responses to selected questions. This allows students to see how others are interpreting a particular selection. However, the basic intent is to have students begin asking themselves these questions as they become more accomplished readers.

1. List all the words you can think of to describe _____.

2. What are all the possible solutions for _____?

3. List as many _____ as you can think of.

4. How would _____ view this?

5. What would _____ mean from the viewpoint of _____?

6. How would a _____ describe _____?

7. How would you feel if you were _____?

8. What would _____ do?

9. You are a _____. Describe your feelings.

10. How is _____ like _____?

11. I only know about _____. Explain _____ to me.

12. What ideas from _____ are like _____?

13. What _____ is most like a _____?

14. What would happen if there were more _____?

15. Suppose _____ happened; what would be the result?

16. Imagine if _____ and _____ were reversed. What would happen?

NOTE: See *Science Verse* and *G Is for Galaxy* for lessons that use this strategy.

Image Makers

Mental imagery helps readers construct "mind pictures" that serve as an aid in comprehension and as a way to tie together predictions, background knowledge, and textual knowledge in a satisfying experience. Once images are created (and colored by a reader's experiences), they become a permanent part of long-term memory. Just as important, they assist in the development of independent readers who are "connected" with the books they read.

Helping students create mental images works particularly well when the following guidelines are made part of the process:

1. Students need to understand that their images are personal and are affected by their own backgrounds and experiences.

2. There is no right or wrong image for any single student.

3. Provide students with sufficient opportunities to create their images prior to any discussion.

4. Provide adequate time for students to discuss the images they develop.

5. Assist students in image development through a series of open-ended questions (e.g., "Tell us more about your image," "Can you add some details?").

> **NOTE:** See *Plantzilla* for a lesson that uses this strategy.

Story Pyramid

The Story Pyramid (Waldo, 1991) helps students focus on main characters, important settings, and the problem/solution of a selected piece of literature. It can be used with individual readers in a reading group or presented as a whole class activity.

The Story Pyramid invites students to complete a triangular outline of story elements using the following information:

Line 1: Name of the main character

Line 2: Two words describing the main character

Line 3: Three words describing the setting

Line 4: Four words stating the problem

Line 5: Five words describing the main event

Line 6: Six words describing a second main event

Line 7: Seven words describing a third main event

Line 8: Eight words stating the solution to the problem

> **NOTE:** See *The Star People* for a lesson that uses this strategy.

Cloze Technique

In the Cloze Technique, you prepare sentences or paragraphs in which selected words have been omitted. You may wish to delete every fifth or every tenth word, for example. Or, you may wish to delete all the nouns or all the adjectives from a chapter in a book.

When you have decided on the words to be deleted from the piece, it is retyped, leaving blank spaces for the deleted words. (It is suggested that each blank be the same length so that students cannot infer words based solely on their length.) The retyped piece can then be used with students as part of an initial introduction to a book or as a summarization technique. The advantage of cloze is that it allows you to focus on specific grammatical concepts within the context of a familiar and contextually appropriate piece of writing. Students are then encouraged to work together or by themselves to replace the missing words with words that "sound right" or that make sense in the selection.

> **NOTE:** See *Around One Cactus* for a lesson that uses this strategy.

Quick-Write

This strategy is particularly useful with expository or nonfiction materials. Not only does it allow students to tap into their background knowledge, it also provides them with active opportunities to generate self-initiated questions based on that knowledge. Here are the steps involved:

1. Prior to inviting students to read a nonfiction book, ask them to write down (in paragraph form) everything they know about the topic of the book.

2. After a few minutes, ask students to revisit their respective paragraphs. Invite them to think of some questions about the topics that are generated by that paragraph. Invite them to record their questions on separate sheets of paper.

3. Provide group members with the titles of the chapters in the book. Ask students to mark which questions on their respective lists they think will be answered in the book. Students may wish to assign a chapter number to each question on their sheet.

4. Provide an opportunity for students to share their questions and their predictions.

5. Invite students to read the book silently and to look for answers to their questions, if possible. After the reading, students may use any unanswered questions to stimulate group discussion. Unanswered questions may also be used for independent research projects.

> **NOTE:** See *The Tarantula Scientist* and *Hidden Worlds* for lessons that use this strategy.

Story Impressions

One way you can assist your students in actively thinking about the materials they are to read is a strategy known as "Story Impressions" (McGinley and Denner, 1987). Story Impressions encourages students to engage in predictive activities utilizing key concepts preselected from a piece of literature. Its advantage lies in the fact that students are provided with realistic opportunities to predict and confirm key elements from the plot of a story. Following are the steps involved in this strategy:

1. Select 10 to 15 key words, ideas, or phrases from a forthcoming book. These key concepts should represent the character, setting, and important points in the plot. These ideas should be printed in sequential order down the left-hand side of a sheet of paper. You may wish to draw an arrow between each listing.

2. Present the sheet to a reading group and tell students that the list represents important concepts from the book.

3. Invite students to read through the list (top to bottom) and encourage them to discuss how the ideas might be related or connect.

4. Using the brainstormed ideas, the group members construct a story. This can be recorded on chart-pack paper or on the chalkboard. As an individual activity, each student can be presented with a duplicated copy of the list of key concepts on which to record his or her original story on the right-hand side of the paper.

5. Encourage students to read the original book and then discuss how the stories compare. The object is NOT to have an exact match, but rather to see how a basic set of ideas can be interpreted differently by two "authors."

NOTE: See *Antarctic Journal* and *Leaf Man* for lessons that use this strategy.

Literature Log

A Literature Log provides students with opportunities to think about what they have read and to organize that information into a systematic piece of writing. These should not be interpreted as "worksheets," since there are no right or wrong answers. They can be used by individuals or small groups of students as a way to record information and thoughts about a particular book. You may find them important as assessment tools or as summary sheets to be maintained in each student's portfolio.

Literature Logs are appropriate for use at the conclusion of a book or can be used by students prior to or during the reading of a book.

NOTE: See *The Tsunami Quilt* for a lesson that uses this strategy.

K-W-L

K-W-L (Ogle, 1986) is a three-step framework that helps students access appropriate information in expository writing. It takes advantage of students' background knowledge and helps demonstrate relationships between that knowledge and the information in text.

K-W-L (What I <u>K</u>now, What I <u>W</u>ant to Learn, What I <u>L</u>earned) involves students in three major cognitive steps: accessing their background knowledge about a topic, determining what they would like to learn about that subject, and evaluating what was learned about the topic. The following steps provide an outline through which teachers and students can begin to read expository text:

1. Invite students to talk about what they already know about the topic of the text. This information should be freely volunteered and written on the chalkboard (K—what we Know).

2. Encourage students to categorize the information they have volunteered. This can be done through various grouping strategies such as semantic webbing. These groupings can be recorded on the chalkboard.

3. Invite students to make predictions about the types of information the text will contain. These predictions should be based on their background knowledge as well as the categories of information elicited in step 2.

4. Encourage students to generate their own questions about the text. These can be discussed and recorded in a section of the board entitled "W—What we want to find out."

5. Invite students to read the text and record answers to their questions. Students may wish to do this individually or in pairs.

6. Upon completion of the text, provide students with an opportunity to discuss the information learned and how it relates to their prior knowledge. Talk about questions posed for which no information was found in the text. Help students discover other sources for satisfying their inquiries.

> **NOTE:** See *Near One Cattail* for a lesson that uses this strategy.

Metacognitive Questioning

Helping students begin asking self-initiated questions can be a powerful element in any guided reading session. Students need models to emulate (as in the examples above). The goal of asking students appropriate metacognitive questions is to gradually release responsibility for question asking and place it squarely in the hands of students.

The chart on page 51 is provided to assist you in asking appropriate metacognitive questions during a reading lesson. Teacher-posed questions are listed down the left side of the chart. The objective is to gradually reduce the number of teacher questions and increase the number of student-posed questions—questions that students begin asking themselves as they read. The list on the right can be posted for students or transcribed onto individual index cards, which can be randomly distributed to a group of students and used as discussion starters during or after the reading of an appropriate passage.

Teacher-Posed Questions	Student-Posed Questions
1. Is this story similar to anything you may have read before?	1. Why would this information be important for me to know?
2. What were you thinking when you read this part of the story?	2. Is this character similar to any other(s) I have read about?
3. What have we learned so far?	3. Does this information give me any clues about what may happen later in the story?
4. What is the major point of this section?	4. How does this information differ from other things I know?
5. Did you change your mind about anything after reading this part of the story?	5. Why is this difficult for me to understand?
6. Do you have any personal questions about this book that have not been answered so far?	6. Do I need additional information to help me understand this topic?
7. What did you do when you didn't understand that word in the story?	7. Can I write a summary of this part of the story?
8. What makes you feel your interpretation is most appropriate?	8. What do I know so far?
9. What new information are you learning?	9. What did the author do to make me think this way?
10. How did you arrive at your interpretation?	10. Am I satisfied with this story?

NOTE: See *Red Eyes or Blue Feathers* for a lesson that uses this strategy.

Picture Perfect

Picture Perfect is a reading strategy that stimulates background experiences, ties them in with textual knowledge, and provides you with relevant information upon which to design an effective reading lesson. Its other advantage is that it incorporates the writing process into the reading process and provides students with a glimpse into the interrelationships that exist between the two. This strategy has been used effectively with all ability levels and all grade levels. Here's how it works:

1. Select an illustration, photograph, or picture from the cover of the book or from the inside. The illustration should provide sufficient clues or information about the book in terms of setting, characters, or significant events.

2. Photocopy the illustration and duplicate it at the top of a sheet of paper. Make sufficient copies for each student in two or more guided reading groups to have one.

3. Invite each group to look at the illustration and then generate three to five questions about the illustration. One person in the group records these questions for the group.

4. Invite groups to exchange their questions with another group.

5. Invite each group to write a story that embeds answers to the other group's questions in that story. The story can be fiction or nonfiction, expository or narrative. All members of a group contribute elements of the story, and one member records it.

6. When the stories are completed, invite each group to return the story to the group that originated the questions.

7. Group members can now read the story that was written in response to their questions.

8. Take time to discuss the background knowledge that was tapped as well as the information that was generated as a result of that background knowledge in concert with the selected illustration.

9. Invite students (individually or collectively) to read the book.

10. After the book has been read, invite students to compare the plot of the book with those of the stories.

11. Invite students to modify their 'Before Reading" stories in light of the information in the book. What new information needs to be included in the second draft?

Picture Perfect has proven itself as an effective and lasting strategy that underscores students' active involvement and engagement in the reading process. There are no right or wrong ways to construct the initial stories, and they will reflect the prior experiences students bring to the reading of a book. That information will be helpful for you in directing and shaping the content of any follow-up lessons.

> **NOTE:** See *Song of the Water Boatman* and *Flotsam* for lessons that use this strategy.

COMPREHENSION STRATEGIES AND THE SIX PRINCIPLES

The following chart shows the correlation between the 24 comprehension strategies shared throughout this book and the 6 critical principles of comprehension instruction for grades 1–6 (see Chapter 4).

Principle	Reading Strategies
Tapping into Background Knowledge	• Semantic Webbing • Concept Cards • K-W-L • Anticipation Guide • Quick Write • Reflective Sharing • Chapter Slam • MM & M
Mental Imagery	• Mental Imagery • Possible Sentences • MM & M

Principle	Reading Strategies
Predicting and Inferring	• S.M.A.R.T. • Anticipation Guide • Quick Write • Chapter Slam • Possible Sentences • Story Impressions • DRTA • MM & M
Questioning	• Quick Write • S.M.A.R.T. • Picture Perfect • Divergent Questions • Metacognitive Questions • Answer First • What-If • Question Master
Identifying Important Details	• Concept Cards • Semantic Webbing • Anticipation Guide • Reflective Sharing • Picture Perfect • Chapter Slam • Possible Sentences • Story Impressions • Story Pyramid • Cloze • Literature Log • Story Map
Synthesizing and Summarizing	• K-W-L • Reflective Sharing • Picture Perfect • Story Impressions • Story Pyramid • Answer First • Story Frames • Literature Log • Question Master • Story Map • Cloze

CHAPTER 6

How to Use This Book

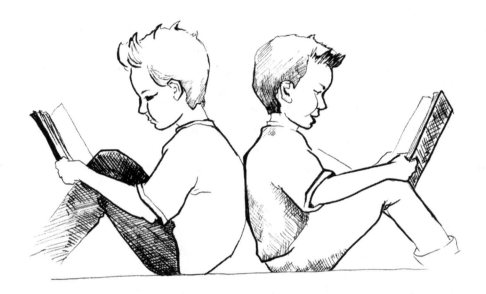

Welcome aboard! Are you ready for some incredible teaching and learning experiences? I hope so. This book is designed to promote the science + reading partnership through exciting, dynamic, and fascinating children's literature. Whether you are a classroom teacher or school librarian, you will discover a wealth of learning opportunities that will actively engage kids in a variety of "hands-on, minds-on" experiences. Let's take a look.

BOOK SELECTION

Part II contains a host of activities and processes designated for some of the best trade books in elementary science. These books have been selected because of their appropriateness to the science curriculum, their adaptability to all grades (K–6) and ability ranges (high-low), and their usefulness in promoting relevant science concepts. Included are

- Caldecott Medalists and Honor Books

- NCTE Orbis Pictus Award (Outstanding Nonfiction for Children)

- Bulletin of the Center for Children's Books

- Outstanding Science Trade Books—Children's Book Council/National Science Teacher's Association

- Teacher's Choice Awards—International Reading Association

- Teacher's Choice Awards—*Learning Magazine*

- Recommendations from numerous children's librarians (school and public library)

- Recommendations from classroom teachers in a variety of schools

- Recommendations profiled in *Book Links, Horn Book, Children's Literature, School Library Journal, Book List, Kirkus Reviews, Science and Children,* and other professional journals

In short, there's something for everyone!

The literature included in this book reflects a range of reading levels. You should feel free to select and use those books that best meet the needs and abilities of students in your classroom or library. An "energized" science curriculum will include literature selections throughout the entire academic year. You will discover innumerable opportunities for developing, expanding, and teaching both science content and reading comprehension using the literature in these pages. In that regard, remember that the readability or difficulty level of a single book should not determine if or how it will be used; rather, the emphasis should be on whether students are interested and motivated to pursue literature-related activities that promote learning in a supportive and holistic curriculum.

COMPREHENSION LESSONS

Each featured book includes an appropriate comprehension lesson for you to share with your students. These lessons are designed to emphasize students' active engagement with science literature, helping them to use reading and language arts strategies in understanding and appreciating the best in science literature.

Each of the lesson plans follows the format described earlier in this book. This format is organized into five separate categories that allow you to "slot" appropriate instructional activities into a dynamic and engaging framework for comprehension development:

1. Setting the Stage

2. Before Reading

3. During Reading

4. After Reading

5. Literature Extensions

The lesson plans use a different comprehension strategy for each designated book. The selection of a particular strategy was arbitrary and was not based on any specific criteria (other than its appropriateness for expository or narrative literature). It is my hope that you will see how the strategies in this book can be combined with a variety of titles to assist students within and throughout their literary encounters. In short, the "assignment" of a designated strategy to a designated book is based more on your decision about what is best for your students than on any preconceived standards established by outside "experts." Simply, all of the comprehension strategies are universal in nature—that is, each can be used with a wide range of children's books throughout the science curriculum as well as the entire elementary program.

You will discover a wide range of instructional possibilities with these strategies, as well as the flexibility that can be part and parcel of your students' comprehension development. Use these lesson plans as guides rather than absolutes. Adapt, modify, and alter these lessons according to the needs of your students and the evolving nature of your classroom. Also, use these plans and blueprints for the design and delivery of your own lessons with your own literature.

HANDS-ON, MINDS-ON ACTIVITIES

Each featured children's book includes a host of potential activities and processes. It is not necessary to use all the activities. Rather, you and the students with whom you work should decide which activities best serve the needs of the science program and students themselves. Undoubtedly you will discover activities that can be used individually, in small groups, in large groups, or as a whole class.

You should also consider providing students with opportunities to make project selections within the context of a work of literature. This can be a powerful and energizing component of your program. When youngsters are given those opportunities, their appreciation of science and their interest in learning important science concepts increase tremendously.

As students become involved in the various trade books and their accompanying activities, I suggest that you guide them in researching or developing other activities based on classroom dynamics and teaching or learning styles. For learning to be meaningful, it must have relevance. I encourage you and your students to make these activities your own. Add to them, adapt them, and allow students to help you design additional activities, extensions, and projects that will challenge them, arouse their natural curiosity, and create a dynamic learning environment.

Teaching science via trade books is not necessarily an "all or nothing" proposition. That is, it is not necessary to use a single trade book for a full lesson or full day. What it does mean is that you have several options to consider in terms of how you can present a book or series of books to your class, how much you want them to dominate your daily curriculum, and how involved you and your students want to be. Here are some options to consider:

- Introduce a single book and provide students with a variety of selected activities (for that book) for one day.

- Teach a unit built on a combination of several related books.

- Design a thematic unit based on selected pieces of literature within a specific science standard (e.g., the characteristics of organisms, populations and ecosystems, natural hazards).

- Design a thematic unit based on selected pieces of literature within a specific science discipline (e.g., life science, physical science, earth science).

- Utilize the activities for one or two books during an entire day and follow up with the regular curriculum on succeeding days.

- Use a book or series of books as a follow-up to information presented in a textbook or curriculum guide.

- Provide students with literature-related activities as independent work upon completion of lessons in the regular textbook.

- Teach cooperatively with a colleague and present a self-designed thematic unit to both classes at the same time (this can be done with two classes at the same grade level or two classes at different grade levels).

- Use a book or group of books intermittently over the span of several weeks.

How you use these books (and their accompanying activities) may be determined by any number of factors. It is safe to say that there is no ideal way to implement literature into your classroom plans. The preceding list is only a partial collection of ideas. The dictates of your own particular teaching situation, personal experience, and student needs may suggest other possibilities.

PROJECT PAGES

Along with each featured children's book is a collection of project pages to duplicate and use in both the classroom and school library. These pages are designed to extend the learning opportunities for students in a variety of ways.

Here you will discover pages to be used as part of each book's comprehension lesson. Students (either as a whole class or in small groups) can use these as an element of the preceding comprehension lesson. In several cases the pages have been designed to be generic—that is, you will be able to use them with several different books throughout the school year; they are not specific to any single piece of literature or any single book.

For each designated children's book there are several additional project pages for you to duplicate and share with students. These pages are primarily designed as independent activities or science experiments. You may wish to assign these to students (either in small groups or independently) for completion during a science lesson or during available "free time." Although these pages are designed for specific books and specific science and/or language arts standards, you should feel free to modify or adapt them in keeping with your classroom science curriculum or library program

Most project pages are open-ended; that is, there are no right or wrong responses. Rather, students are afforded opportunities to investigate the dynamics of a book or the elements of a topic with the emphasis more on the processes of learning rather than on the products. Consider the following suggestions for using these pages:

- Use a single project page with multiple books in the same unit of study.

- Use a project page as a regular feature of varying units throughout the school year.

- The project pages may be used in whatever sequence or order you deem appropriate. They are not arranged in any specific order, and you should feel free to distribute them according to the dictates of your science curriculum.

- It is suggested that the project pages not be graded. Rather, they should be promoted as learning extensions rather than as homework assignments.

- Both teachers and librarians should be involved in selecting appropriate project pages for any book. That way a coordinated process is ensured—one that can be promoted and completed in both venues.

• As appropriate, encourage parents to work with their children in completing selected project pages. Again, this should be presented not as a homework assignment, but rather as an opportunity for students and their parents to engage in a dialogue about what is taking place in the science program and the types of literature shared in that program.

Please keep in mind that it is not necessary to use a project page for every book or every unit of study. They are but one item in your instructional repertoire. Used judiciously, they can add an additional element of excitement and enthusiasm for the literature integrated into your science curriculum.

READERS THEATRE

Part III contains several readers theatre scripts for you to duplicate and use with students. These scripts have been coordinated with specific science topics. You are free to use these scripts with whatever concepts and books you wish. Here are a few suggestions:

• Use a readers theatre script as part of a larger science unit.

• Use a readers theatre script as a classroom project to be supplemented with literature obtained in the school library.

• Use a readers theatre script as a library project to be followed up with selected classroom activities.

• After students have participated in several hands-on, minds-on activities, invite them to create their own readers theatre script.

• After students have participated in a readers theatre production in the library, invite them to identify related books and activities for classroom use.

• Invite students—in a classroom or library project—to create their own readers theatre production based on a single science book.

Presenting a readers theatre script need not be an elaborate or extensive production. As children become more familiar with and polished in using readers theatre, they will be able to suggest a multitude of presentation possibilities for future scripts. It is important to help students assume a measure of self-initiated responsibility in the delivery of any readers theatre. In so doing, you will be helping to ensure their personal engagement and active participation in this most valuable of science activities.

Keep in mind that *MORE Science Adventures with Children's Literature* is designed to provide you with instructional options, based on the best in children's literature. You should feel free to modify these creative suggestions in keeping with the interests, needs, and inclinations of the students with whom you work. If these ideas spark additional extensions or possibilities for your classroom or library, then so much the better! The result will be an incredible array of teaching possibilities and a fantastic plethora of learning possibilities.

References

Cooper, D. J., and N. D. Kiger. 2003. *Literacy: Helping Children Construct Meaning*. Boston: Houghton Mifflin.

Fowler, G. L. 1982. "Developing Comprehension Skills in Primary Grades Through the Use of Story Frames." *The Reading Teacher* 36, no. 2: 176–79.

Fredericks, A. D. 2001. *Guided Reading in Grades 3–6*. Austin, TX: Harcourt Achieve.

Fredericks, A. D. 2006. *Teaching Comprehension in Grades 1–2*. Austin, TX: Harcourt Achieve.

Fredericks, A. D., and D. Cheesebrough. 1993. *Science for All Children*. New York: HarperCollins.

Fredericks, A. D., B. Blake-Kline, and J. V. Kristo. 1997. *Teaching the Integrated Language Arts: Process and Practice*. New York: Longman.

Harvey, S., and A. Goudvis. 2000. *Strategies That Work: Teaching Comprehension to Enhance Understanding*. Portland, ME: Stenhouse Publishers.

McGinley, W. J., and P. R. Denner. 1987. "Story Impressions: A Pre-reading/writing Activity." *Journal of Reading* 31: 248–53.

Moore, D. W., and S. A. Moore. 1986. "Possible Sentences." In *Reading in the Content Areas: Improving Classroom Instruction*, 2nd ed., edited by E. K. Dishner, T. W. Bean, J. E. Readance, and D. W. Moore, 174–79. Dubuque, IA: Kendall/Hunt.

National Research Council (NRC). 1996. *National Science Education Standards*. Washington, DC: National Academy Press.

Ogle, D. 1986. "K-W-L: A Teaching Model That Develops Active Reading of Expository Text." *The Reading Teacher* 39: 564–70.

Pearson, P. David, J. A. Dole, G. G. Duffy, and L. R. Roehler. 1992. "Developing Expertise in Reading Comprehension: What Should Be Taught and How Should It Be Taught?" In *What Research Has to Say to the Teacher of Reading*, 2nd ed., edited by J. Farstup and S. J. Samuels. Newark, DE: International Reading Association.

Pressley, G. M. 2000. "What Should Comprehension Instruction Be the Instruction Of?" In *Handbook of Reading Research*, edited by M. K. Kamil, P. B. Mosenthal, P. D. Pearson, and R. Barr, vol. 3, 545–62. Mahwah, NJ: Lawrence Erlbaum Associates.

Stauffer, R. 1969. *Directing Reading Maturity as a Cognitive Process*. New York: Harper & Row.

Vacca, R., and J. Vacca. 1989. *Content Area Reading*. New York: HarperCollins.

Waldo, B. 1991. "Story Pyramid." In *Responses to Literature*, edited by J. M. Bacon, D. Bewell, and M. Vogt, 23–24. Newark, DE: International Reading Association.

Part II

Activities, Projects, and Experiments: Literature Selections

The Dinosaurs of Waterhouse Hawkins

Barbara Kerley

New York: Scholastic Press, 2001

SELECTED CITATIONS

- **2002 Caldecott Honor Book**—American Library Association

- **2002 Outstanding Science Trade Book**—Children's Book Council/National Science Teachers Association

- **2002 Orbis Pictus Honor Book**—National Council of Teachers of English

SUMMARY

In the mid-nineteenth century an artist named Waterhouse Hawkins brought dinosaurs to life—through his drawings and three-dimensional models. He stunned the citizens of two countries—England and the United States—with his realistic and true-life depictions of these ancient creatures. This is a book that must be part of any exploration into the world of dinosaurs and the scientists who study them.

SUGGESTED GRADE LEVELS: 3–5

LESSON OBJECTIVES

Science Standards

- Content Standard A: Science as Inquiry

    Understandings about science inquiry (K–4, 5–8)

- Content Standard D: Earth and Space Science

    Earth's history (5–8)

• Content Standard G: History and Nature of Science

Science as a human endeavor (K–4, 5–8)

CRITICAL THINKING QUESTIONS

1. Why do scientists keep changing their minds about how dinosaurs looked?
2. Which of the dinosaurs depicted in the book do you want to learn more about?
3. Why do we know more about dinosaurs now than in the time of Waterhouse Hawkins?
4. What do you enjoy most about dinosaurs?
5. What questions would you like to ask Waterhouse Hawkins (if you could)?

COMPREHENSION LESSON (ANTICIPATION GUIDE)

Setting the Stage

Distribute copies of the book to students. Invite students to look at the cover illustration and describe what they see. How does that illustration compare with what they may already know about dinosaurs?

Before Reading

Duplicate the Anticipation Guide and distribute copies to students. Invite students to agree or disagree with each of the Anticipation Guide statements. They should mark their responses in the BEFORE column.

During Reading

Invite students to read the entire book (or to listen to it as a read-aloud). Invite students to look for (or listen for) confirmation of the Anticipation Guide statements.

After Reading

After students have completed the book, ask them to re-read the Anticipation Guide statements and decide which are correct and which are incorrect. They should mark their post-reading responses in the AFTER column. Plan time for students to verify their decisions by re-reading appropriate passages. Ask students to talk about changes between their pre-reading knowledge and their post-reading knowledge.

LITERATURE EXTENSIONS

Invite students to select one or more of the following activities:

1. Invite students to brainstorm for all the adjectives they can think of that could be used to describe dinosaurs. After a sufficient list of adjectives has been generated, divide the class into several small groups. Each group is charged with the responsibility of de-

ciding on the "Top Ten" dinosaur adjectives. After each group has come up with a list, invite the groups to share and to arrive at a mutually agreeable list of "Top Ten Dinosaur Adjectives."

2. Provide students with empty shoe boxes, various pieces of colored construction paper, glue, scissors, and other art materials. Using these materials, students (individually or in small groups) can design dioramas of selected scenes from this book.

3. Invite a paleontologist from a nearby college or university to visit your classroom. Ask the visitor to discuss some of the theories about the extinction of the dinosaurs (e.g., Yucatan meteor, disease, significant environmental changes, etc.). Help students prepare a list of questions to be sent to the visitor beforehand.

4. Ask students to create a time line on a large sheet of butcher paper. The periods in which the dinosaurs lived (Mesozoic, Triassic, Jurassic, and Cretaceous) may be recorded along the bottom of the paper. Encourage students to draw illustrations of the dinosaurs represented in this book and fasten each illustration in its proper place on the mural (additional research will be necessary). Students may also wish to add some of their favorite dinosaurs (those not depicted or described in the book) to this mural, too.

5. Students may wish to create a dinosaur alphabet book, using words and terms from this book as well as other books in the school or public library. For example:

   A = Allosaurus

   B = Bones in Mongolia

   C = Cold-blooded

6. Invite students to become newspaper reporters who have been transported back to the time of Waterhouse Hawkins. Encourage them to prepare a series of newspaper articles on some of the events that were described in the book. For example, they may wish to offer an interview with Mr. Hawkins, a description of the night his models were destroyed in New York, the opening of his exhibit in Crystal Palace Park, or the dinner party with the world's top scientists.

7. Provide each student with a piece of modeling clay. Invite students to create a model of a favorite dinosaur (using an illustration in this book or another dinosaur book). After a sufficient amount of time, ask students to discuss some of the challenges, problems, or difficulties they had in constructing their dinosaur models. Would these be some of the same challenges Waterhouse Hawkins faced as he created his life-sized models of dinosaurs? What were some of the things he had to consider when building his models?

8. Invite students to each pretend to be a specific species of dinosaur (either one mentioned in the book or another species). Ask students to describe their dinosaur bodies, outlining their size, configuration, dimensions, skeletal structure, and other important features. Invite each individual to explain why his or her dinosaur body is different from those of other dinosaurs.

9. Divide the class into various groups. Invite the groups to put together some (or all) of the following lists, using a variety of resources at school and at home:

- The best dinosaur books for kids
- The best dinosaur Web sites for kids
- The best dinosaur museums in the country
- The best dinosaur sites to visit in the country
- The best colleges or universities to attend to become a dinosaur expert

ANTICIPATION GUIDE

Look at the sentences on this page. The statements are numbered from 1 to 6. Read each sentence; if you think that what it says is right, print "Yes" on the line under the word BEFORE. If you think the sentence is wrong, print "No" on the line under the word BEFORE. Do the same thing for each sentence. Remember how to do this, because you will do it again after reading *The Dinosaurs of Waterhouse Hawkins* (except that you will write "Yes" or "No" on each line under the word AFTER).

BEFORE   AFTER

_____   _____   1. Dinosaurs lived in London many years ago.

_____   _____   2. Everybody loves dinosaurs.

_____   _____   3. A model of a dinosaur would be very large.

_____   _____   4. People know more about dinosaurs today than they did in the 1800s.

_____   _____   5. Several dinosaurs have been discovered in the United States.

_____   _____   6. Benjamin Waterhouse Hawkins was a well-known scientist.

From *MORE Science Adventures with Children's Literature: Reading Comprehension and Inquiry-Based Science* by Anthony D. Fredericks. Westport, CT: Teacher Ideas Press. Copyright © 2008.

THE SIZE OF DINOSAURS

How big were dinosaurs? How does the size of these ancient creatures compare with you? Let's find out.

Materials:

- roll of string or yarn
- measuring tape
- a helper

Directions:

1. Go outside to a large area such as a neighborhood playground, baseball field, or vacant lot.
2. Ask your helper (a parent, adult, or relative) to measure your height with the measuring tape.
3. Cut a piece of string that is the same length as your height. Lay that string on the ground.
4. Measure different lengths of string using the dinosaur measurements below.
5. Lay those pieces of string on the ground side by side.
6. Take a look at the various pieces of string. How does your height compare with the height and length of different dinosaurs?
7. Consult other dinosaur books and add some other species of dinosaurs to this list. Make sure to include your favorite dinosaur(s).

Dinosaur	Length	Height
Tyrannosaurus rex	32 feet	14 feet
Brachiosaurus	67 feet	27 feet
Stegosaurus	28 feet	13 feet
Plateosaurus	20 feet	7 feet
Camptosaurus	18 feet	8 feet
Velociraptor	8 feet	3 feet
Protoceratops	8 feet	3 feet

From *MORE Science Adventures with Children's Literature: Reading Comprehension and Inquiry-Based Science* by Anthony D. Fredericks. Westport, CT: Teacher Ideas Press. Copyright © 2008.

THE THIGH BONE'S CONNECTED TO THE . . .

NOTE: This activity requires assistance from an adult. Do not do this on your own.

Paleontologists are scientists who study dinosaur bones. When dinosaur bones are discovered, one of the things paleontologists often want to do is assemble the bones into a skeleton that scientifically represents the actual dinosaur. Here's an activity in which you can be a paleontologist, too.

Materials:

- fresh whole chicken (from your local grocery store)
- large pot
- water
- vinegar
- stove
- sheet of newsprint or large piece of paper

Directions:

1. Ask an adult to put the whole chicken into a pot. Add enough water to cover the chicken and add a cup of vinegar. Boil the chicken. (The chicken should be boiled until the meat begins to fall off the bones. The meat can be saved and eaten later.)

2. Remove the chicken from the pot and allow it to cool.

3. After the chicken has cooled sufficiently, begin to pull the meat off the bones (if the meat does not come off the bones easily, return the chicken to the pot and boil it a little longer).

4. Strip as much meat off the bones as you can.

5. When you have all the meat off the bones, ask an adult to break the skeleton apart at all the joints. Ask the adult to place all the chicken bones randomly into a plastic container.

6. Spread out a sheet of newsprint or a large sheet of paper. Take all the chicken bones from the container and lay them on the paper.

7. Now, try to reconstruct the chicken skeleton into its original configuration.

From *MORE Science Adventures with Children's Literature: Reading Comprehension and Inquiry-Based Science* by Anthony D. Fredericks. Westport, CT: Teacher Ideas Press. Copyright © 2008.

THE THIGH BONE'S CONNECTED TO THE . . .
(CONTINUED)

Description:

You may find this activity more challenging than you thought. Even though you may be familiar with chickens (you've eaten chicken, you've seen live chickens, or you have seen photos of chickens in magazines or books), you might find it difficult or challenging to reassemble a chicken skeleton.

When paleontologists discover some new dinosaur bones, they often don't find an entire skeleton—there may be many missing pieces. So, putting a dinosaur skeleton together is somewhat of a challenge. Couple that with the fact that nobody (not even scientists) has ever seen a live dinosaur, and you can see why putting a dinosaur skeleton together is a real challenge.

From *MORE Science Adventures with Children's Literature: Reading Comprehension and Inquiry-Based Science* by Anthony D. Fredericks. Westport, CT: Teacher Ideas Press. Copyright © 2008.

AN INVITATION

Waterhouse Hawkins wasn't able to set up his dinosaur models in Central Park in New York City. Pretend that you are the mayor of your town or city. Write an imaginary letter to Mr. Hawkins inviting him to set up his dinosaur models in your town. Be sure to share with him the various reasons why your town would be an excellent location for his models. What would you need to say that would convince him to build his models where you live?

_____

(date)

Dear Mr. Hawkins:

_____

_____

_____

_____

_____

_____

_____

_____

_____

_____

_____

_____

Sincerely,

_____

Mayor

From *MORE Science Adventures with Children's Literature: Reading Comprehension and Inquiry-Based Science* by Anthony D. Fredericks. Westport, CT: Teacher Ideas Press. Copyright © 2008.

Actual Size

Steve Jenkins

Boston: Houghton Mifflin, 2004

SELECTED CITATIONS

- **2005 Orbis Pictus Honor Book**—National Council of Teachers of English

- **2004 Blue Ribbon Nonfiction Book Award**—*The Bulletin of the Center for Children's Books*

SUMMARY

Using striking torn-and-cut paper collages, 18 animals are profiled in actual size. Included is the eye of a giant squid, the hand of a gorilla, a Goliath frog, a saltwater crocodile, and a mouse lemur. The large and the small, the big and the little inhabit the pages of this dynamic book, which offers budding scientists an "up close and personal" look at the size and dimensions of select creatures. The end matter offers full pictures of the creatures and more details about their habitats and habits. This is a great book for any examination of animals in the wild.

SUGGESTED GRADE LEVELS: 1–4

LESSON OBJECTIVES

Science Standards

- Content Standard A; Science as Inquiry

    Abilities necessary to do science inquiry (K–4; 5–8)

- Content Standard C: Life Science

    The characteristics of organisms

CRITICAL THINKING QUESTIONS

1. What was the most amazing animal in the whole book?

2. Which of the animals would you like to see "in person"?

3. What are some other large animals that should be in this book?

4. What are some other small animals that should be in this book?

5. What did you enjoy most about the illustrations?

COMPREHENSION LESSON (ANSWER FIRST!)

Setting the Stage

Provide a copy of the book for each student (or do a read-aloud). Invite students to "thumb" through the book and closely observe the illustrations (and their respective sizes). What do they notice about each illustration? How are these illustrations similar to (or different from) those found in other books?

Before Reading

Invite students to discuss the title of this book. How did the author/illustrator arrive at this particular title? After looking at the illustrations, what will be found in the text of the book? What does the term "Actual Size" really mean?

During Reading

Invite students to read the entire book on their own or to listen to it as part of a read-aloud. Ask them to take note of interesting information, unusual facts, or fascinating data.

After Reading

Provide students with copies of the Answer First! project page. Invite students—either individually or in small groups—to generate a question for each of the five answers on that page. After they have had sufficient time, ask students to share the questions they generated and why they believe those questions to be appropriate for this book. Afterward, point out to students that the answers were arranged in a hierarchical order—from easy to more challenging. Let them know that the later questions (more challenging) are the kinds of questions that good readers (and good scientists) always ask themselves as they read.

LITERATURE EXTENSIONS

Invite students to select one or more of the following activities:

1. Divide the class in half. One half can be predators and the other half can be prey. A predator is matched up with a prey. Invite each pair to construct a book on the life of a predator trying to catch its prey and the prey's attempts to escape. Illustrations should also be included.

2. Encourage students to keep an "Animal Journal." This can be a record of all the animals they see during the week. It should include pets, wild animals, insects, and animals seen on television. Hang posters for mammals, fish, birds, reptiles and amphibians, etc. Students can add to the charts daily.

3. Ask youngsters to create "Wanted" posters for some of the animals in the book. What information should be included on each poster? What are some of the "vital statistics" that students would want to share with others via their posters? If possible, obtain one or more "Wanted" posters from your local post office and use them as models for your students' posters.

4. Invite youngsters to locate animal tracks in soft dirt or mud (these can be cat or dog tracks, or deer or some other wild animal in your area). Place a circle of cardboard around the track and push it partway down into the soil (be careful not to disturb the track). Mix up some plaster of Paris according to the package directions. Pour it into the mold up to the top of the cardboard strip. Wait until the plaster cast hardens and then remove the cast from the ground print. Take off the cardboard strip and clean off the bottom. Students may wish to make several of these (each a separate animal) and display them in the classroom along with pertinent research notes.

5. Ask students to imagine that they are one of the creatures in the story. Encourage them to create a poster that says "Save Our Home." They can include a full-color drawing of the selected creature and write a convincing ad for saving the ecosystem represented by the animal.

6. Invite students to imagine that they can be the size of one of the animals in the book. Which animal would they choose? How would their lives be different if they were the same size at that animal? What accommodations would they have to make? What accommodations would others have to make?

7. Ask students to discuss the advantages and disadvantages of size. In the wild, is it better to be a large animal or a small animal? Is size an advantage in the wild? You may wish to divide the class into two groups—pro and con—and engage students in a friendly debate about this issue. Is there a satisfactory answer?

8. Students may wish to do some library or Internet research and identify the following:
   - The largest creature that has ever lived on Earth.
   - The largest creature on Earth today.
   - The smallest creature that has ever lived.
   - The smallest creature on Earth today

9. Students may wish to conduct a survey of individuals in the school (both adults and children) to determine the following:
   - Who has the largest feet? Smallest feet?
   - Who has the largest hand? Smallest hand?
   - Who has the largest teeth? Smallest teeth?
   - Who has the largest eye? Smallest eye?
   - Who has the largest head? Smallest head?

10. Invite students to locate a variety of animals in their neighborhood or community. These can be pets as well as wild animals. After students have a sufficient list, ask them to create a book similar to *Actual Size* in which they detail the measurements of the local animals. What is the largest animal in the community? The smallest animal? Which animal has the largest teeth? The smallest teeth? What is the heaviest animal? The lightest animal?

ANSWER FIRST!

Using the book *Actual Size,* write a question for each answer below:

Question 1: _____

_____

Answer 1: _____ It's the largest bird. _____

Question 2: _____

_____

Answer 2: _____ The huge gorilla and the pygmy mouse lemur. _____

Question 3: _____

_____

Answer 3: _____ It's a way of protecting themselves. _____

Question 4: _____

_____

Answer 4: _____ They are effective in capturing prey. _____

Question 5: _____

_____

Answer 5: _____ "Survival in the Wild" _____

From *MORE Science Adventures with Children's Literature: Reading Comprehension and Inquiry-Based Science* by Anthony D. Fredericks. Westport, CT: Teacher Ideas Press. Copyright © 2008.

LARGE TO SMALL

As you discovered in *Actual Size,* animals come in all sizes, from large to small. Using just the animals profiled in the book, arrange them in the chart below, from the longest creature down to the shortest creature.

atlas moth	dwarf goby	giant squid
Alaskan brown bear	ostrich	giant anteater
Goliath birdeater	tarantula saltwater crocodile	Goliath frog
great white shark	gorilla	pygmy mouse lemur
Siberian tiger	Goliath beetle	giant walking stick
African elephant	giant Gippsland	earthworm

	Animals (longest to shortest)	**Length**
1.		
2.		
3.		
4.		
5.		
6.		
7.		
8.		
9.		
10.		
11.		
12.		
13.		
14.		
15.		
16.		
17.		

From *MORE Science Adventures with Children's Literature: Reading Comprehension and Inquiry-Based Science* by Anthony D. Fredericks. Westport, CT: Teacher Ideas Press. Copyright © 2008.

LARGE TO SMALL (CONTINUED)

Reorder the animals, this time from the heaviest animal down to the lightest animal.

	Animals (heaviest to lightest)	Weight
1.		
2.		
3.		
4.		
5.		
6.		
7.		
8.		
9.		
10.		
11.		
12.		
13.		
14.		
15.		
16.		
17.		

From *MORE Science Adventures with Children's Literature: Reading Comprehension and Inquiry-Based Science* by Anthony D. Fredericks. Westport, CT: Teacher Ideas Press. Copyright © 2008.

WHAT DO YOU THINK?

Consider the book *Actual Size.* What did you think about that book? Here's an evaluation form you can use to evaluate the book. Take some time to fill it in. Then discuss your evaluation of the book with other students. Do you all agree? Are there some points over which you disagree?

Feature	Evaluation
The title was original and fresh.	☐ WOW! ☐ Very Strong ☐ Strong ☐ O.K. ☐ Not very good
The information was interesting.	☐ WOW! ☐ Very Strong ☐ Strong ☐ O.K. ☐ Not very good
The illustrations were distinctive and unusual.	☐ WOW! ☐ Very Strong ☐ Strong ☐ O.K. ☐ Not very good
I was interested throughout the entire book.	☐ WOW! ☐ Very Strong ☐ Strong ☐ O.K. ☐ Not very good
The notes in the back added to my enjoyment of the book.	☐ WOW! ☐ Very Strong ☐ Strong ☐ O.K. ☐ Not very good
I was satisfied when I finished the book.	☐ WOW! ☐ Very Strong ☐ Strong ☐ O.K. ☐ Not very good

From *MORE Science Adventures with Children's Literature: Reading Comprehension and Inquiry-Based Science* by Anthony D. Fredericks. Westport, CT: Teacher Ideas Press. Copyright © 2008.

JUST IMAGINE!

Just imagine if you were the size of one of the animals in this book. How would your life be different? What would you be able to do that you can't do now? What wouldn't you be able to do that you can do now?

Select any two animals from this book (one large, one small). Write a brief paragraph (for each one) on how your life would be different if you were the size of that animal. Think about how your (new) size would affect how you played, how you ate, what you did in school, or how your parents or friends would treat you. Please remember that there are no right or wrong answers.

1. If I was a _____

I would be able to _____

_____

_____

_____

_____

_____

_____

2. If I was a _____

I would be able to _____

_____

_____

_____

_____

_____

_____

 From *MORE Science Adventures with Children's Literature: Reading Comprehension and Inquiry-Based Science* by Anthony D. Fredericks. Westport, CT: Teacher Ideas Press. Copyright © 2008.

Under One Rock: Bugs, Slugs and Other Ughs

Anthony D. Fredericks

Nevada City, CA: Dawn Publications, 2001

SELECTED CITATIONS

- **2002 Ecology and Nature Award**—*Skipping Stones Magazine*

- **2003 Teacher's Choice Award**—*Learning Magazine*

SUMMARY

In this creatively illustrated book, readers make some amazing discoveries about an ecosystem right in their own back yard. They'll journey with a youngster as he lifts up a single rock to find an amazing collection of creatures that take up residence on and in the ground. Using a rhythmic verse, this book introduces youngsters to some delightful inhabitants of this community of critters. ("This is the spider with her eight-eyed face/Who builds a home in this cool dark place.")

SUGGESTED GRADE LEVELS: 1–4

LESSON OBJECTIVES

Science Standards

- Content Standard A: Science as Inquiry

    Abilities necessary to do science inquiry (K–4, 5–8)

    Understandings about science inquiry (K–4, 5–8)

- Content Standard C: Life Science

   The characteristics of organisms (K–4)

   Organisms and environments (K–4)

   Populations and ecosystems (5–8)

   Diversity and adaptations of organisms (5–8)

- Content Standard F: Science in Personal and Social Perspectives

   Characteristics and changes in populations (K–4)

- Content Standard G: History and Nature of Science

   Science as a human endeavor (K–4, 5–8)

CRITICAL THINKING QUESTIONS

1. Which of the creatures was most amazing?

2. How did the illustrations help you learn about the animals in this book?

3. Which of the animals would you like to learn more about?

4. How are so many different animals able to live together in one place?

5. What other animals do you think could be found under a single rock?

6. If you could tell the author one thing, what would you like to say?

COMPREHENSION LESSON (CONCEPT CARDS)

Setting the Stage

Invite students to share what they know about insects and bugs. Where did they get their information? How accurate is their information? What uncertainties do they have about the topic?

Duplicate the Concept Cards on sheets of card stock (65 paper). Cut the cards apart into four to six sets of 25 cards each. Place each set of cards inside a zipper-closing sandwich bag.

Before Reading

Divide the class into four to six small groups. Provide each group with a set of Concept Cards. Invite each group to arrange the cards into several categories. Inform students that there are no right or wrong answers for this activity. There is no set numbers of categories nor is there a set number of words within a category. That is entirely up to each individual group. After allowing sufficient time, invite each group to describe its various categories and some of the words those students placed in each category (there are often significant differences).

During Reading

After students have arranged their cards into categories and shared the words in each category, invite them to read the book. Encourage students to look for the words they saw on the Concept Cards.

After Reading

Invite students to return to their Concept Cards and rearrange them according to information learned in the book. What new categories do they need to create? What words need to be shifted from one category to another? Are there any new words that could be added to a category? Plan time for students to discuss the changes they made.

LITERATURE EXTENSIONS

Invite students to select one or more of the following activities:

1. Invite students to each choose an animal from the book to study. Students can pretend that they are writing a newspaper birth announcement for the birth of their animals. They will need to do some research to collect necessary information. Provide the birth announcement section of daily newspapers for students to use as a reference for writing their articles. Decorate a bulletin board to look like a section of a newspaper, and hang the animal birth announcements there. Students can include illustrations of the new "babies."

2. As a class, brainstorm about what Earth would be like if there were no insects. For example, imagine no more mosquito bites or bee stings, no more honey, no more flowers, no more butterflies, and so on. Invite students to list the positive and negative effects of insects on the chalkboard. They can also write and illustrate stories about the planet with no insects.

3. Invite students in the class to each select one of the animals illustrated in the book. Encourage each child to conduct necessary library research on his or her identified species. Then, invite each student to write a series of diary entries told from the perspective of the creature, for example, "A Day in the Life of a Slug" or "My Life as an Ant."

4. Ask youngsters to keep a journal of the activities, habits, travels, and motions of a single animal. Kids may want to select a house pet or some other animal that can be observed quite regularly throughout the day. Provide youngsters with a "Field Journal," a simple notebook that wildlife biologists frequently use to track the activities of one or more wild animals over the course of an extended period of time.

5. Invite students to select a rock near the school. Encourage them to take photographs of the rock throughout the year and maintain a diary or journal of the events or changes that take place around the rock. Who comes to visit the rock (animals)? What does the rock look like when it rains, snows, or is sunny outside? Periodically, talk with students about any changes in the surrounding environment and how those changes may be similar to or different from some of the events in the story.

6. Talk with students about some of the "Fantastic Facts" included in the back of this book. Which ones did they find most amazing? Why did the author include those facts?

7. Invite children to make a large chart (on an oversized piece of poster board, for example) listing the speeds at which selected animals (from the book or in your neighborhood) travel. The chart can rank order animals from the fastest to the slowest or vice versa. Be sure to encourage kids to add additional animals with which they are very familiar (dogs, cats, guinea pigs, etc.). How much faster are their pets than the slowest animal on the chart? What is the fastest animal found in *Under One Rock*?

8. Ask students to keep a logbook of the numbers of selected bugs located in a specific area (a room in their houses, a section of the classroom, a plot of land in their back-yards). Encourage students to record numbers of bugs observed during a designated part of each day (from 3:30 to 4:00 P.M., for example) over a selected period of time (one week, for example). Invite students to create a chart or graph that records those numbers and that can be displayed.

9. People in this country live in a wide variety of houses or dwellings—so do animals. Invite youngsters to create a chart and investigate the wide variety of homes and dwellings used by animals. They may wish to use some of the following examples and add to the list through their library readings:

   nest   burrow
   cave   tunnel
   branch   ledge

   Invite students to discuss the similarities between human dwellings and animal homes. What are some of the things that determine where an animal lives? Are those conditions or features similar to the considerations of humans in selecting a living site? Invite youngsters to create a chart of animal homes and examples of the animals that might live in or on those spaces. Do animals have more options for living spaces than humans do?

10. Ask students to each select one of the critters mentioned in the book. Ask each child to demonstrate the movement of that insect in a designated area. For example, for an earthworm, students can slither across the floor on their bellies; for a cricket, students can leap on their hands and knees. Provide opportunities for students to describe their movements and why they may be unique to the selected animal.

CONCEPT CARDS

insects	turtles	birds	lizards	creatures
village	earthworms	squiggly	soil	ground
ants	spider	beetle	crickets	millipede
slugs	critters	boy	lad	rock
crowd	neighbors	army	dirt	slime

From *MORE Science Adventures with Children's Literature: Reading Comprehension and Inquiry-Based Science* by Anthony D. Fredericks. Westport, CT: Teacher Ideas Press. Copyright © 2008.

WORD WISE

Seven primary animals were featured in the book *Under One Rock*. Each of the animals was described using specific adjectives. For each of the animals in the column on the left side of this chart you will note two specific adjectives. After conducting some additional research (library, Internet, classroom encyclopedia, etc.), you are invited to add two more adjectives that could be used to describe each creature.

Afterward, insert five more animals in the blank spaces in the left-hand column. For each animal that you include, locate four specific adjectives that could be used to describe that creature.

ANIMAL	ADJECTIVE	ADJECTIVE	ADJECTIVE	ADJECTIVE
Earthworms	squiggly	round		
Ants	tiny	diggers		
Spiders	eight-eyed	busy		
Beetles	shiny	black		
Field Crickets	singers	leapers		
Millipedes	many feet	sensitive		
Slugs	slimy	creepers		

From *MORE Science Adventures with Children's Literature: Reading Comprehension and Inquiry-Based Science* by Anthony D. Fredericks. Westport, CT: Teacher Ideas Press. Copyright © 2008.

WONDER WORMS

Worms are some of the most surprising creatures on earth. This activity will help you make some fascinating discoveries about these creatures.

Materials:

- large, wide-mouthed jar
- tin can
- gravel or small pebbles
- soil
- 5 or 6 earthworms (also known as nightcrawlers), from your garden, the bait shop, or a local pet store
- dark construction paper

Directions:

1. Stand the can in the middle of the glass jar.
2. Place a layer of gravel or small pebbles about ½ inch deep on the bottom of the jar, between the can and the jar sides.
3. Fill the jar with garden soil up to the height of the tin can.
4. Place the worms on top of the soil.
5. Wrap the dark construction paper around the outside of the jar to keep out the light. (Check the condition of the soil every so often and moisten it as needed.)

Description:

The worms will begin burrowing into the soil. After several days, they will have dug a series of tunnels. You will be able to see these tunnels by carefully removing the construction paper from the sides of the jar. (Replace the construction paper after observing their work so the worms will continue to tunnel in the darkness.) You should be able to watch the worms' behavior without harming them, for three or four weeks, but then you should put them back outside.

Worms feed by taking soil through their bodies, creating tunnels as they go. These tunnels aerate the soil, providing plants with the oxygen they need to grow. If it weren't for earthworms, many varieties of plants would not be able to survive.

From *MORE Science Adventures with Children's Literature: Reading Comprehension and Inquiry-Based Science* by Anthony D. Fredericks. Westport, CT: Teacher Ideas Press. Copyright © 2008.

OBSERVATION RING

Here's an interesting activity that you can do any time and any place.

Materials:

- 4 sharpened pencils
- string
- magnifying lens

Directions:

1. Go outside and select a section of grassy area (part of a yard, lawn, or playground).
2. Push four sharpened pencils into the soil in a one-foot square pattern.
3. Tie string around the pencils, making a miniature "boxing ring" on the ground.
4. Get on your hands and knees and look closely inside the square.

Description:

If you look carefully enough and long enough, you'll begin to see many different critters. You may want to keep some "Field Notes" of all the different types of animals you see inside the ring. Note the movements, habits, or behaviors of any animals (ants, grasshoppers, caterpillars, worms) as they travel (jump, crawl, slither) through the ring. You might want to visit your "ring" frequently over a period of several weeks.

From *MORE Science Adventures with Children's Literature: Reading Comprehension and Inquiry-Based Science* by Anthony D. Fredericks. Westport, CT: Teacher Ideas Press. Copyright © 2008.

Hurricanes

Seymour Simon

New York: Collins, 2007

SELECTED CITATIONS

- "Pairing a simply phrased narrative with arresting, eye-catching color photos, Simon explains what hurricanes are and imparts a vivid sense of their destructive potential." —*Booklist*

- "The full-color photos, including a satellite image of a storm and scenes of devastation, are not only spectacular, but also informative. The writing is precise and accurate and the format is appealing. A natural selection for any library."—*School Library Journal*

SUMMARY

This book will take readers on an incredible journey inside the science of hurricanes and inside the hurricanes themselves. Known by many names—hurricanes, typhoons, cyclones, "willy willies"—these formidable and devastating storms are one of nature's most destructive natural disasters. Dramatic accounts of Hurricane Andrew and Hurricane Katrina supplement the awe-inspiring text. Full-color photographs and satellite images bring the wonder of hurricanes to life. This is a book that will be re-read many times.

SUGGESTED GRADE LEVELS: 3–5

LESSON OBJECTIVES

Science Standards

- Content Standard B: Physical Science

    Position and motion of objects (K–4)

    Motions and forces (5–8)

    Transfer of energy (5–8)

- Content Standard D: Earth and Space Science

    Changes in Earth and sky (K–4)

- Content Standard E: Science and Technology

    Abilities of technological design (K–4, 5–8)

    Understanding about science and technology (K–4, 5–8)

- Content Standard F: Science in Personal and Social Perspectives

    Natural hazards (5–8)

    Risks and benefits (5–8)

CRITICAL THINKING QUESTIONS

1. What was the most amazing photograph in this book?

2. What scares you the most about a hurricane?

3. Why are hurricanes so destructive?

4. What are some things you would do if a hurricane was approaching?

5. How do you think people dealt with hurricanes a hundred years ago?

COMPREHENSION LESSON (POSSIBLE SENTENCES)

Setting the Stage

Pass out copies of the book, one for each student (or show the class the book as part of a read-aloud). Invite students to look at the cover illustration and the title. What can they infer from these two items? Does the photograph give any information about the contents of the book? Take a few moments to discuss students' perceptions.

Before Reading

Engage students in a Possible Sentences strategy. Provide them with copies of the Possible Sentences project page. Before students read the book, invite them to select two words from the list and use them in a complete sentence. Tell them that the sentence should be one that they think might appear in the book. Invite students to repeat this sentence construction (using other words from the list) two to three additional times. After students have created their sentences, take time to discuss the sentences and how they might relate to the plot of the book.

During Reading

Remind students to watch for the words from the project page (which were selected from the book) as they read (or as they listen to the book being read aloud).

After Reading

Invite students to revisit their Possible Sentences. What changes do they need to make to those sentences? Can they write some new sentences using those words? How did their original ideas about the book change after reading the book? What would be some appropriate sentences to share with others who have not read the book?

LITERATURE EXTENSIONS

Invite students to select one or more of the following activities:

1. When a hurricane is predicted for a specific area of the country (e.g., the Gulf Coast, Florida, the Eastern Seaboard), have students track the "history" of the storm. They may wish to consult the daily newspaper, a weekly newsmagazine, television or radio broadcasts, or firsthand accounts from meteorologists or weather forecasters. They can collect the "life story" of a hurricane into an album or PowerPoint™ presentation.

2. As a class, students may wish to create a weather dictionary containing all the "hurricane words" they have learned from this book, other books, Web sites, or other library materials. They may wish to complement the definitions with their own illustrations or with pictures from magazines and/or newspapers.

3. Before reading *Hurricanes*, invite students to discuss what they would do if a hurricane were to strike their part of the country (if applicable) or if they were caught in a hurricane while on vacation. Ask students to focus on personal emotions (scared, frightened, challenged) and on how a hurricane would affect their families (flooded house, belongings ruined, temporary housing). After reading the book, revisit the earlier conversation and invite students to discuss any change(s) in their perceptions or attitudes about the short- or long-term effects of a hurricane on family life.

4. The author includes information on the wind speeds of the five categories of hurricanes. Ask students to post these speeds on the bulletin board. Encourage them to locate the speeds of other objects (car, train, cheetah, blue whale, jet plane, etc.) and post

their fastest speeds on the bulletin board, too. Ask students to rank order (from low to high) the relative speeds of various categories of hurricanes in concert with the speeds of the other items.

5. Invite students to log on to the following Web site: http://www.hurricanehunters.com/. At this site, teachers and students can pose questions to the people known as "hurricane hunters"—individuals who fly over and into developing hurricanes. Once students are familiar with this site, encourage them to develop a short list of potential questions to pose to the hurricane hunters. What criteria will they use to determine the best questions? Which of the questions is most critical to their understanding of hurricanes?

6. Invite a representative of the local chapter of the American Red Cross to visit your classroom. Ask the individual to share emergency preparedness procedures and information about rescue operations that the Red Cross uses in hurricanes. The person may wish to recount the efforts of the Red Cross during a recent hurricane.

7. Ask students to create a chart similar to the one below. Over the course of a hurricane season, they can record and graph various aspects of all the hurricanes for any respective year.

Name	Atlantic/Pacific	Landfall	Highest Wind Speed	Duration

8. A hurricane watch is issued when a hurricane may strike within 36 hours. A hurricane warning is issued if a hurricane is likely to strike within the next 24 hours. Take time to discuss with students the difference between these two terms. Ask students to form two separate lists, one of the preparations that people should make when a hurricane watch is in effect and the other of what people should do when a hurricane warning is issued. Students may obtain the necessary information for these two lists from the National Hurricane Center (www.nhc.noaa.gov) as well as from other hurricane-related sources.

9. Invite students to log on to the National Hurricane Center's Web site (www.nhc.noaa.gov). The NHC issues watches, warnings, and forecasts on tropical events in both the Atlantic and Pacific regions. Included on the site are the latest forecasts, storm names, historical storm data, and more. During hurricane season, invite students to track the progression of selected storms across the ocean. They can transfer data from this site to a large wall map for daily viewing.

POSSIBLE SENTENCES

The words below are from the book *Hurricanes* by Seymour Simon. Use two of these words to create a sentence you think could be part of the book. Keep in mind that you are making a prediction (also known as an "educated guess") about a possible sentence. After you have created one sentence (using two words from the list) try to create two or three additional sentences (using two words from the list for each additional possible sentence).

storm	destruction
spinning	Atlantic
ocean	clouds
forecast	surge
killed	energy
category	tornadoes
flooding	evacuation

Sentences:

1. _____

   _____.

2. _____

   _____.

3. _____

   _____.

4. _____

   _____.

TOP TEN HURRICANES

The *South Florida Sun Sentinel* Web site (http://www.sun-sentinel.com/news/weather/hurricane/sfl-hc-canehistory1,0,3352010.special) includes various time lines of the "greatest" hurricanes in history, from the time of Christopher Columbus to the present. Log on to the site and read the various sections. The sections are as follows:

Hurricane Timeline: 1495–1800

Hurricane Timeline: The 1800s

Hurricane Timeline: 1900–1950

Hurricane Timeline: 1950–1990

Hurricane Timeline: 1990–2000

After viewing the various lists, select the "Top Ten" hurricanes of all time. You can select the hurricanes for your list based on one of the following criteria:

- amount of damage
- lives lost
- wind speed
- area destroyed
- dollar amount of damage
- category

Top Ten

1.

2.

3.

4.

5.

6.

7.

8.

9.

10.

 From *MORE Science Adventures with Children's Literature: Reading Comprehension and Inquiry-Based Science* by Anthony D. Fredericks. Westport, CT: Teacher Ideas Press. Copyright © 2008.

BLOW HARD

Here's an interesting activity: Create a chart of the number of hurricanes that have struck the United States for each month of the hurricane season (June to November in the northern Atlantic) for the past ten years.

For example, the following chart lists the number of hurricanes that struck the United States during the period from 1900 to 1994:

Month	Number of U.S. Hurricanes
June	12
July	16
August	40
September	61
October	23
November	6

Using resources in your school or public library as well as Web sites, complete the chart below:

Month	Number of U.S. Hurricanes in the Last Ten Years
June	
July	
August	
September	
October	
November	

Why does September seem to be "hurricane month?"

What factors or conditions seem to "produce" more hurricanes in September than in any other month?

From *MORE Science Adventures with Children's Literature: Reading Comprehension and Inquiry-Based Science* by Anthony D. Fredericks. Westport, CT: Teacher Ideas Press. Copyright © 2008.

SURVIVOR LETTER

Imagine that you know someone who has just gone through a hurricane. In the space below, write an imaginary letter to your friend. What would you want to say to your friend? How could you comfort that individual? What could you say that would help that person feel better?

Dear _____:

_____

_____

_____

_____

_____

_____

_____

_____

_____

_____

_____

_____

_____

Sincerely,

_____

From *MORE Science Adventures with Children's Literature: Reading Comprehension and Inquiry-Based Science* by Anthony D. Fredericks. Westport, CT: Teacher Ideas Press. Copyright © 2008.

Rocks in His Head

Carol Otis Hurst

New York: Greenwillow, 2001

SELECTED CITATIONS

- **2002 Outstanding Science Trade Book**—Children's Book Council/National Science Teachers Association

- **2001 Nonfiction Honor Book**—*Boston Globe-Horn Book*

SUMMARY

This is a touching story that truly brings science to life and life to science. It's a story about the author's father and his lifelong passion for collecting rocks—of every size, shape, and dimension. Through good times and bad, he would gather rocks wherever he could find them, carefully catalog them, and share them with friends and family. Eventually a science museum decided that a man "with rocks in his head" would be the perfect individual to curate its geological exhibits. This book would be an ideal read-aloud in advance of any earth science unit.

SUGGESTED GRADE LEVELS: 2–4

LESSON OBJECTIVES

Science Standards

- Content Standard A: Science as Inquiry

    Abilities necessary to do science inquiry (K–4, 5–8)

    Understandings about science inquiry (K–4, 5–8)

- Content Standard D: Earth and Space Science

    Properties of Earth materials (K–4)

- Content Standard G: History and Nature of Science

    Science as a human endeavor (K–4, 5–8)

CRITICAL THINKING QUESTIONS

1. How is the author's father similar to anyone else that you know?

2. What did you enjoy most about the author's father?

3. Why do you think he spent his whole life collecting rocks?

4. Why do people enjoy rocks so much?

5. What is the most unusual rock you have ever seen?

COMPREHENSION LESSON (STORY MAP)

Setting the Stage

Ask students to discuss a hobby or an activity that they engage in on a regular basis. Provide opportunities for them to share those events as well as their feelings about the events. Why do they participate in selected events? What pleasure do they derive from those events?

Before Reading

Provide students with copies of the Story Map. Inform them that they will be completing this form after they have finished reading (or listening to) the book. Take a few minutes to go over the elements of the map with students.

During Reading

Invite students to read (or listen to) the book. Ask them to focus in on the necessary information that will be used to complete the Story Maps.

After Reading

Upon completion of the book, ask students to fill in the appropriate information on the Story Maps. Students may wish to complete these on an individual basis or in pairs. Take time afterward for students to share their maps. What similarities are there between maps? What differences are there? It is not essential that students all arrive at the same conclusions, but rather that they have adequate opportunities to talk about their perceptions and conclusions.

LITERATURE EXTENSIONS

Invite students to select one or more of the following activities:

1. Ask students to create a "Rock Dictionary" of terminology and phrases that are associated with rocks or geology. Students may wish to create a page for each letter of the alphabet. For example, A = All over the ground; B = Basalt; C = Carbon; D = Dirt.

2. Invite students to write their own personal newspaper articles about favorite rocks or minerals. Afterward, encourage students to assemble the articles into a classroom newspaper, newsletter, or PowerPoint presentation. Make plans to distribute the final piece to other classes.

3. Encourage students to work in small groups and research other books about rocks. Each group may wish to contact the school librarian or the children's librarian at your local public library. Each group may prepare a brief summary on its findings and present the discoveries to the rest of the class.

4. Invite a geologist from the local college or university to visit your classroom. Ask the visitor to share geological samples or a collection of rocks and minerals that might be found in the local area. Invite students to generate a series of questions for the visitor.

5. Students may wish to take a mini field trip around the school to collect as many different samples of rocks as they can find. When a sufficient quantity of different rocks have been gathered, invite students to construct a "Rock Museum" in the classroom. Sample rocks can be placed inside empty shoeboxes, each with an appropriate label and description. The shoeboxes can be decorated similarly to what might be found in a museum. Be sure to invite other classes to visit the "Museum."

6. Invite students to create a readers theatre production (see Part III of this book) that focuses on one of the following: a day in the life of a geologist, a single rock, the story of how a single rock was created, or a most incredible discovery. Provide an opportunity for students to present their script to another class.

7. Just for fun, ask students to put together an oversized poster or collage of various phrases, colloquialisms, or sayings that involve the word "rock" (or its derivations). Examples: "Rock on," "You really rock me," "Do you have rocks in your head?," "Rock and Roll," and "Like a rock."

8. Invite students to each write a fictitious letter to the author of this book asking for more information about her father. What else did he do besides collect rocks? Where did he travel? What are some of the places he lived? What kinds of books did he enjoy reading? Where did he go to school?

9. Ask students to write a sequel to the story that focuses on what happened to the father after he got the job as curator of mineralogy. What were some of the things he did in his new job? What did he learn? What were some of the challenges he faced?

10. Invite students to check the Web sites of several colleges and universities that offer degrees in geology. What are some of the courses that students must take to become a geologist? What are some of the challenges they face? What types of jobs can someone with a geology degree get?

STORY MAP

Title: *Rocks in His Head* by Carol Otis Hurst

Setting:

```
┌──────────────────────────────────────────────────────┐
│                                                      │
│                                                      │
│                                                      │
│                                                      │
└──────────────────────────────────────────────────────┘
```

Characters:

_____

_____

_____

Problem:

```
┌──────────────────────────────────────────────────────┐
│                                                      │
│                                                      │
│                                                      │
│                                                      │
└──────────────────────────────────────────────────────┘
```

Event 1: _____

Event 2: _____

Event 3: _____

Event 4: _____

Solution:

```
┌──────────────────────────────────────────────────────┐
│                                                      │
│                                                      │
│                                                      │
│                                                      │
└──────────────────────────────────────────────────────┘
```

From *MORE Science Adventures with Children's Literature: Reading Comprehension and Inquiry-Based Science* by Anthony D. Fredericks. Westport, CT: Teacher Ideas Press. Copyright © 2008.

CRACKING UP

Here's a neat experiment that demonstrates a powerful force that breaks large boulders into small rocks, pebbles, and even sand!

Materials:

- pieces of sandstone (from your local hardware store or building supply store)
- sealable plastic freezer bags
- water

Directions:

1. Soak pieces of sandstone in water overnight.

2. The next day, place several pieces of the wet sandstone in plastic freezer bags and seal them tightly.

3. Place the bags in the freezer overnight.

4. The next day, take them out and examine them.

Description:

You will notice that the sandstone has cracked into several pieces. That's because when water freezes, it expands. The sandstone absorbs some of the water, taking it up into the air spaces between the sand particles. When the stone was placed in the freezer, the water in it froze and expanded.

In nature, water seeps into the cracks of rocks, freezes in winter, and causes the rocks to break apart. After a while (thousands of years), the rocks are reduced to very small pebbles and eventually to sand.

From *MORE Science Adventures with Children's Literature: Reading Comprehension and Inquiry-Based Science* by Anthony D. Fredericks. Westport, CT: Teacher Ideas Press. Copyright © 2008.

ROCK ON!

Locate a rock somewhere on the school grounds, in your neighborhood, or around your house. Bring it in to school and observe it for a while. Afterward, create a brochure that "advertises" your rock. Try to get others interested in your particular rock. This is an opportunity to let your creativity "go wild." Here are a few suggestions you may wish to include in your advertisement (it's not necessary to include all of them):

1. Three reasons why people would be interested in your rock.

2. A catchy slogan that will grab the attention of anyone passing by your rock.

3. A map showing the location of your rock.

4. An "endorsement" from a famous movie star or recording artist.

5. A drawing or photograph of your rock.

6. The life story of your rock—its "birth," events that happened during its "life," places it's been.

7. The future of your rock—what will happen to it in the years to come?

8. The benefits of owning this particular rock.

From *MORE Science Adventures with Children's Literature: Reading Comprehension and Inquiry-Based Science* by Anthony D. Fredericks. Westport, CT: Teacher Ideas Press. Copyright © 2008.

WHAT DO YOU DO?

Interview an adult about her or his hobby or free time activity. You may wish to consider some of the questions below. Also, think about other questions you can ask the individual to learn more about what she or he does.

What is your hobby? _____

How long have you been doing it? _____

What skills are needed for this hobby? _____

_____

What interesting things have you learned? _____

_____

How many other people participate in this hobby? _____

What do you enjoy most? _____

_____

What do you find most challenging? _____

_____

How much time can you devote to your hobby each week? _____

What do you need to do to get better at your hobby? _____

_____

What suggestions can you offer me to get into this hobby? _____

_____

_____

From *MORE Science Adventures with Children's Literature: Reading Comprehension and Inquiry-Based Science* by Anthony D. Fredericks. Westport, CT: Teacher Ideas Press. Copyright © 2008.

Song of the Water Boatman and Other Pond Poems

Joyce Sidman

Boston: Houghton Mifflin, 2005

SELECTED CITATIONS

- **2006 Caldecott Honor Book**—American Library Association

- **2006 Outstanding Science Trade Book**—Children's Book Council/National Science Teachers Association

SUMMARY

This is a wonderful collection of poems about life in the pond—from the first days of spring to the chilly signals of winter. Painted turtles, peepers, diving beetles, ducks, and dragonflies all inhabit this fascinating ecosystem that pulsates with life. The poetry is fresh, engaging, and always inviting. This is a delightful book to add to any unit on ecosystems, environments, or the web of life.

SUGGESTED GRADE LEVELS: 2–5

LESSON OBJECTIVES

Science Standards

- Content Standard C: Life Science

    Life cycles of organisms

Organisms and environments

Diversity and adaptations of organisms

CRITICAL THINKING QUESTIONS

1. Which of the animals would you like to learn more about?

2. What would you like to discover in a visit to a pond?

3. How are all the animals able to live together?

4. What other pond animals could have been included in this book?

5. What did you learn from the illustrations in this book?

COMPREHENSION LESSON (PICTURE PERFECT)

Setting the Stage

Invite students to briefly discuss some of the things they would discover if they visited a pond. What types of plants would be growing there? What types of animals would be living there?

Before Reading

Use a piece of paper to cover over the words on the cover of this book. Then create a transparency of the cover illustration. Project the transparency for the entire class. Then divide the class into several groups. Ask each group to generate three to five questions about the illustration and record them on the Picture Perfect project page. Afterward, ask each group to exchange its list of questions with another group. Then invite each group to write a story that has answers to the other group's questions embedded in the story (one member of each group records the story that is contributed by all the other members of the group). After allowing sufficient time, invite the groups to share their completed stories with each other.

During Reading

Invite students to read the book (or to listen to it as part of a read-aloud session). Ask them to pay attention to the details, facts, and information shared in each of the poems as well as the data presented in the expository sidebars.

After Reading

Invite each of the groups to return to its original "Picture Perfect" story and edit it in light of the information gathered from the book. What changes will the groups need to make in a second or third draft?

LITERATURE EXTENSIONS

Invite students to select one or more of the following activities:

1. Invite students to compare the illustrations in this book with photographs in nonfiction books about ponds or wetlands ecosystems. What similarities do they notice? What were some of the things the artist had to consider in drawing the pictures for this book?

2. Ask students to write and assemble a collection of their poetry about a local ecosystem. Using the poems in *Song of the Water Boatman* as examples, invite students to create their own book about a field, puddle, tree, yard, lake, stream, or some other nearby ecosystem. Be sure the finished product is appropriately displayed in the classroom or library.

3. Provide students with an assortment of magazines that contain pictures of pond creatures (e.g., *National Geographic, Ranger Rick, National Wildlife*). Encourage students to bring in some old magazines from home, too. Invite students to make a large class collage of a pond ecosystem by pasting pictures of various creatures and plants on a large sheet of newsprint. The completed sheet can be hung along one wall of the classroom.

4. Invite students to create posters or advertisements to attract other students to this book. What information or illustrations should be included? Students may wish to hang their creations throughout the school or in the school library.

5. Ask students to research and gather some examples of nature art (remind them that this book was a 2006 Caldecott Honor Book). If possible, show students a selection of paintings that represent things in nature. Work with the school art teacher to obtain books of prints containing artwork created by nature artists (e.g., Frederic Church, Claude Monet). Are there any artists or paintings that would be representative of a pond ecosystem?

6. Invite students to brainstorm what a pond ecosystem would be like if there were no creatures living in it. For example, imagine no more water boatmen, no more dragonflies, no more ducks, no more painted turtles. Invite students to discuss the implications of a creature-less pond.

7. Cut off the fingers of several pairs of inexpensive work gloves. Invite students to use a variety of art materials (crayons, yarn, felt-tip markers, sequins, etc.) to turn each "finger" into a puppet representing one of the creatures in the book. Students can then use these puppets as part of one or more finger plays during a retelling of one or more of the poems.

8. Invite students to create charts and graphs that record the number of species of each of the animals described in the book. Which species has the greatest number of members around the world? Which has the smallest number of members? Based on the number alone, which species has the greatest likelihood of being placed on an "endangered species" list?

9. Ask students to research other poetry books about nature. Ask them to each collect three nature poems from those resources. Students may wish to assemble the collection of poems into a "Pond Poetry Book" or PowerPoint presentation. Or, invite students to share their poems each day in a read-aloud.

10. Invite students to create a large wall chart divided into several sections: Mammals, Birds, Fish, Amphibians, Reptiles, and Insects. Ask them to place each of the creatures featured in the book in its appropriate category on the chart. Then ask students to select other animals that might be discovered in a pond ecosystem and add them to the chart as well. Take time to discuss the various species found in a "typical" pond. Which species or classification seems to predominate?

PICTURE PERFECT

Write three to five questions about the illustration:

1.

2.

3.

4.

5.

Write a story that contains answers to the questions above:

| |
| |
| |
| |
| |
| |
| |
| |
| |
| |
| |
| |

POLLUTION PROBLEM

Pollution can be very dangerous for a pond. Here's an activity that will demonstrate that process.

Materials:

- 4 small jars, without lids
- tape
- felt-tip marker
- water
- pond soil
- pond water with scum (algae)
- liquid plant fertilizer
- liquid detergent
- motor oil (use vegetable oil as a substitute)
- vinegar

Directions:

1. Leave the water out in a container for three to four days to let any chlorine dissipate.
2. When the water has "aged," label the four jars A, B, C, and D.
3. Prepare the jars as follows: fill each jar halfway with the aged water, put in a ½-inch layer of pond soil, add 1 teaspoon of liquid plant fertilizer, then fill the jar the rest of the way with pond water.
4. Allow the jars to sit in a sunny location for two weeks.
5. Next, treat the jars as follows: to jar A add 2 tablespoons of liquid detergent; to jar B add enough drops of motor oil or vegetable oil to cover the surface; to jar C all ½ cup of vinegar; and leave jar D as it is.
6. Allow the jars to sit for at least four weeks.

Description:

With the addition of the detergent, motor oil, and vinegar to the first three jars, the healthy growth that took place in the jars during the first two weeks of the experiment has severely changed. In fact, those jars now probably show little or no growth taking place, while the organisms in jar D continue to grow.

Detergent, motor oil, and vinegar are pollutants that prevent organisms from obtaining the nutrients and oxygen they need to grow. The jar with the detergent shows what happens when large quantities of soap are released into a pond; the one with the motor oil shows what happens to organisms after an oil spill; and the jar with the vinegar shows what can happen when high levels of acids are added to a pond ecosystem.

From *MORE Science Adventures with Children's Literature: Reading Comprehension and Inquiry-Based Science* by Anthony D. Fredericks. Westport, CT: Teacher Ideas Press. Copyright © 2008.

LIKE AND UNLIKE

What are the similarities when you compare a pond with other aquatic ecosystems? In each box below, write three similarities (you may need to consult other books or some Web sites.)

Pond + Ocean

```



```

Pond + Swamp

```



```

Pond + River

```



```

Pond + Swimming Pool

```



```

From *MORE Science Adventures with Children's Literature: Reading Comprehension and Inquiry-Based Science* by Anthony D. Fredericks. Westport, CT: Teacher Ideas Press. Copyright © 2008.

POND POEM

Use the diagram below to help you create your own "pond poem." Write one word on each blank line. The first line has five blanks, the second line has four blanks, and so on. You may want to read some of the poems in *Song of the Water Boatman* to help you get ideas. Remember, your poem doesn't have to rhyme—it can include thoughts, feelings, words, and any ideas you care to use. There is no right or wrong way to build your "pond poem."

_____ _____ _____ _____ _____

_____ _____ _____ _____

_____ _____ _____

_____ _____

_____

From *MORE Science Adventures with Children's Literature: Reading Comprehension and Inquiry-Based Science* by Anthony D. Fredericks. Westport, CT: Teacher Ideas Press. Copyright © 2008.

Parts

Tedd Arnold

New York: Puffin Books, 2000

SELECTED CITATIONS

- **2000 Pennsylvania Young Reader's Choice Award Masterlist**

- "Trying to make sense of one's 'parts' is a common childhood concern, and [the author's] comical hyperbole will set children at ease about fears they might hesitate to share."—*Publishers Weekly*

SUMMARY

This book will have students rolling in the aisles with laughter. It is a genuinely funny book that looks at our body parts through the innocent eyes of a young child. With a delightful rhyming pattern and an infectious dose of creativity, this is a read-aloud that will beg to be told over and over again. Be sure to get the follow-up books in the series so that students get a "well-rounded" perspective on the humor evident in their own bodies.

SUGGESTED GRADE LEVELS: 1–4

LESSON OBJECTIVES

Science Standards

- Content Standard A: Science as Inquiry

    Abilities necessary to do science inquiry (K–4, 5–8)

- Content Standard C: Life Science

    The characteristics of organisms (K–4)

    Structure and function in living systems (5–8)

- Content Standard F: Science in Personal and Social Perspectives

    Personal health (K–4, 5–8)

- Content Standard G: History and Nature of Science

    Science as a human endeavor (K–4, 5–8)

CRITICAL THINKING QUESTIONS

1. Do you think that the style of writing the author used in the book helped to make the story more effective?

2. What events that the main character went through in the story can you relate to?

3. If you were a parent, how would you explain that the various things that are happening to your child's body are normal?

4. What was the funniest part of *Parts*?

5. Has something funny happened to your body in the last year? If so, what was it?

COMPREHENSION LESSON (WHAT IF)

Setting the Stage

Before distributing copies of the book to students (or reading it aloud to the class), share the title and the cover illustration. Invite students to make predictions about the story. What will it be about? Who will be in it? How will it turn out?

Before Reading

Engage students in a What If activity. Ask students to imagine that their bodies are falling apart. What parts would they be losing? What would be happening? What would they notice? Stir the pot a little by providing students with a copy of the What If project page and invite them to respond to the questions (in writing or orally).

During Reading

Provide a copy of the book for each student. Ask students to read the book silently on their own (or it can be used as a class read-aloud).

After Reading

Encourage students to talk about the humor in this book. What does the author/illustrator do to make this a funny book? How do the illustrations contribute to the humor? Did anything happen that you didn't expect? You may want to follow the reading by asking students some of the same questions you did in the "Before Reading" stage. Invite students to share reasons for any changes in their responses.

LITERATURE EXTENSIONS

Invite students to select one or more of the following activities:

1. Ask students to write additional pages to the story, using the same figurative language that Arnold used. These additional pages can include other things that students have noticed that change on people throughout their lives. Have students create illustrations to go along with their additional pages.

2. Encourage students to study the specific body parts that the main character notices throughout the story. Afterward, invite students to assemble their information into appropriate pamphlets, brochures, or booklets for display in the classroom or library.

3. Encourage students to create a time line of normal things that will change and happen to their bodies throughout their lives. They may wish to interview the school nurse or their family doctors to collect the necessary information.

4. Give students a picture of an outline of a body. Ask them to label and circle the different parts that the main character noticed throughout the story.

5. Inform students that the human tongue has four different types of taste buds (sour, bitter, salty, and sweet). Students can "map out" portions of their tongues as follows: Obtain several cotton swabs and ask students to dip each swab into the following solutions and then touch those swabs to various portions of their tongues:

   – lemon juice (sour)

   – salt water (salty)

   – sugar water or corn syrup (sweet)

   – tonic water (bitter)

   Students may wish to draw an oversized illustration of a human tongue and "plot" the location of the four major types of taste buds.

6. Push a wooden kitchen match into a small piece of modeling clay. Flatten the bottom of the clay. Lay your wrist, palm side up, on a table. Place the clay on your wrist near to the thumb side. The match will begin vibrating with your heartbeat (you may need to adjust the location of the clay or match). Invite students to count your heartbeat in beats per minute. Repeat this activity with students and invite them to calculate their own heartbeats. Afterward, invite them to participate in some form of physical activity (jumping jacks for one minute) and then repeat the activity. What did they notice?

7. Invite students to read all the books in this series. Ask them to evaluate each in terms of the "funny factor." Which was the funniest? Which made them laugh the most? Students may wish to rank order the books in terms of the "funny factor."

8. Students may obtain some props for a retelling of the story, for example cotton for belly button stuffing, marbles for eyeballs, string for pieces of hair, or tablet-type gum for teeth. Retell the story and invite students to act it out using the selected props.

9. Invite students to survey other students in the school, asking them to identify the most important part of the human body. Gather the information together and ask students to create one or more charts or graphs that summarize and record the results of their survey. Before sending them out to do the survey, you may want to ask them "What do you think most people would say is the most important body part?"

WHAT IF

Respond to each of the following "What If" questions. Keep in mind that there are no right or wrong responses to these questions—anything is possible.

What if all your hair fell out one day?

What if your insides started to ooze out of your belly button?

What if your skin suddenly started to peel off your body?

What if your brain started to leak out of your nose?

What if all your teeth fell out all at once?

What if your arm fell off while throwing a ball?

What if you lost your head? (no, really)

From *MORE Science Adventures with Children's Literature: Reading Comprehension and Inquiry-Based Science* by Anthony D. Fredericks. Westport, CT: Teacher Ideas Press. Copyright © 2008.

BODY PERFECT

The human body has lots of interesting parts. Many of those parts also have some very interesting measurements. Here are some of the most interesting body measurements you're likely to find. Please keep in mind that most of these measurements apply to adults, rather than kids, simply because your body is still growing and developing. You may wish to "test" these measurements on adult family members—parents, relatives, neighbors, etc.

- A person's height should equal about 6 to 7.5 times the length of his or her head (from the chin to the top of the head).

- For most adults, the distance from fingertip to fingertip (with arms outstretched side to side) is roughly equal to one's height.

- The distance around a closed fist (over the knuckles) and the length of a foot (from end of heel to end of big toe) is approximately equal.

- The distance from the shoulder to the elbow and the elbow to the wrist is about equal.

- The bottom of one's ears line up with the base of his or her nose.

- The width of an adult's mouth (from corner to corner) is the same as the distance between the middle of one eyeball and the middle of the other eyeball.

- The length of a human hand (including the wrist) is approximately equal to the height of the person's head.

- A person's eyebrows are on the same level as the tops of his or her ears.

- The eyes are in the middle of the head—halfway between the top of the head and the tip of the chin.

- The width of the mouth (from corner to corner) is the same as the distance between the middle of one eyeball and the middle of the other eyeball.

- The width of the nose (at its base) is the same as the width of an eye.

 From *MORE Science Adventures with Children's Literature: Reading Comprehension and Inquiry-Based Science* by Anthony D. Fredericks. Westport, CT: Teacher Ideas Press. Copyright © 2008.

ANCIENT MEASUREMENTS

- In ancient Rome, the width of a man's thumb was called an *uncia* (the English word "inch" comes from this word). The width of an average man's thumb (across the cuticle) is one inch.

- Twelve *uncia* equaled a foot, which was about the same length as a man's foot.

- Three feet equaled a yard. A yard was defined as the distance from the end of a man's nose to the tip of the middle finger of his outstretched arm (you can quickly see that measurements in ancient times were not as accurate as they are today).

- The *cubit* was the length of a man's arm from his elbow to the tip of his middle finger. Today, the *cubit* is defined as 18 inches long.

Complete the chart below using one or more adults in your family. You may wish to select several different adult members of your family for comparison purposes.

	Actual	Child	Adult Female	Adult Male
Uncia	1 inch			
Foot	12 inches			
Cubit	18 inches			
Yard	36 inches			

From *MORE Science Adventures with Children's Literature: Reading Comprehension and Inquiry-Based Science* by Anthony D. Fredericks. Westport, CT: Teacher Ideas Press. Copyright © 2008.

MY PARTS

Listed below are the body parts that the character in *Parts* was worried about. For each one, list something that has happened to you regarding a specific part. For example, for "teeth" you might mention when you lost your first tooth.

Hair:

Belly Button:

Skin:

Nose:

Teeth:

Ears:

Eyes:

Arm:

Head:

 From *MORE Science Adventures with Children's Literature: Reading Comprehension and Inquiry-Based Science* by Anthony D. Fredericks. Westport, CT: Teacher Ideas Press. Copyright © 2008.

W Is for Wind: A Weather Alphabet

Pat Michaels

Chelsea, MI: Sleeping Bear Press, 2005

SELECTED CITATIONS

- **2007 Teachers' Choice Award**—*Learning Magazine*

- "[The illustrator] does an excellent job capturing the audience's attention with her detailed, realistic paintings that often include children experiencing the various conditions. A useful and attractive addition."—*School Library Journal*

SUMMARY

This creative book illustrates and describes 26 facts about the weather. Filled with fascinating information and engaging descriptions, it assures readers of a complete and thorough introduction to meteorology. Each letter of the alphabet (H is for Hurricane; V is for Vapor) includes a short poem (for younger readers) in addition to a brief section of exposition (for older readers). This book is an ideal resource tool for any youngster interested in the "how's" and "why's" of weather.

SUGGESTED GRADE LEVELS: 3–6

LESSON OBJECTIVES

Science Standards

- Content Standard A: Science as Inquiry

    Understandings about science inquiry (K–4, 5–8)

- Content Standard B: Physical Science

    Position and motion of objects (K–4)

    Motions and forces (5–8)

- Content Standard D: Earth and Space Science

    Changes in Earth and sky (K–4)

- Content Standard E: Science and Technology

    Abilities of technological design (K–4, 5–8)

CRITICAL THINKING QUESTIONS

1. What fascinates you the most about the weather?

2. What was the most interesting fact you learned in this book?

3. Why do so many people enjoy the field of meteorology?

4. How many forms of weather (described in the book) have you seen or experienced?

5. What is one weather-related question that was not answered in the book?

COMPREHENSION LESSON (REFLECTIVE SHARING)

Setting the Stage

Show students the illustration on the cover of the book. Invite them to make some predictions about the information they will learn in this book.

Before Reading

Inform students that you will involve them in a comprehension strategy known as Reflective Sharing. In the middle of a chalkboard, write the word "weather." Invite students to brainstorm as many ideas, concepts, or items that could be included within that topic as they can in three to five minutes. Ask students to each select one of the brainstormed items from the list on the board, then write about her or his selected item for about five minutes. Arrange the students into groups of four and assign each person a role (Person 1, Reader; Person 2, Summarizer; Person 3, Teller; Person 4, Liker). Invite students to repeat the process of sharing (according to the chart on the project page) until they have gone through all four rounds.

During Reading

Ask students to read the book independently. You may wish to have them read three or four sections each day over a period of several days.

After Reading

After students have finished the book, invite them to discuss some of their favorite parts. Which "letters" were most informative? Which "letters" had the most interesting information? Was there any weather-related information that was excluded from this book? What did students learn that they didn't know before?

LITERATURE EXTENSIONS

Invite students to select one or more of the following activities:

1. Use a nail to dig out a hole in the center of a cork. Fill a bottle all the way to the brim with colored water and push the cork into the neck of the bottle. Push a straw halfway into the hole in the center of the cork. Pack some modeling clay around the straw to seal any potential leaks. Mark a line on the straw (with a felt-tip pen) where the water line is. Set the bottle outside in the shade. Note the temperature on a regular thermometer and mark that on a narrow strip of paper glued next to the straw. Take measurements over several days, noting the temperature on a regular thermometer and marking that at the spot where the water rises in the straw on the strip of paper. After several readings, students will have a fairly accurate homemade thermometer. (Note: Liquids expand when heated [water rises in the straw] and contract when cooled [water lowers in the straw]).

2. Invite a local TV meteorologist to visit your classroom or library. Ask the visitor to talk about her or his job, the instruments or tools used, the challenges faced, and the education and training necessary for the job. Brief your students beforehand so they can generate appropriate questions for the guest.

3. Ask students to gather newspaper or magazine articles about weather or bring in information from daily weather forecasts from local newspapers, television news shows, or the Internet. Articles can be filed in appropriate folders and shared in a "Weather News" area. Encourage students to examine all the clippings and compile a list comparing and contrasting the various forecasts.

4. Designate a "Weatherperson of the Day" to forecast the next day's weather. Invite that student to write her or his prediction on a card and post it on the bulletin board or the class's Web page. Be sure to talk about current weather conditions and how they might affect the weather the following day.

5. Invite students to make weather word cutouts. Begin by cutting out shapes of clouds, the sun, raindrops, and snowflakes. On each shape, write one or more appropriate weather-related words. Display the weather words on a bulletin board and add new cutout words as they are learned.

6. Students may wish to create a supplemental weather-related alphabet book. For example, the author used the word "atmosphere" for the letter "A." What other weather words could be used with the letter "A?" You may wish to divide students into small

groups and invite each group to develop alternate lists of weather words for a selection of letters (e.g., A–F, G–L, etc.)

7. Students may enjoy making their own rain. You will need a large glass jar, very hot tap water, 10 to 12 ice cubes, a foil pie pan, and a flashlight. Fill the jar halfway with very hot tap water. Fill the pie pan with ice cubes. Put it on top of the jar. Turn out the lights. Shine a flashlight into the jar. Have students note what happens inside the jar. After completing the demonstration, students can research and write about what happened and why.

8. Invite students to each imagine that she or he is a particular form of weather (a raindrop, a gust of wind, a snowflake, etc.). Encourage students to write about the imaginary life cycle of that item from its perspective (e.g., "My life as a hailstone" or "Round and Round: My Life as a Hurricane"). What are some of the things it observes? What distances are traveled? How long is its "life span"?

9. Obtain a copy of *USA Today*. Show students the color weather map on the back of the first section. Invite students to note the various designations used to record weather information. Encourage students to read through the weather section and note the predictions for their area of the country. Invite students to create a special weather map similar to the *USA Today* map, but specifically tailored to their geographic region (as opposed to the entire country).

REFLECTIVE SHARING

You will be participating in a reading comprehension strategy known as Reflective Sharing. Before you read the book *W Is for Wind,* you will be divided into small groups of four students each. Each student in the group will write a story about some aspect of the weather. Then, in your group you will have an opportunity to share your story with the other members of that group. You will also have opportunities to react to the stories shared by the other members of the group.

Here's how it works:

Role	Round 1	Round 2	Round 3	Round 4
Reader Reads (to the entire group) what he or she wrote.	Person 1 (Reader)	Person 2 (Summarizer)	Person 3 (Teller)	Person 4 (Liker)
Summarizer Summarizes what the Reader read to the group.	Person 2 (Summarizer)	Person 3 (Teller)	Person 4 (Liker)	Person 1 (Reader)
Teller Tells the Reader what he or she liked about what was read.	Person 3 (Teller)	Person 4 (Liker)	Person 1 (Reader)	Person 2 (Summarizer)
Liker Tells the Reader something else he or she would like to know about the topic.	Person 4 (Liker)	Person 1 (Reader)	Person 2 (Summarizer)	Person 3 (Teller)

From *MORE Science Adventures with Children's Literature: Reading Comprehension and Inquiry-Based Science* by Anthony D. Fredericks. Westport, CT: Teacher Ideas Press. Copyright © 2008.

WEATHER SAYINGS

Over the centuries people have always tried to predict the weather. As a result, there is much folklore and numerous sayings about the weather—particularly about the approach of specific kinds of weather.

Here are a few of those sayings. For each one, write a brief explanation of what it means. You may need to consult other books and/or Web sites.

Red sky at morning, sailor take warning. Red sky at night, sailor's delight.

Explanation: _____

_____

A January fog will freeze a hog.

Explanation: _____

_____

When smoke descends, good weather ends.

Explanation: _____

_____

Ring around the sun, time for fun; ring around the moon, storm coming soon.

Explanation: _____

_____

Which of these is true? Which of these is false?

From *MORE Science Adventures with Children's Literature: Reading Comprehension and Inquiry-Based Science* by Anthony D. Fredericks. Westport, CT: Teacher Ideas Press. Copyright © 2008.

FOLKLORE

Because ancient people did not always understand the weather, they had many beliefs about the conditions or situations that cause weather patterns. Here are a few beliefs that people have had through the ages:

- Sea fog was once thought to be the breath of an underwater monster.
- In Germany, some people believed that a cat washes itself just before a rain shower.
- The Aztecs believed that the sun god could be kept strong and bright only through human sacrifices.
- The Norse peoples thought that weather was created by the god Thor, who raced across the sky in a chariot pulled by two giant goats.

Consult other books on weather as well as some Web sites. What other beliefs, superstitions, or folklore can you discover that could be added to the list above? What were some of the other weather beliefs of ancient cultures, civilizations, and individuals?

- _____
  _____

- _____
  _____

- _____
  _____

- _____
  _____

- _____
  _____

- _____
  _____

From *MORE Science Adventures with Children's Literature: Reading Comprehension and Inquiry-Based Science* by Anthony D. Fredericks. Westport, CT: Teacher Ideas Press. Copyright © 2008.

WEIRD WEATHER

Many strange and out-of-the-ordinary weather events have occurred over the years. Some of these are unexplainable, while others have scientific explanations. For each event listed below, try to discover how and why it happened. Check the many resources in your school and public library.

On October 14, 1755, red snow fell on the Alps.

Explanation:

In June 1940, a shower of silver coins fell on the town of Gorky, Russia.

Explanation:

On June 16, 1939, it rained frogs at Trowbridge, England.

Explanation:

In 1917 a tornado in Connecticut picked up a jar of pickles and dropped it, unbroken, in a ditch 25 miles away.

Explanation:

From *MORE Science Adventures with Children's Literature: Reading Comprehension and Inquiry-Based Science* by Anthony D. Fredericks. Westport, CT: Teacher Ideas Press. Copyright © 2008.

Antarctic Journal: Four Months at the Bottom of the World

Jennifer Owings Dewey

Honesdale, PA: Boyds Mills Press, 2001

SELECTED CITATIONS

- **2002 Outstanding Science Trade Book**—Children's Book Council/National Science Teachers Association

- "A great deal of fascinating information is included in the text, which flows easily from fact bites to narrative."—*School Library Journal*

SUMMARY

With sketchbook in hand, the author/illustrator traveled to one of the most barren and most desolate places in the world—Antarctica. Here she spent four months observing the wildlife, experiencing the elements, and sailing past building-sized icebergs. In a series of letters home to her family she described this incredible wilderness and the equally incredible adventures she had almost every day. This book is a delightful exploration of a land few will visit, but all will admire.

SUGGESTED GRADE LEVELS: 3–6

LESSON OBJECTIVES

Science Standards

- Content Standard A: Science as Inquiry

    Abilities necessary to do science inquiry (K–4, 5–8)

    Understandings about science inquiry (K–4, 5–8)

- Content Standard D: Earth and Space Science

    Properties of Earth materials (K–4)

    Structure of the Earth system (5–8)

- Content Standard E: Science and Technology

    Understanding about science and technology (K–4, 5–8)

- Content Standard G: History and nature of science

    Science as a human endeavor (K–4, 5–8)

CRITICAL THINKING QUESTIONS

1. What did you enjoy most about this book?

2. Based on the author's adventure, would you like to visit Antarctica?

3. Which of the animals was most interesting to you?

4. Why do scientists spend so much time and money studying Antarctica?

5. If you could ask the author one question, what would it be?

COMPREHENSION LESSON (STORY IMPRESSIONS)

Setting the Stage

Make enough copies of the project page for Story Impressions for all students in the class. You may also wish to provide students with an opportunity to discuss some of the background information they have about Antarctica. Some of this information can be listed on the chalkboard.

Before Reading

Present the sheet to individuals or small groups of students. Tell students that the list represents important concepts from the book *Antarctic Journal*. Invite students to read through the list (top to bottom) and encourage them to discuss how the ideas might be related or connect.

Ask students to construct a story using all of the printed concepts (in the order in which they are listed). This can be done as an individual story or a story crafted and written by a small group of students. Make sure students understand that they are making predictions about the plot of the story based simply on a few of the facts from that story.

During Reading

Provide students with individual copies of the book (or use it as a read-aloud) and invite them to read it silently.

After Reading

After completing a reading of the book, offer students an opportunity to discuss how their original story and the actual story in the book compare. The object is *not* to have an exact match, but rather to see how a basic set of ideas can be interpreted differently by two separate "authors."

LITERATURE EXTENSIONS

Invite students to select one or more of the following activities:

1. If possible, obtain a copy of the DVD entitled *March of the Penguins* (2005). Show this movie (or parts of the movie) to students. Afterward, invite students to create an oversized poster of a penguin and post it on one wall of the classroom or library. Ask students to record various facts and information about penguins inside the borders of the penguin illustration.

2. As a variation of the activity above, invite students to create a large illustration of the continent of Antarctica. Post this on a wall of the classroom or library. Encourage students to collect factual information about Antarctica (they may wish to begin with the data on pages 16–17 of the book) and write that information across the illustration. New facts can be added periodically.

3. Encourage students to create a large Venn diagram that compares Antarctica with the United States (or any other country). What are some of the similarities? What are some of the differences? Are there more similarities, or are there more differences?

4. Invite students to talk about how Palmer Station might be similar to or different from the town in which they live. What do they have in their town that they wouldn't find at Palmer Station (e.g., a movie theater, a car wash, a grocery store)? What would Palmer Station have that they wouldn't find in their town (e.g., science labs, permanent ice cover, penguins)?

5. Ask students to select favorite scenes or illustrations from the book. Invite them to create dioramas of their selections. They may wish to create original drawings and use clay, construction paper, pipe cleaners, and wire to construct three-dimensional objects to be placed in the diorama. The dioramas may be displayed in the classroom or school library.

6. Provide students with opportunities to act out selected pages or chapters of the book. Divide a large group of students into several smaller groups. Ask each group to select a chapter or an event described in the book. Invite a narrator to read the events as they happen as each group mimes the appropriate actions.

7. Invite students to consult various weather information sources (e.g., http://www.wunderground.com/). Ask them to record the daily weather in Antarctica over a period of two to three weeks. They can record the temperature, wind conditions, thickness of

the ice pack, cloud cover, and other factors. Students may wish to create a chart that records daily weather conditions in Antarctica and daily weather conditions in their home town. What differences do they note?

8. Provide students with several library resources on continents. Ask them to make a list of the elements or features of a continent. Based on their listing, does Antarctica constitute a continent? You may invite students to form two debate groups—one that argues that Antarctica is a continent; the other that Antarctica is not a continent. Be sure students are able to substantiate their positions with relevant data.

9. For up-to-the-minute information about Antarctica, students may log on to www.antarcticconnection.com. You may wish to divide students into various "teams" and invite each to put together an informational packet about a certain aspect of the "continent at the bottom of the world." The packets could deal with wildlife, climate, history, scientific explorations, famous explorers, the South Pole, or other topics. Students may wish to assemble their information into a PowerPoint presentation for another class.

STORY IMPRESSIONS

Several selected ideas and concepts from the book *Antarctic Journal: Four Months at the Bottom of the World* are listed on the left-hand side of this sheet. Read through this list and imagine how a story with these concepts might be constructed. Then begin to write a story using all the concepts from top to bottom. Remember, your story may be different from the actual one—that's OK. We'll discuss any differences and similarities when we finish reading the book.

	Your Story:
↓ **Depart from home**	
The ship heaves	
↓ **At Palmer Station**	
Alone on Litchfield Island	
↓ **Penguins care for chicks**	
Orcas in the water	
↓ **A raging storm**	
Fell in a crack	
↓ **Christmas in Antarctica**	
Towers of ice	
↓ **Iceberg rolling**	
Lemon-yellow sky	
↓ **Headed home**	

From *MORE Science Adventures with Children's Literature: Reading Comprehension and Inquiry-Based Science* by Anthony D. Fredericks. Westport, CT: Teacher Ideas Press. Copyright © 2008.

LETTERS HOME

Imagine that you are a resident of Palmer Station. Write an imaginary letter back home to your parents and family members about some of your adventures. What do you see every day? What kind of weather conditions do you experience? What are some of the various animals you encounter regularly?

Dear _____:

_____

_____

_____

_____

_____

_____

_____

_____

_____

_____

_____

_____

_____

_____.

Sincerely,

_____

From *MORE Science Adventures with Children's Literature: Reading Comprehension and Inquiry-Based Science* by Anthony D. Fredericks. Westport, CT: Teacher Ideas Press. Copyright © 2008.

A FROZEN ADVENTURE

Imagine that you are a travel agent. You have been invited to prepare some travel plans for a group of people who wish to visit Antarctica. They would like to do one of the following:

- A trip to the South Pole
- A three-day trip across Weddell Sea.
- An all-day trip to Litchfield Island
- A snowmobile trip across the Ross Ice Shelf
- A visit to Cormorant Island

Using the book *Antarctic Journal* and any other reference material, plan an itinerary for the group: form of transportation, time frame, sights to see, food to eat, lodging, etc.

BY THE NUMBERS

Of the 17 species of penguins in the world, only four breed on the Antarctic continent—the *Adelie*, the *Emperor*, the *Chinstrap*, and the *Gentoo*. Using library resources and appropriate Web sites plot the population of each species on the chart below. Which species has the most individuals? Which of the four species of Antarctic penguin has the fewest number of individuals?

Number (in millions)	
15	
14	
13	
12	
11	
10	
9	
8	
7	
6	
5	
4	
3	
2	
1	
.5	

Adelie   **Emperor**   **Chinstrap**   **Gentoo**

From *MORE Science Adventures with Children's Literature: Reading Comprehension and Inquiry-Based Science* by Anthony D. Fredericks. Westport, CT: Teacher Ideas Press. Copyright © 2008.

The Tarantula Scientist

Sy Montgomery

Boston: Houghton Mifflin, 2004

SELECTED CITATIONS

- **2005 Outstanding Science Trade Book**—Children's Book Council/National Science Teachers Association

- "Informative, yes, but even more important, this is a vivid look at an enthusiastic scientist energetically and happily at work, both in the field and in the lab, questioning, examining, testing, and making connections."—*School Library Journal*

SUMMARY

This book, filled with incredible photographs, will dazzle, amaze, and delight any young scientist or scientist-to-be. Readers follow tarantula scientist Sam Marshall as he slogs his way through the rain forests of French Guiana looking for these elusive critters. Fascinating details and captivating explanations will keep readers on the edge of their seats as they examine the lives, anatomy, and characteristics of an animal surrounded by misinformation and fear. The scientific process is well documented in this book, along with lots of surprises and revelations. This is a book not to be missed!

SUGGESTED GRADE LEVELS: 4–6

LESSON OBJECTIVES

Science Standards

- Content Standard A: Science as Inquiry

   Abilities necessary to do science inquiry (K–4, 5–8)

   Understandings about science inquiry (K–4, 5–8)

- Content Standard C: Life Science

   The characteristics of organisms (K–4)

   Life cycles of organisms (K–4)

   Populations and ecosystems (5–8)

   Diversity and adaptations of organisms (5–8)

- Content Standard G: History and Nature of Science

   Science as a human endeavor (K–4, 5–8)

CRITICAL THINKING QUESTIONS

1. Prior to reading this book, what were some of your thoughts or feelings about tarantulas?

2. Would you enjoy doing the work of Sam Marshall?

3. What features about tarantulas would make them good pets?

4. What was the single most amazing thing you learned about these creatures?

5. What subjects would you need to study to be a tarantula scientist?

COMPREHENSION LESSON (QUICK WRITE)

Setting the Stage

Before inviting students to read an expository or nonfiction book, show them the cover of this book. Point out the illustration or photograph on the cover along with the book's title.

Before Reading

After viewing the book's cover, ask students to write (in paragraph form) everything they know about the topic of the book. After a few minutes, ask students to revisit their respective paragraphs, inviting them to think of some questions about the topics generated by that paragraph. This step may be done in small groups or on an individual basis. Invite them to record their questions on separate sheets of paper.

Provide students with the titles of the chapters in the book, asking students to mark which questions on their respective lists they think will be answered in the book. Students may wish to assign a chapter number to a respective question on their sheet. Provide opportunities for students to share their questions and their predictions.

During Reading

Invite students to read the book silently and to look for answers to their questions, if possible.

After Reading

After the reading, students may use any unanswered questions to stimulate group discussion or for independent research projects.

LITERATURE EXTENSIONS

Invite students to select one or more of the following activities:

1. Invite students to each write an imaginary letter to Sam Marshall. What would they like to know about his life? What else would they like to know about his life's work—tarantulas? What do they enjoy most about the work that he does? If they could travel with him on one expedition, what would they like to learn? If they would like to eventually become tarantula scientists themselves, what should they study in school? Take time for students to share their respective letters with each other.

2. As a modification of the activity above, invite some students to write imaginary letters to the real stars of the book—tarantulas. If possible, what would they like to say to a tarantula? What is it about a tarantula's life that they appreciate? What amazes them about tarantulas? What did they learn that they didn't know before? What do they think about this scientist who is spending his whole life studying them? Do they have any secrets that he hasn't learned yet? Why should people know more about tarantulas? Again, allow time for students to share their missives.

3. If possible (and practical), invite a representative from a local pet store to visit your classroom and bring along one or two tarantulas for "show and tell." Before the visit, encourage students to generate an appropriate list of questions from reading the book. What new information can they learn from the visitor that was not included in the book?

4. Tarantulas can be found in many different countries. Post an oversized map of the world on one wall of the classroom or library. Invite students to conduct some library or Internet research on the various tarantula species. Ask them to record information on individual index cards and affix those cards to the world map. Ask students to thread a length of yarn (using thumbtacks) from each card to a country on the map in which a species lives. (Note: One card may have several lines, depending in the number of countries in which it lives.)

5. Invite students to conduct some Internet or library research on endangered species of tarantulas. Why are some species more endangered than others? What can humans do to protect tarantulas from endangerment? Why should tarantulas be protected in the first place?

6. Ask students to survey other students, friends, relatives, and family members on their perceptions about tarantulas. Do most people have a favorable impression about tarantulas? Do most have a negative perception of tarantulas? Students may wish to investigate why many people seem to have negative reactions to tarantulas. What are some of the leading causes? Can students conclude that lack of knowledge and insufficient information is a leading cause of negative reactions to tarantulas?

7. Just for fun, invite selected students to create a "Wanted" poster for a tarantula. Bring in sample "Wanted" posters from your local post office (or take photographs of them) and share them with your students. Then ask students what critical information about a tarantula should be included on their "Wanted" poster. This poster creation can be fun, but it should also have a purpose—that is, protecting tarantulas in the wild, saving endangered species, and educating the public about these fascinating creatures.

8. The tarantula has generated many myths and superstitions over the years. Invite students to create some posters or other appropriate displays depicting some of these beliefs (whether they are true or not). They can survey people in their neighborhood or check out information on the Web. What are some of the most persistent superstitions or myths? Why have these beliefs persisted over the years?

9. Students may also wish to extend the activity above by looking into beliefs and superstitions about other animals in nature. What are some of the other animals about which myths and superstitions have been generated? How did some of those beliefs come to be? Why do they still persist?

10. Here are a few Web sites that students may wish to check out for additional information about tarantulas:

> http://www.nationalgeographic.com/tarantulas/index2.html
> http://www.desertusa.com/july96/du_taran.html
> http://exoticpets.about.com/cs/tarantulas/a/tarantulasaspet.htm
> http://www.birdspiders.com/main.html
> http://www.extremescience.com/BiggestSpider.htm

QUICK-WRITE

Look at the cover of the book *The Tarantula Scientist*. Write (in paragraph form) everything you know about tarantulas:

_____

_____

_____

_____

_____

_____

_____

_____

_____

_____

_____

Based on your paragraph above, what are some questions you have about tarantulas?

1.

2.

3.

4.

5.

6.

From *MORE Science Adventures with Children's Literature: Reading Comprehension and Inquiry-Based Science* by Anthony D. Fredericks. Westport, CT: Teacher Ideas Press. Copyright © 2008.

QUICK-WRITE (CONTINUED)

Following are the titles of the chapters and chapter sections in the book *The Tarantula Scientist*. Circle the questions on your list above that you think will be answered in these chapters (write the chapter number after each question). Remember that you are only making predictions, so there are no right or wrong responses.

1. Queen of the Jungle

   When Is a Tarantula a Tarantula?

2. Science and Spiders

3. Secrets of the Burrow

   Arachnids All Around

4. Expedition to Les Grottes

   Got Silk?

5. Hairy Mats and Hissing Fits

6. Tarantula Frontiers

7. "Elle Est Belle, le Monstre"

After completing the book, what are some of your unanswered questions (from your list above)?

A. _____

B. _____

C. _____

D. _____

From *MORE Science Adventures with Children's Literature: Reading Comprehension and Inquiry-Based Science* by Anthony D. Fredericks. Westport, CT: Teacher Ideas Press. Copyright © 2008.

SPIDER MAN

You may wish to "capture" your own spider web—here's how:

Materials:

- transparent self-adhesive plastic (e.g., clear Contac™ paper)
- dark-colored construction paper
- masking tape
- aerosol hair spray

Directions:

1. Go outside with the hair spray, masking tape, and construction paper.
2. Locate a spider web.
3. Make five rings of masking tape and slip them over the fingers of one hand.
4. Press the construction paper to your hand so that it sticks to the rings of the masking tape (this allows you to hold the construction paper vertically so that it doesn't fall).
5. Carefully hold the construction paper just behind a spider web.
6. With your other hand (or a friend can assist), gently spray the web with the hairspray from the other side (this will cause the web to stick to the construction paper).
7. Carefully remove the web and it will stick to the face of the construction paper.

Description:

When you return to the classroom, you can place a sheet of the transparent self-adhesive plastic over the web (or laminate it) and seal it (this will preserve the spider web). You can then use this web as the cover for a notebook or journal about all discoveries in a "Spiders and Insects" unit in science.

You may wish to collect several different examples of spider webs from around the school or neighborhood. A scrapbook of different webs can be put together.

NOTE: This activity takes some practice, so don't get discouraged if you can't do it the first time.

From *MORE Science Adventures with Children's Literature: Reading Comprehension and Inquiry-Based Science* by Anthony D. Fredericks. Westport, CT: Teacher Ideas Press. Copyright © 2008.

FACT BY FACT

Select five random facts from the book *The Tarantula Scientist.* Write each on one of the "Fact" lines below. Then check off the appropriate boxes after each fact. Remember, these are your opinions—there are no right or wrong ways to respond. After you have completed this sheet, take some time to discuss your views with other students in the class.

1. Fact: _____

  ☐ I didn't know this before I began reading the book.
  ☐ This is really interesting.
  ☐ This is fresh and original.
  ☐ This is relevant to the theme of the book.

2. Fact: _____

  ☐ I didn't know this before I began reading the book.
  ☐ This is really interesting.
  ☐ This is fresh and original.
  ☐ This is relevant to the theme of the book.

3. Fact:_____

  ☐ I didn't know this before I began reading the book.
  ☐ This is really interesting.
  ☐ This is fresh and original.
  ☐ This is relevant to the theme of the book.

4. Fact: _____

  ☐ I didn't know this before I began reading the book.
  ☐ This is really interesting.
  ☐ This is fresh and original.
  ☐ This is relevant to the theme of the book.

5. Fact: _____

  ☐ I didn't know this before I began reading the book.
  ☐ This is really interesting.
  ☐ This is fresh and original.
  ☐ This is relevant to the theme of the book.

 From *MORE Science Adventures with Children's Literature: Reading Comprehension and Inquiry-Based Science* by Anthony D. Fredericks. Westport, CT: Teacher Ideas Press. Copyright © 2008.

THE SPIDER IN ME

Imagine that you are a tarantula. Write a short story describing yourself—particularly for those who have never seen a tarantula before. What are your features? What are your eating habits? Where do you live? Who are some of your enemies? What are some of the challenges you face every day?

You may wish to draw a picture of (a) your home, (b) you eating your dinner, (c) an approaching enemy, or (d) yourself.

_____

_____

_____

_____

_____

_____

_____

_____

_____

Outside and Inside Mummies

Sandra Markle

New York: Walker & Company, 2005

SELECTED CITATIONS

- **2006 Outstanding Science Trade Book**—Children's Book Council/National Science Teachers Association

- "What makes this book stand out are the actual scanned images of the mummies reproduced in the book. These give the reader a much clearer and more in-depth picture of what a mummy is and what can be learned from them about ancient cultures."—*Children's Literature*

SUMMARY

In this captivating and fascinating book, readers will get an "inside look" into mummies from around the world. Preservation techniques, ancient rites, and the scientific process are all detailed in this "can't put it down" book. The dynamic and mesmerizing text is complemented by awesome "inside" photographs. This is a book that will command the attention of even the most reluctant scientist in your classroom. Best of all, students can create their own mummy.

SUGGESTED GRADE LEVELS: 2–5

LESSON OBJECTIVES

Science Standards

• Content Standard A: Science as Inquiry

> Abilities necessary to do science inquiry (K–4, 5–8)
>
> Understandings about science inquiry (K–4, 5–8)

• Content Standard C: Life Science

> Structure and function in living systems (5–8)

• Content Standard E: Science and Technology

> Abilities of technological design (K–4, 5–8)

• Content Standard G: History and Nature of Science

> Science as a human endeavor (K–4, 5–8)
>
> History of science (5–8)

CRITICAL THINKING QUESTIONS

1. Which of the mummies did you find most interesting?

2. What would you enjoy most about being a mummy expert?

3. What are some things scientists are discovering about mummies?

4. How has this book inspired you to read more about mummies?

5. If you could ask a mummy one question, what would it be?

COMPREHENSION LESSON (MM & M)

NOTE: This is a *modeling strategy*—one in which you select a reading selection and begin to "think out loud" for students—verbalizing what is going on inside your head as you read. The verbalization process allows students to "see" what happens inside the head of accomplished readers. As such, this is a "passive" strategy—students observe rather than participate. Later, they will be able to replicate your thought processes with their own reading materials.

Setting the Stage

Show students the cover of the book *Outside and Inside Mummies*. Based on the title and cover photograph, make a prediction or two about the plot or theme of the book (as illustrated on the appropriate project page).

Before Reading

Talk about some of the mental images that are taking place inside your head as you consider the title and the cover photograph.

During Reading

Begin reading the book out loud to students. Stop at an appropriate place (a suggestion is provided on the project page) and show how the information in the book is related to something in your own background knowledge.

Continue reading and stop at another appropriate spot in the book to verbalize a confusing point (demonstrating how you keep track of your level of comprehension as you read). Verbalize a "fix-up" strategy—a way in which you "repair" any comprehension problems as you consider the information at that particular point in the reading.

After Reading

After completing the book and the modeling process, invite members of the class to duplicate the five stages of MM & M in other reading materials. You may need to model the five stages of MM & M several times so that students "see" how you think as you read in a variety of reading materials. After each modeling session, encourage students to replicate your actions in their own reading materials.

LITERATURE EXTENSIONS

Invite students to select one or more of the following activities:

1. Invite students to pretend that they are mummies. Encourage them to write "Life Stories" about the time in which they lived (before they became a mummy), some of the things they did, people they knew, or historical events that took place. Students may wish to post their stories alongside self-designed illustrations of themselves before they "died" as well as what they look like as a mummy.

2. Ask students to craft a quiz about the book. What questions would they want to ask to see if those taking the quiz truly understood the information in this book? Students may wish to assemble a written quiz to share with another class.

3. Invite students to create their own mummy using the directions listed on pages 36–37 of the book. How is this mummification process similar to the mummification process used by ancient Egyptians? How is it different? What did they learn as a result?

4. Invite a doctor or nurse to visit your classroom and discuss X-ray technology with students. She or he may wish to bring along some X-rays and discuss how they were taken and what they reveal. Plan time beforehand for students to generate an appropriate list of X-ray-related questions. They may also wish to generate some queries related to the information in *Outside and Inside Mummies*.

5. If possible, invite a local storyteller to visit your classroom or library. Names of individuals can be obtained through the local phone book, the children's librarian at a local public library, an independent bookstore in your area, or a local storytelling troupe. Ask if someone could share one or more stories from one of the areas mentioned in the book—North Africa, Europe, or South America. Students may be interested in learning about the origin of a particular story and its various renditions.

6. Just for fun, provide students with the yellow pages of your local phone book. Ask them to look at the various listings, the display ads, and the variety of goods and services offered. Then encourage students to create a special set of "yellow pages" especially for mummies; for example, listing skin care products, dentists, fashion designers, orthopedic surgeons, etc. How might some of the "businesses" advertise their services in the yellow pages? Students may wish to assemble their display ads into a scrapbook or some other published format to include with a copy of *Outside and Inside Mummies*.

7. Students may be interested in reading some of the other 'Outside and Inside" books by this author. What themes does she include in most of her stories? Are her books always about scientific topics? What do readers (and critics) enjoy most about her books?

8. Invite students to write journal entries about how their lives would be different if they lived in the time of the mummies. What would they miss most? What would be the greatest change? What would they have the greatest difficulty living without?

9. Ask students to assemble a listing of Web sites related to mummies. They may wish to create an attractive poster for display in the school library. Here are a few sites to get them started:

   http://www.site-ology.com/egypt/

   http://www.si.umich.edu/CHICO/mummy/

   http://www.nationalgeographic.com/inca/

   http://www.virtual-egypt.com/newhtml/mummies/

MM & M

NOTE: Since this is a teacher modeling strategy, the quotes indicated for each stage of MM&M below are suggestions only. Please feel free to develop your own comments as appropriate. Also, the "stopping points" indicated below are suggestions, too. You are welcome to select alternate "stopping points" in accordance with your own background knowledge as well as knowledge of the students in your class.

1. **Make Predictions** (Demonstrate the importance of making hypotheses.)

   "From the title, I predict that this book will be about all those old mummies in Egypt."

   "When I look at the photograph on the cover, I think that this will be a book about all that stuff that was found in the pyramids."

2. **Describe your mental images** (Show how mental pictures are formed in your head as you read.)

   "I can see a picture of lots of kings and other important people walking around the pyramids about 5,000 years ago."

   "I'm getting a picture in my mind of some attendants standing around a table with a dead person on it. They are spreading some ointments and jellies over the body to help preserve it."

3. **Share an analogy** (Show how the information in the text may be related to something in your background.)

   [after the first three pages] "This is similar to the time I had to go to the hospital with my son when he broke his arm and needed an X-ray."

   "This is like the time my doctor took an X-ray of my chest when I had to get a physical exam for my first teaching job."

4. **Verbalize a confusing point** (Show how you keep track of your level of comprehension as you read.)

   [after the first four pages] "I'm not sure why the scientists had to take the X-ray of the mummies while they were still in the pyramid. Couldn't they do it in the laboratory?"

5. **Demonstrate "fix-up" strategies** (Let students see how you repair any comprehension problems.)

   "Maybe that part is explained later in the book. Perhaps I need to read more of the book to find the answer to my question."

 From *MORE Science Adventures with Children's Literature: Reading Comprehension and Inquiry-Based Science* by Anthony D. Fredericks. Westport, CT: Teacher Ideas Press. Copyright © 2008.

I WONDER . . .

After you complete this sheet for the book *Outside and Inside Mummies* by Sandra Markle, take some time to discuss your reactions with other students.

1. I wonder why . . .

2. Why did . . .

3. I really liked . . .

4. I didn't understand . . .

5. I don't believe . . .

6. I was surprised . . .

7. I found myself thinking about . . .

8. When I finished the book, I thought . . .

9. I wish the author would . . .

10. I think . . .

AROUND THE WORLD

Mummies have been discovered in many countries around the world. In each of the boxes below, identify one country where mummies have been discovered and two interesting facts about the mummification process used in that country. For example, if you listed Egypt as one of the countries, you might write that during the mummification process in that country the brains were removed and replaced with pieces of cloth.

Country:	Mummification Facts: 1. 2.

Country:	Mummification Facts: 1. 2.

Country:	Mummification Facts: 1. 2.

Country:	Mummification facts: 1. 2.

 From *MORE Science Adventures with Children's Literature: Reading Comprehension and Inquiry-Based Science* by Anthony D. Fredericks. Westport, CT: Teacher Ideas Press. Copyright © 2008.

MUMMY QUESTIONS

Scattered around the illustration of the mummy below are eight lines. At the end of each line, write a mummy-related question that was answered in the book *Outside and Inside Mummies*. For example, you might write: "Did people in ancient Egypt have any diseases?" Write some other appropriate questions.

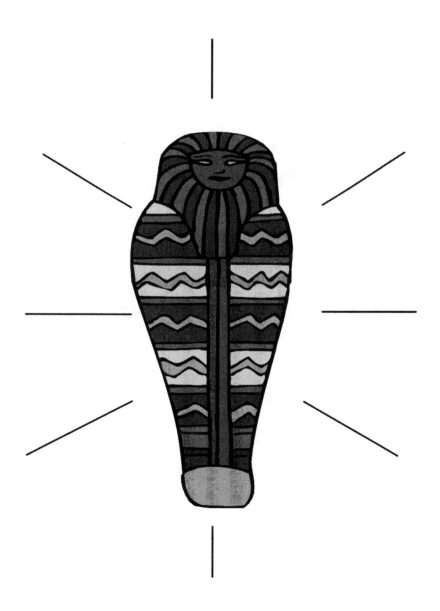

From *MORE Science Adventures with Children's Literature: Reading Comprehension and Inquiry-Based Science* by Anthony D. Fredericks. Westport, CT: Teacher Ideas Press. Copyright © 2008.

Over in the Jungle

Marianne Berkes

Nevada City, CA: Dawn Publications, 2007

SELECTED CITATIONS

- "This is a handsome book on an important subject, and it can serve as recreational reading as well as an introduction to a basic unit on the rain forest."—*School Library Journal*

- "If the fun rhythm and pictures were not enough, other back matter, including information about each animal mentioned, the rainforest in general, a finding game, and recommendations to encourage child participation both from the author and the artist, make this picture book an excellent teaching tool on many levels."—*Children's Literature*

SUMMARY

Here is a delightful story that is a treat for both the eyes and the ears. The author has crafted a tale about the animals of the rain forest—based on the tune 'Over in the Meadow"—that will have students laughing and learning about some amazing creatures. The rhymes in the book are supplemented with factual information, a sing-along section, movement activities, and notes on the incredible artwork (created from skillfully designed polymer clay by Jeanette Canyon). This book is a perfect introduction to life in the rain forest ecosystem and will be treasured for many years as a "staple" of any rain forest unit.

SUGGESTED GRADE LEVELS: 1–3

LESSON OBJECTIVES

Science Standards

• Content Standard C: Life Science

> The characteristics of organisms (K–4)
> Life cycles of organisms (K–4)
> Organisms and environments (K–4)

CRITICAL THINKING QUESTIONS

1. What did you find most enjoyable about this book?

2. What was the most amazing rain forest animal?

3. Which of the animals would you like to learn more about?

4. What did you enjoy about the artwork in this book?

5. How is the rain forest similar to or different from where you live?

COMPREHENSION LESSON (CHAPTER SLAM)

Setting the Stage

Invite students to list everything they know about the rain forest or a jungle. Students may wish to do this individually or in small groups.

Before Reading

Ask students to group all the items on their lists into various categories (students select the category titles or designations). After students have assigned a name to each group of items, ask them to arrange the categories as though they were a table of contents for a book. Again, this can be done on an individual basis or in small groups.

Invite students to write a "book" about the topics "The Rain Forest" or "The Jungle" using the categories (above) as chapter titles. Encourage students to write as much about each topic as they can, summarizing what each section is about. If students get stuck, allow them to make up what they don't know.

During Reading

Ask students to read the book (or to listen to a read-aloud). Encourage them to listen for specific information that may (or may not) be compatible with the pre-reading categories they selected earlier.

After Reading

After students have finished reading *Over in the Jungle,* invite them to write another "book" and compare it (orally) with the one generated at the beginning of the lesson. Students will undoubtedly discover that some of their previous perceptions about rain forests and the animals that live there have changed.

LITERATURE EXTENSIONS

Invite students to select one or more of the following activities:

1. This activity will illustrate how rapidly nutrients are depleted from rain forest soil. Add ¼ teaspoon of blue tempera paint (dry) to ½ cup of dry dirt and mix thoroughly. Place a coffee filter in a funnel and set the funnel in a large jar. Put the colored dirt into the filter in the funnel. Pour water into the funnel and note the color running into the jar. Keep adding water and note how quickly the color fades.

2. Encourage students to imagine that they are each one of the creatures in the book. Ask them to create posters that say "Save Our Home." They may wish to include full-color drawings of their creatures and write convincing ads for saving the rain forest.

3. As an extension of the activity above, invite students to assume the role of one of the creatures in the book. Encourage students to each write a "thank you" note to humans for their efforts in preserving the creature's environment.

4. Invite students to make a collage of all the animals listed in the book. They may wish to cut out photographs and illustrations from a collection of old magazines or environmental catalogs. The collages can be posted throughout the classroom, library, or school.

5. The rain forest is filled with an enormous variety of birds. Students may wish to create a series of bird feeders and compare the types of birds in their part of the country with the types of birds that inhabit the rain forest. Here are some simple feeders students can build:

    – Cut a half-circle from the plastic lid of a coffee can. Nail or tape a small board to the side of the can and put some birdseed inside. Put the lid back on, so that it covers the bottom half of the can, and lay the feeder outside.

    – Cut an orange in half. Scoop out the insides and make four small holes around the edge. Tie pieces of string to the holes around the orange half, fill it with birdseed. and hang it in a tree.

    – Tie a string to a pinecone. Fill the crevices in the cone with peanut butter and roll the cone in some birdseed. Hang the cone from a tree branch.

    – Tie a string to the stem of an apple. Roll the apple in some fat or bacon grease and then roll it in some birdseed. Hang it from a tree branch.

6. Divide the class in half. One half can be "predators" and the other half can be "prey." A "predator" is matched up with a "prey." Encourage the pair to construct a book or poster on the life of a rain forest predator trying to catch its prey and the prey's attempt at escape. Illustrations should also be added.

7. This book lends itself to a delightful readers theatre adaptation (see Part III of this book). Invite students to create a readers theatre script using the creatures in this book along with a narrator. They may wish to use the actual rhymes from the book or create their own original dialogue for the critters.

8. Several Internet sites are ideal for students seeking additional information about rain forests. Invite your students to check out some of the following:

    http://www.prekinders.com/rainforest_kids.htm

    http://www.kathimitchell.com/rainfor.html

    http://kids.mongabay.com/

    http://www.kiddyhouse.com/Rainforest/

    http://www.rainforest-alliance.org/programs/education/kids/index.html

9. Ask students to pretend that they are moving to a rain forest region somewhere in the world. Encourage them to write a postcard about their life in the rain forest to a family member who stayed behind.

CHAPTER SLAM

Make a list of all the words you know that would pertain to the rain forest:

_____ _____ _____ _____ _____

_____ _____ _____ _____ _____

_____ _____ _____ _____ _____

Now, organize those words into various categories. Create a name or title for each category.

Category 1 Name:
Words:

Category 2 Name:
Words:

Category 3 Name:
Words:

Using the category names above as chapter titles, write a "book" about the rain forest. If you get stuck, you can make up what you don't know. You'll be able to revise your "book" after reading *Over in the Jungle*.

From *MORE Science Adventures with Children's Literature: Reading Comprehension and Inquiry-Based Science* by Anthony D. Fredericks. Westport, CT: Teacher Ideas Press. Copyright © 2008.

STORE-HOUSE

With your parents, visit your local grocery store or supermarket. Look for some of the following rain forest fruits, vegetables, and plants in the aisles, display counters, and produce section. How many can you find?

Product	Description
Chocolate	found in cocoa, cookies, cakes, drinks, and candies
Coffee	the most popular beverage in the world
Banana	the most popular fruit eaten in the United States
Pineapple	grown in many tropical areas, including Hawaii
Avocado	grown in California; used in many Mexican dishes
Rice	a staple food for many people around the world
Corn	grown as a food source for humans and animals
Sweet potato	a staple of rain forest people for hundreds of years
Manioc	used to make tapioca; a food staple for more than 300 million people around the world
Sugar cane	used primarily as a food sweetener
Orange	most oranges eaten in the United States come from California, Florida, and Brazil
Mung bean	a low-calorie vegetable often used in salads
Guava	a popular tropical fruit
Mango	a tropical fruit often used in fruit salads
Papaya	a popular tropical fruit
Peanut	most peanuts used in the United States come from Georgia or Africa
Cinnamon	a flavoring taken from the bark of the cinnamon tree
Cardamom	a popular spice used in cooking
Clove	used as flavoring for food
Cashew nut	a popular nut
Tomato	a popular fruit grown throughout the United States
Tea	a popular drink throughout the world
Grapefruit	a popular breakfast food and drink
Kiwi fruit	originally known as Chinese gooseberry
Brazil nut	a popular nut found in canned nut mixes

From *MORE Science Adventures with Children's Literature: Reading Comprehension and Inquiry-Based Science* by Anthony D. Fredericks. Westport, CT: Teacher Ideas Press. Copyright © 2008.

PLENTY OF PLANTS

You may wish to grow some rain forest plants right in your own home. Visit a large supermarket, garden shop, or nursery and look for one or more of the following rain forest plants:

- African violet

- Begonia

- Bird's-nest fern

- Bromeliad

- Christmas cactus

- Corn plant

- Croton

- Dumb cane

- Fiddle-leaf fig

- Orchid

- Philodendron

- Prayer plant

- Rubber plant

- Snake plant

- Umbrella tree

- Zebra plant

You should know that the plants you grow at home will be somewhat smaller than the plants normally found throughout the rain forest.

From *MORE Science Adventures with Children's Literature: Reading Comprehension and Inquiry-Based Science* by Anthony D. Fredericks. Westport, CT: Teacher Ideas Press. Copyright © 2008.

ANIMAL SCRAMBLE

Listed below are all of the animals featured in *Over in the Jungle*. For each one, look in other books or on the Internet to obtain the requested information.

Marmoset

Where it lives:

Food it eats:

Size/dimensions/colors:

Fascinating fact:

Morpho Butterfly

Where it lives:

Food it eats:

Size/dimensions/colors:

Fascinating fact:

Parrot

Where it lives:

Food it eats:

Size/dimensions/colors:

Fascinating fact:

Leaf Cutter Ant

Where it lives:

Food it eats:

Size/dimensions/colors:

Fascinating fact:

Honey Bear

Where it lives:

Food it eats:

Size/dimensions/colors:

Fascinating fact:

From *MORE Science Adventures with Children's Literature: Reading Comprehension and Inquiry-Based Science* by Anthony D. Fredericks. Westport, CT: Teacher Ideas Press. Copyright © 2008.

ANIMAL SCRAMBLE (CONTINUED)

Boa Constrictor

Where it lives:

Food it eats:

Size/dimensions/colors:

Fascinating fact:

Poison Dart Frog

Where it lives:

Food it eats:

Size/dimensions/colors:

Fascinating fact:

Ocelot

Where it lives:

Food it eats:

Size/dimensions/colors:

Fascinating fact:

Sloth

Where it lives:

Food it eats:

Size/dimensions/colors:

Fascinating fact:

Howler Monkey

Where it lives:

Food it eats:

Size/dimensions/colors:

Fascinating fact:

From *MORE Science Adventures with Children's Literature: Reading Comprehension and Inquiry-Based Science* by Anthony D. Fredericks. Westport, CT: Teacher Ideas Press. Copyright © 2008.

The Flower Hunter: William Bartram, America's First Naturalist

Deborah Kogan Ray

New York: Farrar, Straus & Giroux, 2004

SELECTED CITATIONS

- **2005 Outstanding Science Trade Book**—Children's Book Council/National Science Teachers Association

- "Required reading for young students of nature or American history."—*Kirkus Reviews*

SUMMARY

Told in the form of diary entries, this engaging book will open up students' eyes to the majesty of nature around them as well as to opportunities to explore that nature. This book is inquiry-based science at its finest, as we travel with a youngster and his father in search of strange and unusual botanical specimens. Questions are asked and many are answered as this duo travels throughout the East to discover and examine some of nature's most wondrous plants. This book is also a perfect complement to the writing curriculum as it demonstrates the ways in which stories can be shared in a dynamic and captivating fashion.

SUGGESTED GRADE LEVELS: 4–6

LESSON OBJECTIVES

Science Standards

- Content Standard A: Science as Inquiry

    Abilities necessary to do science inquiry (K–4, 5–8)

    Understandings about science inquiry (K–4, 5–8)

- Content Standard C: Life Science

    The characteristics of organisms (K–4)

    Organisms and environments (K–4)

    Populations and ecosystems (5–8)

    Diversity and adaptations of organisms (5–8)

- Content Standard G: History and Nature of Science

    Science as a human endeavor (5–8)

    Nature of science (5–8)

    History of science (5–8)

CRITICAL THINKING QUESTIONS

1. If you could ask William Bartram one question, what would it be?

2. What did you enjoy most about the travels of William and his father?

3. How is the region they searched similar to (or different from) the region in which you live?

4. Why do you think scientists are always asking so many questions?

5. Which of the places that William traveled to would you like to explore?

COMPREHENSION LESSON (STORY FRAMES)

Setting the Stage

Invite students to discuss what they know about botany (the study of plants) or botanists (scientists who study plants). Why would someone want to study plants? What kinds of things would a botanist discover in her or his work? Why is botany an important area of science?

Before Reading

Provide each student with a copy of the Story Frame in the project pages. Take a few minutes to discuss the frame and the information that will need to be written in the appropriate spaces. Indicate to students that this frame will help them organize their thoughts about the book.

During Reading

Ask students to read the book silently (or to listen to it as part of a read-aloud session). Encourage students to visualize some of the settings and events of the story as they are reading. This will aid them in completing the frame.

After Reading

Upon finishing the book, ask students to complete their Story Frames. Allow sufficient time for students to share and discuss their respective frames. How were their perceptions similar? How were they different?

LITERATURE EXTENSIONS

Invite students to select one or more of the following activities:

1. Invite students to interview several of their neighbors and/or relatives. Ask them to gather information on some of their favorite plants. What plants are most often mentioned? What plants are never mentioned? What are some of the qualities of a species of plant that make it particularly desirable to humans? Why do people enjoy gardening so much? What are the benefits?

2. Ask students to write a sequel to the story. Using the information in the "Afterword" in concert with the writing style of the author, encourage students to create a series of fictitious diary entries that might have been penned by William Bartram.

3. Students may enjoy developing the story into a readers theatre script (see Part III of this book). Using the events of this story, a narrator (William), and selected characters, students may reenact the book for class members or another class.

4. Invite students to create a collage (pictures and words cut from old magazines and glued to a sheet of poster board) of plants that are indigenous to your part of the country. What are some of the more common plants in your area? Are those plants found in other parts of the country?

5. Ask students to create posters on the value of plants to people. If possible, obtain permission from a local garden center or nursery to display the posters throughout their establishment. Every so often students may wish to create new posters and rotate them.

6. Invite an employee of a local garden center or nursery to visit your class and discuss some of the plants the nursery has for sale. What are some good gardening tips? What plants are most popular in your area? How should new plants be taken care of? If possible, the visitor may bring several samples of plants to share with students.

7. Students may wish to establish and maintain a classroom garden somewhere on the school grounds. Obtain appropriate permission from your building principal or grounds crew to set up a garden area. Talk with students about some of the vegetables and other plants that could be raised in the garden. You may be able to solicit help from parent volunteers to establish and care for the plants.

8. Invite students to create a bulletin board display of some of the plants described and illustrated in this book. They may use a botanical guide to identify specific species and the features or characteristics of those particular species.

9. Encourage students to pretend that they are television reporters assigned to interview William Bartram for a special TV program. What questions should they ask as part of that interview? What information would the viewers be most interested in knowing? How could they capture Bartram's life in just seven minutes (an average interview length)?

STORY FRAME

Complete the Story Frame below for *The Flower Hunter* by Deborah Kogan Ray:

This is a story about _____.

The author has included _____

and _____. This is important

because _____. I feel

that the author _____

because _____.

I think that _____ is _____

_____

because _____

_____.

Something I especially like is _____

_____.

One suggestion I have for the author is _____ because

_____.

Finally, the author has _____

_____.

From *MORE Science Adventures with Children's Literature: Reading Comprehension and Inquiry-Based Science* by Anthony D. Fredericks. Westport, CT: Teacher Ideas Press. Copyright © 2008.

WHAT I SEE

Look at the illustration on the cover of the book. You see a smiling boy standing behind a flowering bush. He is wearing a red vest and a brimmed hat. Based on what you see, you could make the following inferences (educated guesses):

- The boy is enjoying what he is doing.
- He lives in another time (probably more than 100 years ago).
- He is outdoors.

Scientists do two things quite frequently—they observe and they make inferences. The inferences they make help them ask questions, and those questions sometimes lead to scientific experiments and discoveries.

Select one of the first five illustrations in the book. Fill in the chart below with three observations and three inferences about your selected illustration.

Describe the illustration:

_____

_____

_____

_____

Observation	Inference

From *MORE Science Adventures with Children's Literature: Reading Comprehension and Inquiry-Based Science* by Anthony D. Fredericks. Westport, CT: Teacher Ideas Press. Copyright © 2008.

MY PLANTS

Go outside and locate two plants that you particularly like. Draw an illustration of each plant, describe the plant, and then try to discover the name of the plant using library or Internet resources.

Description:

_____

_____

_____

_____.

Plant Name: _____

Description:

_____

_____

_____

_____.

Plant Name: _____

WATER IN, WATER OUT

Plants take in water in order to grow, but they also give off water.

Materials:

- small potted plant
- clear plastic bag (one gallon)
- water
- tape or string

Directions:

1. Water the plant thoroughly.
2. Place the plastic bag over the green, leafy part of the plant and close it up gently around the stem with tape or string.
3. Place the plant in a sunny location for several hours.

Description:

You will note that water droplets form on the inside of the bag. That's because plant leaves have tiny openings called **stomata** in them. In most plants, stomata are located on the underside of the leaves. During a plant's food-making process, air is taken in and released through these openings. Water, in the form of water vapor, is also released through the stomata into the atmosphere. You can see that water as it condenses and forms water droplets on the inside of the plastic bag. The amount of water a plant loses varies with the weather conditions as well as the size and shape of its leaves.

From *MORE Science Adventures with Children's Literature: Reading Comprehension and Inquiry-Based Science* by Anthony D. Fredericks. Westport, CT: Teacher Ideas Press. Copyright © 2008.

The Tsunami Quilt: Grandfather's Story

Anthony D. Fredericks

Chelsea, MI: Sleeping Bear Press, 2007

SELECTED CITATIONS

- "WOW—What an incredible story! This is a must-read book—a great way to help children understand that there are traditions that should be honored in any family."—Caryn P., teacher

- "For remembrance, education and hope [the author has] created a story that deals with difficult themes in a sensitive and poignant manner."—*The Garden Island News*

SUMMARY

Young Kimo loves his grandfather very much—they go everywhere together, sharing Hawaiian stories and experiences. But there is one story his grandfather has yet to share, and that is the reason behind their yearly pilgrimage to Laupâhoehoe Point. Here, in silent remembrance, Grandfather places a flower lei atop a stone monument. It is only after his grandfather's sudden death that Kimo learns the story behind their annual visit and the reason for the sadness that has haunted his grandfather throughout the years.

SUGGESTED GRADE LEVELS: 3–6

LESSON OBJECTIVES

Science Standards

- Content Standard A: Science as Inquiry

    Abilities necessary to do science inquiry (K–4; 5–8)

• Content Standard B: Physical Science

  Motions and forces (5–8)

  Transfer of energy (5–8)

• Content Standard D: Earth and Space Science

  Changes in Earth and sky (K–4)

• Content Standard F: Science in Personal and Social Perspectives

  Science and technology in local challenges (K–4)

  Natural hazards (5–8)

CRITICAL THINKING QUESTIONS

1. What did you enjoy most about Kimo? About his grandfather?

2. Why do you think tsunamis are so dangerous?

3. If you could ask a tsunami survivor one question, what would it be?

4. What do you enjoy most about this book?

5. What is one question you would like to ask the author?

COMPREHENSION LESSON (LITERATURE LOG)

Setting the Stage

Before distributing copies of the book to members of the class, read aloud the inside front flap on the dust cover. Afterward, invite students to make some predictions about the story. What do they think will happen in the story? What do students think is Grandfather's secret? What kind of person is Kimo? Take a few minutes to discuss and share all predictions.

Before Reading

Provide each student with a copy of the Literature Log. Take a few minutes to discuss the components of the log and the information that needs to be written in each of the appropriate spaces. Indicate to students that this form will help them summarize the major elements of the story as well as summarize the story after it is read. Ask students to complete the "Before" section of the log.

During Reading

Invite students to begin reading the book. When they have gotten to the halfway point in the story, ask them to complete the "During" section of the log. As necessary, assist individual students with difficult vocabulary or complex concepts. Encourage students to visualize some of the settings and events of the story as they are reading. This will aid them in completing their logs.

After Reading

Upon completion of the book, ask students to fill in the "After" section of the log. Allow sufficient time for students to share and discuss their individual logs (it is not necessary for everyone to do so). How were their perceptions similar? How were they different?

LITERATURE EXTENSIONS

Invite students to select one or more of the following activities:

1. Ask students to imagine that they are in a tsunami-prone area. What types of precautions should they take in advance of a tsunami? What types of actions should they take if a tsunami alarm were sounded in their area? Invite students to assemble a "tsunami safety book" that could be distributed to local schools through a chapter of the American Red Cross or other disaster relief agency.

2. Invite small groups of students to each assemble an almanac of various natural disasters that have struck the United States within the last five years. Students may assemble descriptions of the ten most dangerous and/or deadly natural disasters to strike the United States or to develop a booklet on the worst tsunami, the worst hurricane, the worst tornado, etc. Make these available for sharing in the school library.

3. Ask students to write imaginary letters to the families of children lost in the April 1, 1946, tsunami. What would they say to the parents of children lost in that tsunami? What would they say to the children who survived? What do they think would be a fitting memorial to the people who were lost in that tsunami?

4. Invite students to log on to several Internet sites about tsunamis. Because most of these sites are geared for adults, invite students to create their own tsunami Web site—one that provides specific information about tsunamis for students. This information may include survivor stories, a description of the Southeast Asia tsunami of December 26, 2004, tsunami preparedness, the tsunami warning system, tsunami legends, and other information. Students may wish to use the Web site of the Pacific Tsunami Museum (www.tsunami.org) as a template.

5. Invite students to post an oversized map of the world on one wall of the classroom. Ask them to research major tsunamis that have occurred in the past 100 years. Ask students to write a brief description of each tsunami on an index card and then post the cards around the perimeter of the map. Push a pin in the location of the tsunami and string a length of yarn from the tsunami location to its appropriate index card. What do students notice about the locations of tsunamis? Where do most of them occur?

6. Ask one student to take on the role of Kimo. Place the student in the front of the room and invite other students to pose questions to "Kimo"—questions about his grandfather, the visit to the museum, the Tsunami Quilt itself, or the family. Afterward, discuss some of the responses and whether other responses might also be appropriate.

7. If possible, obtain a copy of the National Geographic Society video *Killer Wave: Power of the Tsunami* (Catalog 51904C). This film is an excellent introduction to the power and force of these natural disasters. Invite students to view the video. Afterward, encourage them to compare the information in the book with that presented in the video. What was similar? What was different? Do students have any unanswered questions after reading the book and viewing the video?

8. Here are some great Web sites on tsunamis, including how they are formed, the destruction they cause, where they occur, simulations and animations, and a host of up-to-date information:

    http://www.germantown.k12.il.us/html/tsunami.html

    http://www.geophys.washington.edu/tsunami/welcome.html

    http://www.pmel.noaa.gov/tsunami/

    http://www.usc.edu/dept/tsunamis/

    http://www.thirteen.org/savageseas/neptune-main.html

9. Students can stay up-to-date on the latest events, discoveries, and news about tsunamis by accessing the Web site of the Pacific Tsunami Museum—http://www.tsunami.org. Here they can learn about latest happenings at the museum, contests, and ongoing displays. They may gather selected information together in the form of descriptive brochures or pamphlets for the classroom library.

10. If possible, obtain a copy of the video *Raging Planet: Tidal Wave* (Catalog 51904C) from the Discovery Channel. Invite students to view the video and to focus on the ways in which buildings (particularly those in Hilo, Hawaii) have been constructed so that they can withstand the force of a tsunami. Ask students to check on selected buildings in their town or community. How are those buildings different from those in a tsunami-prone area? What would have to be done to some of the local buildings to make them "tsunami proof?" Encourage students to create diagrams or illustrations of the necessary changes.

11. Invite students to read another book by this author—*Tsunami Man: Learning about Killer Waves with Walter Dudley* (University of Hawaii Press, 2002). This chapter book examines the science of tsunamis and the life of one of the world's leading tsunami experts, Dr. Walt Dudley, who is also the scientific advisor for the Pacific Tsunami Museum, where the Tsunami Quilt is displayed. Students may construct a "compare and contrast" chart outlining the similarities and differences between these two books, one fiction and one nonfiction.

12. After students have completed a reading of *The Tsunami Quilt*, encourage them to create a sequel. What happens to Kimo? How is his life changed now that he knows his grandfather's secret? Invite students to post their stories throughout the classroom.

13. Students may wish to correspond with an oceanographer at a local college or university. They may obtain some firsthand information about wave formation in general or tsunami propagation specifically. You may be able to make arrangements for the expert to visit your classroom for an extended "Q & A" session.

LITERATURE LOG

Name: _____ **Date:** _____

Book Title: *The Tsunami Quilt: Grandfather's Story*

Author: Anthony D. Fredericks

Publisher: Sleeping Bear Press

Date of Publication: 2007

Before Reading

I want to read this book because _____

_____

Here's what I know about tsunamis: _____

_____

These are some questions I would like to ask before I read: _____

_____

_____

I think I will learn _____

_____

During Reading

Here's what I'm learning as I read this book: _____

_____

This is what I do when I don't understand something in the book: _____

_____

I want to finish this book because _____

_____

This is how I find answers to some of my questions: _____

_____

LITERATURE LOG (CONTINUED)

After Reading

I think the author wrote this book because _____

_____

I am satisfied with this book because _____

_____

I can write a brief summary of the book: _____

_____

_____

_____

_____

There are questions I still need answers to: _____

_____

_____

_____

I will find that information here: _____

_____

Here's what I would like to say to the author: _____

_____

_____

_____

_____

From *MORE Science Adventures with Children's Literature: Reading Comprehension and Inquiry-Based Science* by Anthony D. Fredericks. Westport, CT: Teacher Ideas Press. Copyright © 2008.

MAKING WAVES

This activity will help you understand how waves are created.

Materials:

- 9-by-13-inch cake pan
- straw
- water
- blue food color.

Directions:

1. Place the cake pan on a table and fill it about two-thirds full with water.
2. Tint the water with several drops of food color.
3. Hold the straw at about a 45 degree angle and blow across the surface of the water.
4. Vary the angle of the straw several times and repeat step 2.
5. Vary the force of the "wind" that blows through the straw.

Description:

When you blow through the straw across the top of the water, miniature waves are created. As you change the angle of the straw and as you change the power of the "wind" blowing across the water, you also change the size and shapes of the ripples or "waves" that move across the miniature ocean.

Winds blowing across the ocean's surface create ripples of waves. The size of a wave depends on the speed of the wind as well as how far the wind has been blowing across the ocean. Large waves are created when a steady wind blows great distances across the surface of the sea.

A tsunami is a different type of wave. It is not created by the wind. Tsunamis are often generated as a result of undersea events such as volcanoes, landslides, and earthquakes.

From *MORE Science Adventures with Children's Literature: Reading Comprehension and Inquiry-Based Science* by Anthony D. Fredericks. Westport, CT: Teacher Ideas Press. Copyright © 2008.

TSUNAMI DICTIONARY

Create your own "Tsunami Dictionary." For each of the letters of the alphabet, gather words or phrases related to tsunamis. You may wish to consult several tsunami-related books or Web sites. Can you find at least one word or phrase for each letter of the alphabet? How many words or phrases can you locate for a single letter? A few samples have been filled in for you.

A—Aleutian Islands,

B—

C—Crest, Coast Guard,

D—

E—

F—Five hundred miles per hour,

G—

H—Hilo, Hawaii,

I—

J—

K—

L—

M-

N—

O—

P—Pacific Ocean,

Q—

R—

S—

T—

U—

V—

W—Widespread destruction, "wave in harbor,"

X—

Y—

Z—

From *MORE Science Adventures with Children's Literature: Reading Comprehension and Inquiry-Based Science* by Anthony D. Fredericks. Westport, CT: Teacher Ideas Press. Copyright © 2008.

WAVES IN A BOTTLE

Here's how you can make your own ocean—in a bottle.

Materials:

- empty 1-liter soda bottle (with a screw-on top)
- salad oil
- water
- blue food coloring

Directions:

1. Fill an empty one-liter soda bottle two-thirds of the way with water.
2. Place four or five drops of blue food coloring in the water.
3. Fill the rest of the bottle (all the way to the brim) with salad oil.
4. Screw the top on securely (make sure there is no air in the bottle).
5. Hold the bottle sideways in your hands.
6. Slowly and gently rock the bottle back and forth.

Description:

The oil in the bottle will begin to roll and move just like the waves in the ocean. You will have created a "miniature ocean" inside a soda bottle.

Tsunami waves are quite different from other ocean waves. Ordinary waves are caused by wind blowing over the surface of the ocean. The water movement in those waves rarely extends below a depth of 500 feet. Tsunamis involve water movement all the way to the sea floor; as a result, the depth of the sea controls their speed. Interestingly, normal ocean waves travel at speeds of less than 60 miles per hour, whereas tsunami waves can speed across the ocean at an amazing 500 miles per hour.

From *MORE Science Adventures with Children's Literature: Reading Comprehension and Inquiry-Based Science* by Anthony D. Fredericks. Westport, CT: Teacher Ideas Press. Copyright © 2008.

A Mother's Journey

Sandra Markle

Watertown, MA: Charlesbridge, 2005

SELECTED CITATIONS

- **2006 Outstanding Science Trade Book**—Children's Book Council/National Science Teachers Association

- **2006 Nonfiction Honor Book Award**—*Boston Globe-Horn Book*

SUMMARY

This book will delight readers of all ages. It is a true-life story of how emperor penguins —males and females—work together to ensure the survival of their eggs and eventually their newborn chicks. This is truly a tale of survival in one of the world's harshest environments. It is a story of struggle, hardships, and numerous challenges—but it is equally a story of love and devotion. This is a joyous story to read aloud or independently. It will spark lots of questions and discoveries.

SUGGESTED GRADE LEVELS: 2–4

LESSON OBJECTIVES

Science Standards

- Content Standard C: Life Science

    Life cycles of organisms (K–4)

    Organisms and environments (K–4)

- Content Standard D: Earth and Space Science

    Changes in Earth and sky (K–4)

CRITICAL THINKING QUESTIONS

1. What did you enjoy most about this story?

2. Is penguin behavior similar to the behavior of any other animals?

3. Why do penguins live in such a cold environment?

4. What are some of the first challenges a young penguin faces after birth?

5. What would you enjoy most about living in Antarctica?

6. What would you enjoy least about living in Antarctica?

COMPREHENSION LESSON (POSSIBLE SENTENCES)

Setting the Stage

Pass out copies of the book to all students (or show them the book as part of a read-aloud). Invite students to look at the cover illustration and the title. What can they infer from these two items? Does the illustration give any information about the contents of the book? Plan a few moments to discuss students' perceptions.

Before Reading

Engage students in a Possible Sentences strategy. Provide them with copies of the Possible Sentences project page. Before students read the book, ask them to select two words from the list and use them in a complete sentence. Tell them that the sentence should be one that they think might appear in the book. Invite students to repeat this sentence construction (using other words from the list) two to three additional times. After students have created their sentences, allow time to discuss the sentences and how they might relate to the plot of the book.

During Reading

Remind students to watch for the words from the project page (which were selected from the book) as they read (or as they listen to the book being read aloud).

After Reading

Invite students to revisit their Possible Sentences. What changes do they need to make in those sentences? Can they write some new sentences using those words? How did their initial ideas about the book change after reading the book? What would be some appropriate sentences to share with others who have not read the book?

LITERATURE EXTENSIONS

Invite students to select one or more of the following activities:

1. Invite students to read other books by Sandra Markle (for example, *Outside and Inside Mummies,* which is also profiled in this book). Encourage them to discuss some of the

themes that Markle emphasizes in her books. What messages is she trying to convey? What does she believe? What do you know about this author as a result of reading her books? Why have her books won so many awards?

2. Ask students to create an alphabet book about penguins. Encourage them to consult a variety of resources (both print and nonprint) for information. Ask them to identify at least one important item for each letter of the alphabet (there may not be an item for every letter, however). Be sure these books are appropriately displayed in the classroom or library.

3. Encourage students to write and illustrate their own stories about the sacrifices their mothers (or other caregivers) make for them (or other children). They may wish to comment on the specifics of life in their own families or an imaginary family (if circumstances warrant). As appropriate, invite students to share these stories in a warm and supportive discussion group.

4. It could be said that both father and mother penguins are heroes to their young chicks. Invite students to bring in pictures of their heroes. These heroes can be athletes, actors or actresses, family members, etc. Encourage students to discuss the attributes that all heroes possess—whether they be people or animals.

5. Show part of the DVD *March of the Penguins* (2005) to students. Afterward, invite students to make lists of the similarities between the video and the book. What facts were duplicated in these two descriptions of the emperor penguin? What facts were excluded from the book? What facts were excluded from the movie?

6. Invite students to write a series of newspaper articles about the events described in this book. For example: "Penguins Survive Long, Harsh Journey," "Father Caught Sleeping on the Job, or "The Bravest Mother of All." Students may wish to collect these into a large newspaper, *The Penguin Gazette.*

7. There are collectible cards featuring baseball players (and other sports stars). These cards include a photograph of a designated player, statistics, a short biography, and other relevant facts. Invite students to create a series of "penguin cards," each focusing on one of the 17 species of penguins around the world. Invite students to select the relevant data that should be included on each card. Students may create their "penguin cards" on blank index cards, with a word processing program, or as part of a PowerPoint presentation.

8. Invite students to create a time line of the events in this story—from the time when the female penguin pushes out her egg in mid-May to the time when the father heads off to sea. These time lines can be created on long strips of adding machine tape or a roll of newsprint.

9. Ask students to work with the school librarian or children's librarian at your local public library to assemble an annotated list of books about penguins. How many books are in the school library? How many are in the public library? Students may wish to duplicate and share this list with other classes.

POSSIBLE SENTENCES

The words below are from the book *A Mother's Journey* by Sandra Markle. Use two of these words to create a sentence you think could be part of the book. Keep in mind that you are making a prediction (also known as an "educated guess") about a possible sentence. After you have created one sentence (using two words from the list), try to create two or three additional sentences (using two different words from the list for each additional possible sentence).

winter	egg
pouch	male
warm	storms
ice	food
snow	iceberg
roaring	water
wind	escapes

Sentences:

1. _____
   _____.
   _____.

2. _____
   _____.
   _____.

3. _____
   _____.
   _____.

4. _____
   _____.
   _____.

From *MORE Science Adventures with Children's Literature: Reading Comprehension and Inquiry-Based Science* by Anthony D. Fredericks. Westport, CT: Teacher Ideas Press. Copyright © 2008.

LETTER BY LETTER

For each letter in the word "penguin," provide a detail or quote from the book *A Mother's Journey*. One has already been done for you.

P—Parents both help to raise their young in very difficult conditions.

E—

N—

G—

U—

I—

N—

From *MORE Science Adventures with Children's Literature: Reading Comprehension and Inquiry-Based Science* by Anthony D. Fredericks. Westport, CT: Teacher Ideas Press. Copyright © 2008.

LOOKING BACK

Complete this form for the book *A Mother's Journey* by Sandra Markle. Please keep in mind that there are no right or wrong responses to these uncompleted sentences (or paragraphs). After you complete this form, take time to discuss your responses with other students.

1. I wonder why . . .

2. Why did . . .

3. I really liked . . .

4. I didn't understand . . .

5. I found myself thinking about . . .

6. When I finished the book, I thought . . .

7. I would like to suggest to the author that she . . .

From *MORE Science Adventures with Children's Literature: Reading Comprehension and Inquiry-Based Science* by Anthony D. Fredericks. Westport, CT: Teacher Ideas Press. Copyright © 2008.

TOP 10

Conduct some "penguin research" using a variety of library books, the Internet, animal experts, or other resources. Gather as much information as you can about penguins and their lives. When you have gathered sufficient information, identify the 10 most interesting facts about penguins (from least to most interesting). Record those 10 facts on this sheet. Plan to share your facts with other students. Are there any facts that appear on several lists? Is there one fact everyone can agree on as one of the most interesting of all?

10.

9.

8.

7.

6.

5.

4.

3.

2.

1. (The most interesting)

From *MORE Science Adventures with Children's Literature: Reading Comprehension and Inquiry-Based Science* by Anthony D. Fredericks. Westport, CT: Teacher Ideas Press. Copyright © 2008.

Earthshake: Poems from the Ground Up
Lisa Westberg Peters
New York: Greenwillow, 2003

SELECTED CITATIONS

- "Twenty-two delightful poems with a geological theme, including pieces on tectonic plates, lava, strata, and fossils. Exuberant, silly, and serious by turns, the selections engage imagination with often-humorous wordplay."—*School Library Journal*

- "Readers will be engaged with the lively and witty writing of this geology poetry book."—*Children's Literature*

SUMMARY

With just the right amount of whimsy in concert with "down-to-earth" scientific information, this book is a definite "must-have" for any study of geology. The poems take a look at glaciers, fossils, plate tectonics, volcanic eruptions, and sand, as well as other geological concepts. Students will gain a newfound appreciation for the Earth from this delightful collection.

SUGGESTED GRADE LEVELS: 3–6

LESSON OBJECTIVES

Science Standards

- Content Standard D: Earth and Space Science

     Properties of Earth materials (K–4)

     Earth's history (5–8)

• Content Standard F: Science in Personal and Social Perspectives

Natural hazards (5–8)

CRITICAL THINKING QUESTIONS

1. Which of the poems did you enjoy most? Why?

2. Was there an element of earth science that wasn't represented by a poem?

3. What did you find most interesting in the "Endnotes?"

4. What did you learn that you didn't know before?

5. Do you think that geology really rocks? (Sorry, I couldn't resist.)

COMPREHENSION LESSON (SEMANTIC WEBBING)

Setting the Stage

Provide copies of the book to all students. Invite them to thumb through the book and look at all the illustrations (or look at the illustrations in your copy). What do they know about Earth? What can they share about the planet on which they live? What are some of the components, features, or elements of Earth or earth science (geology)?

Before Reading

Provide students with the Semantic Webbing project page. Let them know that there is a globe in the center of the page—and that the globe represents Earth. Around the globe are several spikes. Invite them to write words, phrases, or concepts related to "earth science" or "Earth" on each of the spokes of the web. Note any misperceptions or biases students may have.

During Reading

Invite students to read the book silently (or listen to it being read aloud).

After Reading

Invite students to return to their original semantic web. Ask students to add words or terms from the book to the original web, using a different color of ink. Allow time for students to discuss any differences in their pre-reading knowledge about earth science and their post-reading knowledge about earth science. How have their perceptions changed as a result of reading the book?

LITERATURE EXTENSIONS

Invite students to select one or more of the following activities:

1. Ask students to look through the daily newspaper (over an extended period of time) for articles regarding changes in the earth (volcanic eruptions, earthquakes, etc.). Encour-

age them to create a bulletin board to display the articles under the heading, "Our Changing Earth."

2. Invite students to create a dictionary booklet entitled, "Earthshakes: A Rockin' Alphabet." Ask students to look through the book *Earthshakes: Poems from the Ground Up* to see if they can locate at least one representative word for each letter of the alphabet, for example, A = Alaska, B = Black, C = Coastline, D = Ditch. Make sure they provide an accompanying illustration for each selected word.

3. Cut an old tennis ball in half (very carefully). Pack the inside of one half of the ball with brown modeling clay (leave a small depression in the middle). Pack the small depression with some red modeling clay. Make sure that the clay is smoothed flat. Show this to students and let them know that it is a model of the earth. The "skin" of the tennis ball represents the crust of the earth. The layer of brown clay represents the mantle of the earth. The red clay represents the core of the earth.

4. Provide each of several small groups of students with a shallow pan of water and a marble. Invite individual students to drop a marble into the pan and describe the ripples that are sent out. Inform students that the ripples that are sent out in their pans are similar to the seismic waves sent out from the epicenter of an earthquake. This is one of the reasons that an earthquake can cause damage over a large area. It's also why those seismic waves can be recorded by scientific instruments thousands of miles away.

5. Invite students to write a fictional story about how they might be affected by an earthquake, volcano, glacier, or meteor in their neighborhood or community. What would be some of the effects of that event on their daily lives? How would they survive? What would they do afterward? Provide opportunities for students to share their creation with the class.

6. Ask students to conduct some library research on famous volcanoes in history (e.g., Krakatoa, Mt. Fuji, Vesuvius, etc.). Collected data can be assembled into a large class book or presented as part of a PowerPoint presentation.

7. Some students may be interested in investigating the myths and legends surrounding selected natural disasters. Various cultures and civilizations around the world have shared legends about these disasters—what initiates them, how they arrive, and how they are generated. For example, here are some selected earthquake legends:

   – In India it was believed that Earth was held up by four elephants standing on the back of a turtle. The turtle was balanced on top of a cobra. When any of these animals moved, Earth trembled and shook.

   – In Mexico, El Diablo, the devil, makes giant rips in the earth from the inside. He and his devilish friends use the cracks when they want to come and stir up trouble on Earth.

   – In New Zealand, Mother Earth has a child within her womb, the young god Ru. When he stretches and kicks, he causes earthquakes.

8. Ask students to look for various types of erosion in and around their homes. Some examples to look for are coins that are smooth from handling, shoes with the heels worn down, old car tires with no tread, and a plate or countertop with the design or finish worn away. Invite students to compare these forms of erosion with those that occur in nature (wind and water erosion).

9. Invite college students from a local university majoring in geology to share specially prepared lessons on the changing earth. Invite students to interview the college students.

10. Ask students to begin a rock collection. Provide time for them to investigate and gather sample rocks from the school playground, a neighborhood park, their own backyards, or a nearby field or vacant lot. How many different kinds of rocks can they find? How many different kinds of rocks can they identify?

SEMANTIC WEBBING

This globe represents Earth. Write words, phrases, or concepts related to "earth science" or "Earth" on each of the spokes around the globe.

From *MORE Science Adventures with Children's Literature: Reading Comprehension and Inquiry-Based Science* by Anthony D. Fredericks. Westport, CT: Teacher Ideas Press. Copyright © 2008.

WEAR AND TEAR

The sand in soil is rock that has been broken up and worn down by erosion. To demonstrate this, you can make your own rocks (most outdoor rocks are much too hard).

Materials:

- clean sand
- mixing bowl
- aluminum foil
- white glue
- plastic spoon
- empty coffee can
- water

Directions:

1. Mix three large spoonfuls of sand together with three large spoonfuls of white glue (it should look like wet concrete).
2. Make small lumps of the mixture and place them on a lightly oiled piece of aluminum foil, so that they will not stick to it.
3. Put the "rocks" in a dry, sunny location for 2 or 3 days, until they are hard.
4. Put some of your "rocks" into the coffee can with some water.
5. Hold the lid on securely and shake the can for four to five minutes. Remove the lid.

Description:

The "rocks" in the can begin to wear down. Some "rocks" may be worn down into sand again. That's because the water running over the "rocks" pushes them against each other, causing erosion that wears them down. In nature, this process takes many years, but the result is the same. Rocks are broken up, become smaller from rubbing against each other, and over time wear down into sandy particles that may eventually become part of the soil near a river or stream.

 From *MORE Science Adventures with Children's Literature: Reading Comprehension and Inquiry-Based Science* by Anthony D. Fredericks. Westport, CT: Teacher Ideas Press. Copyright © 2008.

FILL IN THE BLANKS

Each numbered section below has several blank lines and a selected word on one blank in each row. Create your own poems (similar to those in *Earthshake*) using these blanks. Keep in mind that these are YOUR poems, so there is no right or wrong way to write them.

1. _____ _____ _____ _____ __Earth__

   _____ _____ _____ __Earth__

   _____ _____ __Earth__

   _____ __Earth__

   __Earth__

2. __Rock__ _____ _____ _____

   _____ __Rock__ _____ _____

   _____ _____ __Rock__ _____

   _____ _____ _____ __Rock__

3. __Sand__

   _____ __Sand__

   _____ _____ __Sand__

   _____ _____ _____ __Sand__

   _____ _____ _____ _____ __Sand__

From *MORE Science Adventures with Children's Literature: Reading Comprehension and Inquiry-Based Science* by Anthony D. Fredericks. Westport, CT: Teacher Ideas Press. Copyright © 2008.

AMAZING CRYSTALS

NOTE: The following project should be done by an adult only.

Materials:

- piece of brick
- large metal bowl
- small container (for mixing)
- water
- bluing (from the laundry section of the grocery store)
- ammonia (from the cleaning section of the grocery store)
- measuring cup
- salt

Directions:

1. Soak the brick in water overnight.
2. Place the brick in a large metal bowl.
3. In a separate container, mix together ½ cup of water, ½ cup of bluing, and ½ cup of ammonia.
4. Use a measuring cup to pour some of this mixture over the brick.
5. Sprinkle the brick with salt and let it stand for 24 hours.

Description:

The next day, you will be able to see some crystals forming on the surface of the brick. (Continue to add some more of the water/bluing/ammonia mixture to keep the crystals growing.) What you see is similar to a process in nature known as *crystallization,* in which crystals are formed over a long period of time (hundreds, thousands, and millions of years).

From *MORE Science Adventures with Children's Literature: Reading Comprehension and Inquiry-Based Science* by Anthony D. Fredericks. Westport, CT: Teacher Ideas Press. Copyright © 2008.

Eyes and Ears
Seymour Simon
New York: HarperCollins, 2003

SELECTED CITATIONS

- **2004 Outstanding Science Trade Book**—Children's Book Council/National Science Teachers Association

- "Simply written but absorbing explanations of the major components and functions of these sensory organs are accompanied by stunning photographs and crisp drawings." —*School Library Journal*

SUMMARY

The human body is filled with many wonders—including the eyes and ears. In this clearly written and lucid book, Simon offers young scientists an "inside look" into these two essential body parts. Captivating photographs (a hallmark of Simon's books), in concert with incredibly fascinating text, will keep readers turning the pages. This book goes far beyond the simple explanations offered in science textbooks—it captures the miracles and fascination of these sensory organs as few books can.

SUGGESTED GRADE LEVELS: 2–4

LESSON OBJECTIVES

Science Standards

- Content Standard C: Life Science

    The characteristics of organisms (K–4)

    Structure and function in living systems (5–8)

- Content Standard E: Science and Technology

    Abilities of technological design (K–4, 5–8)

    Understanding about science and technology (K–4, 5–8)

- Content Standard F: Science in Personal and Social Perspectives

    Personal health (K–4, 5–8)

CRITICAL THINKING QUESTIONS

1. What did you find most amazing about the optical illusions?

2. Which is most important to you—your eyes or your ears?

3. Of all five senses, which is the most critical for our day-to-day functioning?

4. Why is the human brain so important to our eyes and ears?

5. What is one question you didn't find the answer to in this book?

COMPREHENSION LESSON (ANSWER FIRST!)

Setting the Stage

Provide a copy of the book for each student (or do a read-aloud). Invite students to "thumb" through the book and closely observe the photographs and illustrations throughout. What do they notice about each photograph or illustration? How are these photographs and illustrations similar to (or different from) those found in other books?

Before Reading

Invite students to discuss the title of this book. What does the title say about the contents of this book? What type of information will be found in this book? What will we learn that we don't know now?

During Reading

Invite students to read the entire book on their own or listen to it as part of a read-aloud. Ask them to take note of interesting information, unusual facts, or fascinating data.

After Reading

Provide students with copies of the Answer First! project page. Invite students—either individually or in small groups—to generate a question for each of the five answers on that page. After allowing sufficient time, ask students to share the questions they generated and why they believe those questions to be appropriate for this book. Afterward, point out to students that the answers were arranged in a hierarchical order—from easy to more challenging. Let them know that the latter questions (more challenging) are the kinds of questions that good readers (and good scientists) always ask themselves as they read.

LITERATURE EXTENSIONS

Invite students to select one or more of the following activities:

1. Invite the school nurse or a local doctor to visit the class and talk to students about the importance of taking care of our eyes and ears. Prior to the speaker's arrival, ask students to compile a list of questions they would like to ask. Encourage students to elaborate on the information in the book (via their questions) or to compare the information the speaker shares with data from other books.

2. Ask students to create an imaginative newspaper with "reporters" providing information from within the human body. Students may wish to divide the newspaper into sections similar to the daily newspaper (e.g., sports—slalom through the auditory canal; fashion—What the well-groomed ear looks like; architecture—the structure of the eye; and horoscope—"Parts of your body will function today without your knowledge. Fear not, for you will continue to enjoy good health.").

3. Invite students to look through several old magazines. Ask them to locate advertisements that relate to or include the eyes and ears. What is the focus of those advertisements? Beauty? Looks? Health? Prevention? Does there seem to be a common theme in most of the advertisements? Does the type of magazine make a difference (e.g., news magazine, woman's magazine, travel magazine, science magazine)?

4. Assign each of several groups a specific disease or ailment of the eyes or ears. Challenge each group to locate as much outside information as possible about the causes and cures for each selected illness. Invite groups to assemble their data in the form of brochures or a PowerPoint presentation. Local health organizations can be contacted for preliminary data.

5. If possible, obtain a copy of the movie *Fantastic Voyage* (in which a group of scientists is miniaturized and injected into a scientist's bloodstream to repair damage to his brain). After viewing about 30 minutes of the film, ask students to create their own

original skit depicting a journey inside a human ear or human eye. What adventures will they have, and what dangers will they encounter?

6. Invite students to select one or more of the following topics and discuss their creative insights. They may wish to write a brief report on their personal interpretation, too. Invite students to use information from the book to arrive at some conclusions or suppositions.

    – Discuss or write a story from the viewpoint of an eye or an ear.

    – Prepare a time line or storyboard on "A Day in the Life of My [eye/ear]."

    – My favorite organ [eye/ear] and why.

    – If I could look inside my [eye/ear] I would like to see _____.

7. Invite a biology teacher from the local high school to visit your classroom. Ask that individual to bring models or preserved specimens of eyes and ears to share with your students. The teacher can explain and demonstrate the different organs in various types of animals, including humans. Ask the teacher to describe the similarities and differences between animal organs and human organs.

8. Invite a representative of a local wellness center to visit the classroom and share information about health care in the local community, county, or parish. What is being done to provide people with information about vision and hearing care? What printed materials are available for the general public?

9. Ask students (in small groups) to assemble a picture book on "Eyes" or "Ears" for use in the lower grades. What information should be included, and how should that information be presented to younger students?

10. Students may enjoy putting together a collection of "Eye and Ear Records"—an assembly of amazing growth and development facts related to these two important body organs. Here are a few to get you started; others can be collected via library or Internet resources:

    – The human eye can distinguish up to 10 million different color shades.

    – Human eyes produce about eight ounces (one cup) of tears a year.

    – In order to hear a sound, the eardrum only has to move 40 billionths of an inch.

    – Humans hear sounds between 20 and 16,000 cycles per second. Dolphins can identify sounds up to 150,000 vibrations per second.

ANSWER FIRST!

Using the book *Eyes and Ears*, write a question for each answer below:

Question 1: _____

_____

Answer 1: _____ The vitreous humor. _____

Question 2: _____

_____

Answer 2: _____ The "hammer," "anvil," and "stirrup." _____

Question 3: _____

_____

Answer 3: _____ This is where seeing finally takes place. _____

Question 4: _____

_____

Answer 4: _____ To prevent any damage. _____

Question 5: _____

_____

Answer 5: _____ "Collecting information from the outside" _____

From *MORE Science Adventures with Children's Literature: Reading Comprehension and Inquiry-Based Science* by Anthony D. Fredericks. Westport, CT: Teacher Ideas Press. Copyright © 2008.

HEAR, HERE!

All around you—every day—there are lots of different sounds. Often we aren't aware of all the sounds our ears pick up. Here's a simple activity that will help you focus on some of the sounds around you.

Stand (by yourself) in the middle of a room (at home or at school). Close your eyes and listen carefully for five minutes. What are all the different sounds you hear? Can you describe each sound? Record what you hear below:

Sound 1: _____

Description: _____

Sound 2: _____

Description: _____

Sound 3: _____

Description: _____

Sound 4: _____

Description:_____

Sound 5: _____

Description: _____

From *MORE Science Adventures with Children's Literature: Reading Comprehension and Inquiry-Based Science* by Anthony D. Fredericks. Westport, CT: Teacher Ideas Press. Copyright © 2008.

HEAR, HERE! (CONTINUED)

Now, go outside and stand in the middle of a large area (a playground, baseball field, vacant lot, your back yard). Repeat the activity above and record your results below:

Sound 1: _____

Description: _____

Sound 2: _____

Description: _____

Sound 3: _____

Description: _____

Sound 4: _____

Description: _____

Sound 5: _____

Description: _____

Did you hear any sounds that were similar?   YES   NO

Did you hear any sounds that you did not expect?   YES   NO

From *MORE Science Adventures with Children's Literature: Reading Comprehension and Inquiry-Based Science* by Anthony D. Fredericks. Westport, CT: Teacher Ideas Press. Copyright © 2008.

OPTICAL ILLUSIONS

Eyes and Ears provides you with some optical illusions—something you think you see, but it is not exactly what is really there. You may be interested in some additional optical illusions—opportunities for you to play some tricks on your own brain.

Here are some great Web sites that you may wish to check out:

- http://kids.niehs.nih.gov/illusion/illusions.htm

- http://www.indianchild.com/3d%20mainpage.htm

- http://www.illusion-optical.com/Optical-Illusions/TopHatTrick.php

- http://www.coolopticalillusions.com/invertedflag.htm

- http://www.scientificpsychic.com/graphics/

NOTE: These were current as of the writing of *MORE Science Adventures with Children's Literature*. Please be aware that the Internet is always changing. Some of these sites may change, some may be eliminated, and some may be different by the time you log on to them. Always check with an adult before accessing any new Web site.

From *MORE Science Adventures with Children's Literature: Reading Comprehension and Inquiry-Based Science* by Anthony D. Fredericks. Westport, CT: Teacher Ideas Press. Copyright © 2008.

POST A POSTER

Join with some other students and form a "Poster Team." Make a poster displaying what you learned about eyes and ears. Be prepared to share your poster with the class.

1. What is some of the most important information you learned in the book?

2. Provide one or more labeled diagrams (of the human eye or human ear).

3. Provide some new information from another book or an Internet site.

4. Include a graph or chart of various scientific facts.

5. Include an illustration, photograph, or drawing.

6. Create an original jingle, slogan, or saying.

7. Offer advice on how humans should protect their eyes and ears.

8. Anything else.

Make a plan for sharing your poster with other members of the class.

Presentation date: _____

The Sea, the Storm, and the Mangrove Tangle

Lynne Cherry

New York: Farrar Straus Giroux, 2004

SELECTED CITATIONS

- **2005 Green Earth Award** (for the best environmentally themed children's book of the year)—Newton Marasco Foundation

- "Teachers will want this for elementary-school units about the environment and the web of life, but children [will] choose it on their own for the rich, underwater scenes of tropical sea life."—*Booklist*

SUMMARY

A mangrove tree harbors a unique collection of creatures—both large and small. This tiny ecosystem is alive with myriad sounds and wide diversity of life. The tree provides shelter and nourishment for many animals of the land, sea, and air. It is a small world—but an extremely important one, for it mirrors the lives that are intertwined in other ecosystems and other environments. In short, this is a classic Lynne Cherry book—full of insights, colorful illustrations, and far-ranging implications for all life on this planet. This is a book that will not be forgotten—a book that harbors valuable lessons for us all.

SUGGESTED GRADE LEVELS: 3–6

LESSON OBJECTIVES

Science Standards

- Content Standard C: Life Science

  The characteristics of organisms (K–4)

  Life cycles of organisms (K–4)

  Organisms and environments (K–4)

  Reproduction and heredity (5–8)

  Regulation and behavior (5–8)

  Populations and ecosystems (5–8)

  Diversity and adaptations of organisms (5–8)

CRITICAL THINKING QUESTIONS

1. How is this ecosystem similar to (or different from) the ecosystem in which you live?

2. Why do so many creatures depend on the mangrove tree for their survival?

3. Which of the animals would suffer the most if mangrove trees were completely eliminated?

4. How can a storm be beneficial to life in and around the mangrove tree?

5. How is this book similar to the author's best-selling *The Great Kapok Tree*?

COMPREHENSION LESSON (DRTA)

Setting the Stage

Invite students to discuss what they know about life in the Caribbean Sea. What's the weather like? What animals live there? You may wish to record some of this information on the chalkboard or a large sheet of newsprint.

Before Reading

Involve students in a Directed Reading-Thinking Activity (DRTA). Begin by inviting them to look at the title of the book and the illustration on the cover. Ask: "What do you think this book will be about?" Encourage students to make predictions and to elaborate on the reasons for making them ("Why do you think so?"). Invite students to read to the end of the double-page spread with the two pelicans (" . . . shore of a faraway lagoon."). (*Note:* The pages in this book are unnumbered.)

During Reading

After students read to the end of the page indicated above, ask them the following questions:

• What do you think will happen next?

• Why do you think so?

• How can you prove it?

After allowing sufficient time for discussion, ask students to read to the end of the double-page spread with the illustration of the approaching storm and the five animals (" . . . hurricane was on the way."). Repeat the three questions from above. Some of the predictions will be refined, some will be eliminated, and new ones will be formulated. Ask students, "How do you know?" to encourage clarification or verification. Repeat this process for the remainder of the book.

After Reading

Invite students to discuss the process of making predictions. How did their perceptions of the mangrove tangle or the plot of the story change as they read? Did the act of making predictions stimulate them to read more of the story? What predictions were "close" and what predictions were "way off the mark"? Help students understand that the act of making predictions is something all accomplished readers do.

LITERATURE EXTENSIONS

Invite students to select one or more of the following activities:

1. As a class, students may wish to create a weather dictionary containing all the words related to hurricanes. They may include definitions and illustrations, finding pictures on the Internet, in the daily newspaper, or in news magazines.

2. Invite students to assemble a time line of the 10 most powerful hurricanes in history. When did they occur? Where did they occur? How much property was destroyed? How many people lost their lives? What were the long-term effects? Make sure students understand that although the United States has experienced many hurricanes over the centuries, other countries have also had their share of hurricanes, too.

3. Ask students to create (either as individuals or in small groups) a letter to be sent to a local congressperson or senator advocating the preservation of mangrove ecosystems. The author has included this suggestion in her Author's Note at the end of the book. Ask students to follow through and request consideration of both national and international coastal area preservation efforts.

4. The author also includes the Web sites of two organizations working to protect mangrove ecosystems: The Industrial Shrimp Action Network (www.shrimpaction.org) and the Mangrove Action Project (www.earthisland.org/map/index.htm). Invite students to log on to these two sites and share the information with other students in the school.

5. Invite students to create a brochure, poster, or other type of "advertisement" that would encourage people to visit intact mangrove habitats. What information should be included? What would encourage individuals to spend their money to visit a remote tropical site?

6. After consulting other resources, invite students to create a list of the "Five Reasons Why We Should Preserve Mangrove Ecosystems" (they act as filters, they retard the movement of silt, they provide shelter for various animals, etc.). Invite students to decide on the five most critical reasons people should do everything they can to ensure the survival of these unique ecosystems.

7. Ask students to write an imaginary letter to the author to thank her for alerting the world to the importance of mangrove ecosystems around the world. You may wish to send a letter to the author (in care of the publisher—Farrar Straus Giroux, 19 Union Square West, New York, NY 10003). Inform students that this author receives many letters from readers, so she may not be able to write a letter in response.

8. Invite students to create and decorate a bumper sticker expressing the main point of the story. Make a car out of construction paper and put it on a bulletin board, then place the bumper stickers around it.

9. Encourage students to write and illustrate their own stories about ecosystem preservation. They may wish to comment on their own efforts or those of their family in helping to preserve the environment—locally or globally. As appropriate, invite students to share these stories with the entire class.

DRTA

Part I: The title and the cover illustration

- What do you think the book will be about?

- Why do you think so?

- How can you prove it?

Part II: From the beginning of the story to the "two pelican spread"

- What do you think will happen next?

- Why do you think so?

- How can you prove it?

Part III: From the "two pelican spread" to the "approaching storm spread"

- What do you think will happen next?

- Why do you think so?

- How can you prove it?

Which predictions were accurate?

Which predictions were inaccurate?

208   From *MORE Science Adventures with Children's Literature: Reading Comprehension and Inquiry-Based Science*
by Anthony D. Fredericks. Westport, CT: Teacher Ideas Press. Copyright © 2008.

FIVE IMPRESSIONS

Certain words can be used to describe a piece of writing—whether in a single paragraph or a long book. Those words can also be used to describe the impression the writing has on a reader. Some of those words are listed in the boxes below. Go through this chart and place a check mark in <u>five</u> individual boxes. Select those words you think would apply to *The Sea, the Storm, and the Mangrove Tangle* by Lynne Cherry. Then use those five words in a brief summary or review of the work. Be sure to use complete sentences.

☐ satisfied	☐ simple	☐ time	☐ sense	☐ detail
☐ puzzle	☐ favorite	☐ setting	☐ great	☐ place
☐ wished	☐ wonder	☐ question	☐ enjoyed	☐ dislike
☐ purpose	☐ ending	☐ character	☐ title	☐ beginning
☐ unknown	☐ author	☐ facts	☐ location	☐ situation

Summary/Review:

_____

_____

_____

_____

_____

_____

From *MORE Science Adventures with Children's Literature: Reading Comprehension and Inquiry-Based Science* by Anthony D. Fredericks. Westport, CT: Teacher Ideas Press. Copyright © 2008.

LEARN AND SHARE

Complete the boxes below with information you learned while reading *The Sea, the Storm, and the Mangrove Tangle*.

Three things I learned while reading this book:

Two things I would like to share with someone else:

One thing I would like to learn more about:

From *MORE Science Adventures with Children's Literature: Reading Comprehension and Inquiry-Based Science* by Anthony D. Fredericks. Westport, CT: Teacher Ideas Press. Copyright © 2008.

IN THE MANGROVE TANGLE

The leaves of a mangrove tree are illustrated below. Around those leaves are eight lines. At the end of each line write the name (and/or draw an illustration of) an animal that was mentioned in the book. When completed, you will have put together a web of creatures that depend on a mangrove tangle for their survival.

From *MORE Science Adventures with Children's Literature: Reading Comprehension and Inquiry-Based Science* by Anthony D. Fredericks. Westport, CT: Teacher Ideas Press. Copyright © 2008.

Science Verse

Jon Scieszka and Lane Smith

New York: Viking, 2004

SELECTED CITATIONS

- **2004 Parents Choice Award (Nonfiction)**—Parents' Choice Foundation

- "A fun read for kids from grade school to college and every science nut in your family."
  —*Children's Literature*

SUMMARY

The laughter spills off the pages of this inviting book. Students will appreciate science in new ways after hearing the poems sprinkled throughout this creatively designed volume of scientific insights, challenges, and perspectives. Using familiar nursery rhymes and Mother Goose tales, the authors have crafted a book that will truly stand the test of time—and the scrutiny of students. Not only will this book spark a rash of creative writing endeavors in your classroom, it will also inspire a new appreciation for science as a fun subject. Run and get a copy right away!

SUGGESTED GRADE LEVELS: 3–6

LESSON OBJECTIVES

Science Standards

- Content Standard A: Science as Inquiry

    Understandings about science inquiry (K–4, 5–8)

- Content Standard B: Physical Science

    Properties and changes in properties of matter (5–8)

- Content Standard C: Life Science

    The characteristics of organisms (K–4)

- Content Standard D: Earth and Space Science

    Objects in the sky (K–4)

    Structure of the Earth system (5–8)

- Content Standard E: Science and Technology

    Abilities of technological design (K–4, 5–8)

- Content Standard G: History and Nature of Science

    Science as a human endeavor (K–4, 5–8)

CRITICAL THINKING QUESTIONS

1. Which of the poems did you enjoy most?

2. What area of science lends itself to poetry?

3. What type of science poem would you like to write?

4. Why is science funny?

5. How did the illustrations help you enjoy this book?

COMPREHENSION LESSON

Setting the Stage

Duplicate the project page for Divergent Questions for the book *Science Verse*. Distribute the sheets to students.

Before Reading

Prior to reading the book (either individually or as part of a series of read-aloud sessions), invite students to review the questions on the Divergent Questions sheet. Inform students that you are not looking for right answers at this point, but are merely tapping into their background knowledge about science in general. After allowing sufficient discussion about the questions (and their responses), inform students that they should look for potential answers to the questions as they read the book.

During Reading

Each day, students may read several poems in the book. They may wish to keep track of selected Divergent Questions (and the possible responses) on a separate sheet of paper.

After Reading

After students have finished reading the book, take time to review the Divergent Questions again. Make note of those questions in which students changed or altered their response as a result of information learned in the book. Ask them: "What new information did you learn?" "Why did you change or alter your initial response?" "What might be some additional Divergent Questions we could add to our list?" "Which question(s) caused you to think the most?"

LITERATURE EXTENSIONS

Invite students to select one or more of the following activities:

1. Invite students to share the poems in *Science Verse* with other students throughout the school. Ask students to take a poll of which poems get the "highest marks"—that is, which poems got the biggest laugh or were appreciated the most? Have students create a chart of the "Top Five" poems from this book (as critiqued by a sampling of students throughout the school).

2. Ask students to work with the school librarian to locate the "original" poems for each of the "modified" poems in this book. Who wrote the original poems? In what book(s) can those original poems be found? Can the original poem for every entry in this book be found in the school library?

3. Invite students to modify a selection of these poems and turn them into social studies poetry. Are the poems just as funny with a social studies theme as they are with a science theme? Are there some poems that just lend themselves to science, but not to social studies? Bottom line: What is funnier—science or social studies?

4. What about math? Is it possible to convert these poems (or the original poetry) into mathematical poems? Is math funny? What would have to be done in order for a mathematically themed poem to be humorous?

5. Invite students to select one of their favorite poems from the book. Ask them to record the poem on a separate sheet of paper and then add one stanza (of their own creation). That is, invite students to create a poetical sequel to a specific poem. Using the rhyme scheme of the author, can students continue a poem and maintain its humor?

6. If possible, invite a local scientist to visit your classroom and discuss some of the reasons she or he decided to enter the field. What does the individual like so much about her or his work? What does he or she like least? What aspects of her or his job are most humorous? Do they know any science-related jokes? What makes science funny?

7. Invite students to create a readers theatre script from this book. Share one or more readers theatre scripts (from Part III of this book) and then ask students to develop an original script using some of the characters, settings, or situations from this book.

8. Ask students to discuss the role of science in everybody's life. Why should people know science? How is science important in our daily lives? Why should people know "stuff" about science? Why should they care? You may wish to organize students into two groups to debate the pros and cons of science education.

9. Share one or more of Shel Silverstein's or Jack Prelutsky's books. How is the poetry in those books similar to or different from the poetry in this book? What makes all that poetry so funny? What topics (in all the books shared with students) are best suited for humorous poetry?

10. As an extension of the activity above, invite students to create posters or bulletin boards of selected examples of their favorite (and most humorous) poetry from a variety of sources. Ask other students to vote on the selected poems to determine the all-time, most humorous and most funny poem of all time. What was the topic, and why was that particular topic so humorous?

11. The illustrations in this book are distinctive and dynamic. Plan time to discuss with students the impact those illustrations had on their enjoyment of this book. Did the illustrations provide them with additional ideas relative to the topic of the poem? Were the illustrations as humorous as the poems? What makes these illustrations different from those found in many children's books—particularly books of poetry?

DIVERGENT QUESTIONS

1. List all the words you can think of that describe science.

2. List as many scientists as you can.

3. How would someone from another country enjoy these poems?

4. What would it mean if we never studied science in school?

5. How would your grandparents describe the school's science program?

6. How would you feel if you were a scientist?

7. What would your grandparents think about all the new science technology?

From *MORE Science Adventures with Children's Literature: Reading Comprehension and Inquiry-Based Science* by Anthony D. Fredericks. Westport, CT: Teacher Ideas Press. Copyright © 2008.

DIVERGENT QUESTIONS (CONTINUED)

8. You are an old person. Describe your feelings about dinosaurs.

9. How are insects like people?

10. I only know about our solar system. Explain some other parts of the universe for me.

11. What ideas from this book are like ideas you've read about in other science books?

12. What is so strange about food chains?

13. What would happen if there were fewer scientists?

From *MORE Science Adventures with Children's Literature: Reading Comprehension and Inquiry-Based Science* by Anthony D. Fredericks. Westport, CT: Teacher Ideas Press. Copyright © 2008.

SLIME TIME

There are lots of icky, gooey, and yucky things in the book *Science Verse*. If you would like to create your own icky, gooey stuff, here is a basic recipe for **Slime**. It's easy to make, but be sure to read through the entire recipe before you begin. (You may need some adult assistance.) Following the directions exactly as they are written here will help ensure that you create the best possible Slime.

Materials:

- sealable plastic sandwich bag or freezer bag
- 1 ounce of white glue (e.g., Elmer's Glue®)
- 3–4 drops of food coloring
- 2 ounces of water
- ½ teaspoon of borax (This is used in washing machines to help get clothes cleaner. It can be found in the laundry section of your local grocery store [20 Mule Team Borax® is a brand name].)
- a measuring spoon

Directions:

1. Pour 1 ounce of white glue into the bottom of a plastic sandwich bag.
2. Drop in 2–3 drops of food coloring (any color).
3. Pour in 1 ounce of water.
4. Use your hands to gently squish the sides of the sandwich bag together until the color is thoroughly mixed in (this will take about 2–3 minutes). Set the bag aside for a while.
5. Put ½ teaspoon of borax into a small cup or container.
6. Pour 1 ounce of water into the cup and stir the borax and water together with a spoon.
7. Quickly pour the borax and water into the plastic sandwich bag (since the borax doesn't dissolve in the water, be sure that all the borax granules go into the bag; you may need to use the spoon to scrape out any leftover borax granules). Begin to gently squish everything together (make sure the bag is sealed at the top.)

From *MORE Science Adventures with Children's Literature: Reading Comprehension and Inquiry-Based Science* by Anthony D. Fredericks. Westport, CT: Teacher Ideas Press. Copyright © 2008.

8. Keep squishing until no liquid remains (this takes about 3–5 minutes). While you're squishing, you'll notice that the ingredients are getting firmer and "rubbery." (If there's still some liquid in the bag, sprinkle in just *a little bit* more borax and continue to squish until all the liquid is gone.)

9. Open the top of the bag and set it aside for about 15–30 minutes (this allows some of the leftover liquid to evaporate and the chemical reaction to complete itself).

10. Now reach in and pull out a handful of homemade Slime.

Important Notes:

a. The amount of borax used in this recipe will determine the viscosity (the "thickness") of the Slime. A little more borax and the liquid will be "thicker;" a little less borax and the liquid will be "thinner."

b. Regular tap water or distilled water can be used for this recipe. Please be aware that tap water varies from place to place (the chemicals and/or minerals in the water differ from city to city and from urban to rural sources). The chemical and minerals will affect the viscosity of your Slime. You may need to compensate for the chemical composition of your own local water supply by adjusting the amount of borax used in the recipe.

c. Although borax is a common and frequently used laundry additive, you should note that there is a warning label on the side of the box. This means that you should never place borax or Slime in or around your mouth.

d. Slime should be kept in a covered container. A plastic sandwich bag, a sealable freezer bag, or a food container with a sealable lid works best.

Description:

When white glue, borax, water, and food coloring are mixed together, Slime is created. Your slime has a special scientific name—it's known as a colloid.

A colloid is a mixture of two or more substances. A colloid could be a liquid in a liquid, a gas in a liquid, a solid in a liquid, a liquid in a solid, a gas in a solid, and so on. Slime is a colloid that combined a solid (borax) with a liquid (glue and water).

From *MORE Science Adventures with Children's Literature: Reading Comprehension and Inquiry-Based Science* by Anthony D. Fredericks. Westport, CT: Teacher Ideas Press. Copyright © 2008.

YOUR TURN

Throughout the book *Science Verse* there are many examples of humorous science poems—each one a modification, alteration, or complete destruction of a popular Mother Goose rhyme or other familiar poem.

Now it's your turn! Select a familiar poem (check in the school library for poetry collections—particularly those with which you may be most familiar, such as Mother Goose). Record the poem below. Then play with the words. How could you change that poem into something that's just a little weird, just a little strange, just a little odd? If you wish, work with a friend to create your new science poem—perhaps one that could be added to a future edition of *Science Verse*.

Name of Poem:

Book or Resource (where poem is located):

Write the entire poem here:

Rewrite the poem in your own words:

Be sure to share your poem with others. Collect several poems together into a new book.

From *MORE Science Adventures with Children's Literature: Reading Comprehension and Inquiry-Based Science* by Anthony D. Fredericks. Westport, CT: Teacher Ideas Press. Copyright © 2008.

I SCREAM, YOU SCREAM, WE ALL SCREAM FOR ICE CREAM!

Are you ready for some more "Science Verse" (I scream, you scream, we all scream for ice cream") ? Below is a basic recipe for ice cream that's easy to make. You can (with a little adult supervision) create your own varieties and flavors of ice cream in only five minutes. A great summertime activity and a delicious treat!!

Materials:

- 1 gallon sealable freezer bag
- 1 pint sealable freezer bag
- 2 cups (approx.) of ice (small cubes or cracked)
- 6 tablespoons of salt (approx.)
- 1 tablespoon of sugar
- ½ teaspoon of vanilla
- ½ cup of whole milk
- measuring spoon
- measuring cup
- spoon

Directions:

1. Put the ice into the large freezer bag. Pour the salt over the ice in the bag. Set this large bag aside for a few moments.
2. Pour the milk into the small freezer bag. Add the sugar and vanilla to the milk. Mix the ingredients thoroughly (the bag can be squished by hand for 20–30 seconds).
3. Remove some of the air from the small freezer bag and seal it tightly.
4. Place the small freezer bag inside the large freezer bag. Seal the large freezer bag.
5. Place the large freezer bag on a flat surface (e.g., table top, kitchen counter) and turn it over and over (by the corners) for approximately five minutes.
6. Carefully open the large freezer bag and remove the small freezer bag.
7. Wipe off the top of the small freezer bag and open it.
8. Spoon out some of the homemade ice cream and enjoy!

From *MORE Science Adventures with Children's Literature: Reading Comprehension and Inquiry-Based Science* by Anthony D. Fredericks. Westport, CT: Teacher Ideas Press. Copyright © 2008.

I SCREAM, YOU SCREAM, WE ALL SCREAM FOR ICE CREAM! (CONTINUED)

Important Notes:

a. Be sure to use whole milk only. The recipe will not work with skim milk or other types of reduced fat milk.

b. Always use name-brand freezer bags. Generic freezer bags may not be completely sealed around the edges. This will cause leaking during the activity.

c. You may wish to experiment later by adding different flavors to the basic recipe. Suggested flavors include peppermint, cinnamon, and cherry. You may also wish to add chocolate chips or coconut sprinkles to your ice cream creations. Add different food colors to create colorful ice cream (blue ice cream?).

Description:

Combine whole milk, some flavoring, some sweetener, and a freezing agent (ice), and you have ice cream (a crude form, to be sure). When you put salt on top of the ice, the ice begins to melt (the temperature of the ice is slightly raised). This cools the milk mixture inside the bag. The milk mixture begins to form ice crystals, and it gets thicker and thicker. Eventually, the milk mixture cools down to the temperature of the ice that surrounds it. When that happens, the milk mixture is thickened (because of the fat molecules in the milk) and becomes ice cream. The sugar and other ingredients (already in the bag) add flavor to the mixture.

From *MORE Science Adventures with Children's Literature: Reading Comprehension and Inquiry-Based Science* by Anthony D. Fredericks. Westport, CT: Teacher Ideas Press. Copyright © 2008.

Near One Cattail:
Turtles, Logs and Leaping Frogs

Anthony D. Fredericks

Nevada City, CA: Dawn Publications, 2005

SELECTED CITATIONS

- **2006 Green Earth Award** (for the best environmentally themed children's book of the year)—Newton Marasco Foundation

- **2006 Ecology and Nature Award**—*Skipping Stones Magazine*

SUMMARY

This book introduces young readers to the wonders of a wetlands environment. Readers journey with the heroine as she discovers an incredible variety of wildlife in this dynamic community. Frogs with big bulging eyes, sunbathing turtles, zip-zipping dragonflies, paddling beetles, and brown-feathered ducks "swim, soar or crawl in this sog-soggy home." The emphasis is on the plants and animals that make this ecosystem such an incredible place to investigate and discover.

SUGGESTED GRADE LEVELS: 1–4

LESSON OBJECTIVES

Science Standards

- Content Standard A: Science as Inquiry

    Abilities necessary to do science inquiry (K–4, 5–8)

    Understandings about science inquiry (K–4, 5–8)

- Content Standard C: Life Science

    The characteristics of organisms (K–4)

    Life cycles of organisms (K–4)

    Organisms and environments (K–4)

    Populations and ecosystems (5–8)

    Diversity and adaptations of organisms (5–8)

- Content Standard F: Science in Personal and Social Perspectives

    Characteristics and changes in populations (K–4)

    Changes in environments (K–4)

    Populations, resources, and environments (5–8)

- Content Standard G: History and Nature of Science

    Science as a human endeavor (K–4, 5–8)

CRITICAL THINKING QUESTIONS

1. Which of the animals did you find most interesting?

2. Which of the animals would you like to learn more about?

3. What would you like to discover in a wetlands environment?

4. How are all the animals able to live together?

5. What did you enjoy most about the book?

6. If you could ask the author one question, what would it be?

COMPREHENSION LESSON (K-W-L)

Setting the Stage

Before distributing copies of the book to the class or a guided reading group, read the opening letter (from "Your big-eyed buddy, Frog") to students. Afterward invite students to make some predictions about the contents of the book. What will take place? What creatures will be featured? Take a few minutes to discuss and share all predictions.

Before Reading

Invite students to participate in a K-W-L activity. Ask students to talk about what they already know about wetlands. Write this information in the K section of the K-W-L chart. Encourage students to categorize the information they have volunteered. Students may wish to create a semantic web of this data. Invite students to make predictions about the types of information the book will contain. Write these predictions on a chalkboard or large sheet of newsprint. Ask students to generate their own questions about the book. These can be discussed and recorded in the W—What we want to find out—section of the chart.

During Reading

Invite students to read the book and record any answers to their questions. Students may wish to do this individually or in pairs.

After Reading

Upon completion of the book, provide students with an opportunity to discuss the information learned and how it relates to their prior knowledge. Talk about questions posed for which no information was found in the book. Help students discover other sources for satisfying their inquiries.

LITERATURE EXTENSIONS

Invite students to select one or more of the following activities:

1. Encourage students to write a fictitious letter to the girl in the story. What would they like to say to her? What would they like to know about her adventures in the wetland ecosystem profiled in the book? What else would they like to know about her?

2. Invite each student in the class to select one of the animals illustrated in this book. Encourage each child to conduct necessary research (in the library, on the Internet) on his or her identified species. Then invite students to each write a series of diary entries told from the perspective of the creature, such as "A Day in the Life of a Frog," or "My Life as a Dragonfly."

3. Provide students with an assortment of magazines that contain pictures of wetland creatures (e.g., *National Geographic, Ranger Rick, National Wildlife*). Encourage them to bring in old magazines from home. Invite students to make a class collage of a wetlands environment by pasting pictures of different critters on a large sheet of newsprint (to be displayed in the classroom).

4. Invite students to read one or more of the other books in this series: *Under One Rock: Bugs, Slugs and Other Ughs* (2001), *In One Tidepool: Crabs, Snails and Salty Tails* (2002), *Around One Cactus: Owls, Bats and Leaping Rats* (2003), and *On One Flower: Butterflies, Ticks and a Few More Icks* (2006). How are the books similar? How are they different?

5. Be sure to check out the following Web site: http://www.cln.org/themes/wetlands. html. Here, students and teachers will find a multitude of curricular resources (information, content, etc.) to help them learn about all about wetlands. In addition, there are lots of links to instructional materials (e.g., lesson plans) that will help you provide instruction in this theme. In a word, this site is SUPER!

6. Provide students with blank maps of North America. After appropriate research, invite them to color in the places in the United States and Canada where wetlands would be found. If more appropriate, consider providing youngsters with a blank map of your state and invite them to locate regional wetland areas.

7. Invite students to put together a "Wetlands Newspaper" that presents interesting facts and observations about wetland creatures. Invite students to use the same sections as the local newspaper (e.g., sports—how fast some wetland animals can move; fashion—what the latest "colors" all the fashionable critters are wearing are; food and health—the different diets of wetland creatures). Students can use a word processing program to assemble the newspaper and then print it for distribution to other classrooms.

8. Invite students to log onto the wildlife page of the National Wildlife Federation: http://www.nwf.org/wildlife/. Students may wish to locate various animals profiled in *Near One Cattail* and learn additional information about them through this all-inclusive site. This site is also appropriate for research on selected wetland and endangered animal species.

9. Discuss with students the similarities and differences between the community of animals in a wetlands environment and the community in which they live. Invite students to create an oversized Venn diagram illustrating those comparisons.

10. Here are three excellent videos (all VHS) about wetlands that you may wish to obtain for your classroom or library (all are available from Amazon.com): *Wetlands, Marshes and Swamps* (1996), *Conserving America: The Wetlands* (1994), and *Wild Wetlands (Animal Safari, Vol. 7)* (2000).

11. Invite students to discuss the similarities between human dwellings and animal homes. What are some of the things that determine where an animal lives? Are those conditions or features similar to the considerations of humans in selecting a living site? Do animals, particularly wetland animals, have more options for living spaces than humans?

K-W-L

K	W	L

From *MORE Science Adventures with Children's Literature: Reading Comprehension and Inquiry-Based Science* by Anthony D. Fredericks. Westport, CT: Teacher Ideas Press. Copyright © 2008.

WRITE ON!

Contact several of the following groups and ask for information about the work they do and the types of printed information they have available for students:

Ducks Unlimited
One Waterfowl Way
Memphis, TN 38120
www.ducks.org

Izaak Walton League of America
707 Conservation Lane
Gaithersburg, MD 20878
www.iwla.org

National Wildlife Federation
11100 Wildlife Center Drive
Reston, VA 20190
www.nwf.org

Wetlands International—North America
c/o USFWS
Division of International Affairs
4401 North Fairfax Dr.
Room 730–ARLSQ
Arlington, VA 22203–1622

From *MORE Science Adventures with Children's Literature: Reading Comprehension and Inquiry-Based Science* by Anthony D. Fredericks. Westport, CT: Teacher Ideas Press. Copyright © 2008.

WANTED

Look through the classified section of your local newspaper. Based on examples in the newspaper, create an original classified advertisement based on information in the book. Following is an example:

> FOR RENT: Lily pad. Sometimes wet, sometimes dry. Lots of neighbors. Lots of plants. Waterfront property with great view. Reasonable rates. Available immediately. Call Freddy Frog at 123-4567 any time after bird migration.

Your Ad

| |
| |
| |
| |
| |
| |
| |
| |
| |
| |

E-E-ECOSYSTEM

Here's how you can create your own miniature ecosystem. Although this is not a wetlands ecosystem, it has many of the same components.

Materials:

- 2- or 3-liter plastic soda bottle
- pebbles
- aquarium charcoal
- soil
- water
- small plants (see below)
- small animals (see below)
- string or rubber band
- piece of lightweight cloth

Directions:

1. Ask an adult to cut off the top of the plastic soda bottle.
2. Cover the bottom of the bottle with a layer of small pebbles mixed with bits of aquarium charcoal.
3. Put in a layer of soil about twice as deep as the first layer.
4. Sprinkle the soil with just enough water to keep it moist (you may have to add water occasionally).
5. Place several plants, such as mosses, ferns, lichens, or liverworts (available from your local garden shop), in the soil.
6. Place several rocks or pieces of wood in the bottom of the bottle.
7. Some small land animals (such as snails, earthworms, a tiny turtle, or a small frog) can also be added.
8. To allow humidity and ventilation, place some lightweight cloth over the top, holding it on with a rubber band or tying it there with some string.
9. Keep the bottle out of direct sunlight and be sure to feed the occupants of your habitat regularly.

Description:

Your miniature ecosystem will grow and flourish as long as you add some moisture occasionally. If you put animals in the bottle, check with your local pet store for an appropriate food supply.

This ecosystem is similar to a wetlands or woodlands ecosystem in nature. Plants and animals are able to survive because they are dependent on each other and because all their needs (air, water, food) are provided in their immediate environment.

230   From *MORE Science Adventures with Children's Literature: Reading Comprehension and Inquiry-Based Science* by Anthony D. Fredericks. Westport, CT: Teacher Ideas Press. Copyright © 2008.

Leaf Man

Lois Ehlert

Orlando, FL: Harcourt, 2005

SELECTED CITATIONS

- **2006 Picture Book Award**—*Boston Globe-Horn Book*

- **2006 Notable Children's Book Award**—American Library Association

SUMMARY

With a most creative use of autumn leaves, the author weaves a story that will be treasured by generations of children (and educators). This delightful and inventive tales recounts the story of the Leaf Man, who travels with the wind. Along his journey there are chickens, ducks, geese, potatoes, carrots, and spotted cows—all dynamically created with an inventive placement of leaves. The simple text complements the illustrations, which will amaze and inspire.

SUGGESTED GRADE LEVELS: 1–3

LESSON OBJECTIVES

Science Standards

- Content Standard A: Science as Inquiry

  Understandings about science inquiry (K–4)

- Content Standard C: Life Science

  Organisms and environments (K–4)

CRITICAL THINKING QUESTIONS

1. Where does the Leaf Man go when the wind blows?

2. What did you like about the illustrations?

3. What other animals do you think should be in this book?

4. What did you like most about the Leaf Man?

5. What are some of your favorite leaves?

COMPREHENSION LESSON (STORY IMPRESSIONS)

Setting the Stage

Duplicate the project page for Story Impressions. Provide enough copies for all students in the class. You may also wish to provide students with an opportunity to discuss some of the background information they have about leaves. Some of this information may be listed on the chalkboard.

Before Reading

Present the Story Impressions sheet to individuals or small groups of students. Tell students that the list represents important concepts from the book *Leaf Man*. Invite students to read through the list (top to bottom) and encourage them to discuss how the ideas might be related or connect.

Invite students to construct a story using all of the printed concepts (in the order in which they are listed). This can be done as a story crafted and written by a small group of students or by the entire class. Make sure students understand that they are making predictions about the plot of the story based simply on a few facts from that story.

During Reading

Provide all students with copies of the book (or use it as a read-aloud) and invite them to read it silently.

After Reading

After completing a reading of the book, offer students an opportunity to discuss how their original story and the actual story in the book compare. The object is *not* to have an exact match, but rather to see how a basic set of ideas can be interpreted differently by two separate "authors."

LITERATURE EXTENSIONS

Invite students to select one or more of the following activities:

1. Ask students to collect a variety of leaves from around the school grounds, their neighborhoods, or their own backyards. Invite them to work in groups and assemble some of the leaves into a "leaf man" or some type of animal. How many different types of ani-

mals can students create? Afterward, students may wish to glue the leaves to sheets of construction paper and post them on the bulletin board.

2. As an extension of the activity above, invite students (again, in small groups) to craft a make-believe story about their animal creations. Where does their leaf animal live? What does it see? Does it travel anywhere? What kind of adventures does it have? Post the stories beside the appropriate "animals" on the bulletin board.

3. Show students how to make a leaf rubbing (lay a piece of tracing paper over a leaf and gently rub a soft-leaded pencil across the leaf—an outline of the leaf will appear). Invite students to create a variety of leaf rubbings (with a variety of leaves). These can be arranged into an attractive display in the classroom or library.

4. Ask each student to imagine that "Leaf Man" was flying over her or his house. What would he see? What would he experience? Invite each student to write a "sidebar" to the book—a brief story about the Leaf Man's travels or experiences over her or his house.

5. Trees for Life Adventure (http://treesforlife.org/teacher/adventure/) provides students with hands-on experiences that help them learn about the role of trees in our ecosystem. For a small fee per student, the organization will send planting cartons and tree seeds for each individual. In addition, you will receive a teacher handbook that includes planting instructions, tree-related activities, arts and craft ideas, tree facts, and a letter to parents. Check this out.

6. The National Arbor Day Foundation (http://www.arborday.org/) has an incredible variety of materials for classroom teachers and their students. There are brochures, planting guides, informational packets, trees for sale, and other "goodies" that no teacher should pass up. Check out the Web site and the offerings.

7. Obtain a leaf identification guide or book from your school library or local public library. Provide opportunities for students to bring in collected leaves from the local area and identify the type of tree each leaf belongs to. You may wish to enlist the aid of some parent volunteers for this identification project. How many different varieties of trees are there in your local area?

8. Invite an employee of a local garden center or nursery to visit the classroom or library and discuss the trees that are native to your area. What planting techniques should be used? How should trees be cared for? Why are some trees easier to grow than others? Students may wish to gather the responses to those questions (as well as their own) into an informational brochure or leaflet to be distributed throughout the school.

9. Ask students to cut out an oversized leaf shape from a sheet of construction paper or newsprint. Ask students to each write one or more facts about leaves inside the shape. Post this on the bulletin board. They may wish to do the same thing on another leaf shape, this time including facts about "Leaf Man" and his adventures in the book.

STORY IMPRESSIONS

Several selected story ideas from the book *Leaf Man* are listed on the left-hand side of this sheet. Read through this list and imagine how a story with these concepts might be constructed. Then, begin to write a story using all the concepts from top to bottom. Remember, your story may be different from the actual one; that's OK. We'll discuss any differences and similarities when we finish reading the book.

	Your Story:
↓ **A pile of leaves**	
The wind blew him away	
↓ **He was headed east**	
Past the chickens	
↓ **Over the ducks**	
Over the pumpkins	
↓ **Past carrots**	
Over the meadows	
↓ **Where the wind blows**	
On a lake breeze	
↓ **Following butterflies**	
With a flock of birds	
↓ **Waiting to go home**	

From *MORE Science Adventures with Children's Literature: Reading Comprehension and Inquiry-Based Science* by Anthony D. Fredericks. Westport, CT: Teacher Ideas Press. Copyright © 2008.

MY LEAF COLLECTION

Go outside and collect 15–25 different leaves (get more if you can). Pick up leaves that are on the ground (don't pluck them from trees). When you get back, try to arrange your collection of leaves into several different categories. Here are a few categories to get you started:

1. **Sort them by color**

   How many red?

   How many green?

   How many brown?

   How many black?

   How many yellow?

   How many purple?

2. **Sort them by size**

   How many large?

   How many medium?

   How many small?

3. **Sort them by edges**

   How many with smooth edges?

   How many with rough edges?

4. **Sort them by veins**

   How many with one long vein down the middle?

   How many with several branching veins?

From *MORE Science Adventures with Children's Literature: Reading Comprehension and Inquiry-Based Science* by Anthony D. Fredericks. Westport, CT: Teacher Ideas Press. Copyright © 2008.

IM-PRESS ME

NOTE: This project requires help from an adult. Do not do it alone.

You can preserve the leaves you collect by using a simple plant press.

Materials:

- hand or machine drill
- 2 sheets of plywood or fiberboard—each 10 x 13 inches
- pieces of cardboard the size of a sheet of paper (8½ x 11 inches)
- white construction paper
- 4 long bolts with wing nuts
- washers for the bolts

Directions:

1. Ask an adult to drill holes (to fit your bolts) in each corner of the two pieces of wood. The hole should be about 1 inch in from the top and side of each corner (if the two boards are placed together, the holes will be sure to match).
2. Put the connecting bolts (with a washer on each one) through one board and lay it down so that the bolts stick upward.
3. Lay a piece of cardboard on top of this board.
4. Next, place a sheet of paper on top of the cardboard and one or more leaves on top of the paper.
5. Put another sheet of paper on top of the leaves, and then another piece of cardboard.
6. Repeat this process, making leaf "sandwiches," until you have a stack of several cardboard pieces.
7. Put the second piece of plywood on top of the last cardboard piece on the stack, threading the bolts through the holes.
8. Put a washer on each bolt and then a wing nut. Tighten the wing nuts until you feel pressure.
9. Carefully tighten each bolt in turn as much as you can, putting even pressure on the stack.

From *MORE Science Adventures with Children's Literature: Reading Comprehension and Inquiry-Based Science* by Anthony D. Fredericks. Westport, CT: Teacher Ideas Press. Copyright © 2008.

IM-PRESS ME (CONTINUED)

Description:

The leaf specimens will be pressed flat and will dry within a few weeks. Later you may want to glue your pressed leaves onto sheets of colorful construction paper and place them in paper frames from a hobby or arts and crafts store for display in your house.

The wooden press puts pressure on the leaf specimens placed in it and keeps them flat. The pressure is gentle but constant. Any "juices" squeezed from the leaves are absorbed by the white paper, so the plant dries out rapidly. These pressed leaves are a way of preserving some of nature's beauty long after the leaves would have blown away.

From *MORE Science Adventures with Children's Literature: Reading Comprehension and Inquiry-Based Science* by Anthony D. Fredericks. Westport, CT: Teacher Ideas Press. Copyright © 2008.

A BEAUTIFUL JOURNEY

Imagine you are a leaf (similar to the leaves in the book *Leaf Man*). Now imagine that you are going to take a trip. The wind is going to blow you far away from your home. You will see many things. You will travel many miles. You will have many exciting adventures.

Use the first box below to draw an illustration of yourself (as a leaf). Use the second box to write a short story about your adventure. Be sure to share your story with other students.

My Picture

My Story

From *MORE Science Adventures with Children's Literature: Reading Comprehension and Inquiry-Based Science* by Anthony D. Fredericks. Westport, CT: Teacher Ideas Press. Copyright © 2008.

Reaching for the Moon
Buzz Aldrin
New York: HarperCollins, 2005

SELECTED CITATIONS

- **2006 Outstanding Science Trade Book**—Children's Book Council/National Science Teachers Association

- "Readers will want to check out this title with its easy reading style, beautiful pictures, and valuable message."—*Children's Literature*

SUMMARY

This book is a compelling chronology of the life of Buzz Aldrin, the second man to step onto the surface of the moon. Events that helped shaped his life and his fascination with space are accurately and carefully detailed in this very readable book. Students will learn much about space exploration as seen through the eyes of one of this country's space pioneers. Coupled with engaging illustrations by Wendell Minor, this is one space book that youngsters will turn to again and again.

SUGGESTED GRADE LEVELS: 3–5

LESSON OBJECTIVES

Science Standards

- Content Standard B: Physical Science

    Position and motion of objects (K–4)

    Motions and forces (5–8)

- Content Standard D: Earth and Space Science

    Objects in the sky (K–4)

- Content Standard E: Science and Technology

    Understanding about science and technology (K–4; 5–8)

- Content Standard G: History and Nature of Science

    History of science (5–8)

CRITICAL THINKING QUESTIONS

1. What would you like to do when you grow up?

2. What do you think would be most interesting about traveling in space?

3. What was the most important lesson Buzz Aldrin learned as a youth?

4. Why do you think Buzz Aldrin wanted to become an astronaut so much?

5. What lesson did you learn while reading this book?

COMPREHENSION LESSON (QUESTION MASTER)

Setting the Stage

Discuss the title of the book and its possible meanings. Why is the word "reaching" part of the title? Invite students to look at the cover illustration and make some interpretations about the content of the book.

Before Reading

Provide all students with copies of the Question Master sheet. Help them understand that the questions on this sheet are those that accomplished readers ask themselves as they read. Invite students to place appropriate check marks (and any necessary personal comments) on the sheets for each of the questions asked in the "Before Reading" section.

During Reading

Invite students to read the book. Ask them to stop at some point (of their own choosing) somewhere in the middle of the book. Ask them to check off the statements (and provide necessary information) for the items on the Question Master sheet in the "During Reading" section.

After Reading

After students have completed the book, invite them to place appropriate check marks on the questions (along with any necessary comments) listed in the "After Reading" section of the sheet. Encourage students to discuss the marks they placed as well as why they checked off certain items. Provide multiple opportunities for students to share their thought processes as they read this book.

LITERATURE EXTENSIONS

Invite students to select one or more of the following activities:

1. Because there is no atmosphere on the moon, sound cannot travel. Invite students to think of 10 different ways they could communicate with each other without the use of sound (e.g., hand signals, flags, etc.). Invite students to demonstrate their ideas to each other.

2. Ask students to check out other books as well as the various Web sites maintained by NASA. What are the requirements to become an astronaut? What special training, college courses, and military experience are necessary to qualify as an astronaut? How many years of training are required? Students may wish to assemble their information into a special brochure that outlines the requirements—especially those students considering this as a career path.

3. Invite students to log on to NASA's Web site for students, NASA for Kids, at http://www.nasa.gov/audience/forkids/home/index.html. There's lots of great information, projects, data, current news, and answers to their questions. Students can even participate in the Ask an Astronaut site and get answers to all their questions directly from a former astronaut. This is a great site for space exploration studies.

4. The last two pages of the book include a time line of some of the more notable space achievements over the course of the past century. Invite students to create a similar time line of space exploration events that have taken place just in their lifetimes. You may wish to post an oversized sheet of newsprint along one wall of the classroom and invite students to record significant events (along with appropriate illustrations) over the course of several days.

5. Invite students to survey a variety of adults (teachers, parents, relative, neighbors, etc.) about what they consider to be the most significant or most important event in space exploration. Charge each student with the task of interviewing at least 10 adults. Ask them to gather the information together and create a chart or graph that records the 10 greatest space exploration events in history (as determined by the local community). How many of those events are included on the time line in the back of this book?

6. Ask students to work with the school librarian or the children's librarian at the local public library to assemble a list of children's books about space exploration. What are some other books that have been published in the past five or six years that detail events of the space program? Students may wish to assemble an annotated bibliography of the best space books in the library.

7. Aldrin mentioned that when he was an astronaut on board *Gemini 12* his spacecraft circled the Earth at 17,500 miles per hour, or 5 miles every second. Invite students to put together a "Speed Chart" that records the speed of various types of transportation, from slow to fast. For example, students could include the the bicycle, family car, train, jet airplane, rocket ship, etc.

8. In the early 1600s people sailed across the Atlantic Ocean to reach the shores of this country. The voyage usually took several months. Ask students to calculate the difference in speed between seventeenth-century sailing vessels and twenty-first-century spacecraft. How much faster are spacecraft? In the time it took a ship to travel from England to the Americas, how many orbits of earth could a spacecraft make?

9. Invite students to investigate some of the things that Buzz Aldrin did after the Apollo 11 mission. Students may wish to investigate various Web sites and books to discover some of his interests and pursuits. They may wish to create a supplemental biography to include with this book in the school library.

10. Ask students to create a fictitious job application to be a lunar explorer. What special talents would applicants be expected to have? What kind of training or college degree? What skills should they have? What personality characteristics should they possess? How detailed should these applications be? Allow sufficient time for students to discuss the talents and attributes of a good lunar explorer.

QUESTION MASTER

Before Reading

_____ Is this similar to anything I have read before?

_____ Why am I reading this?

_____ Why would this information be important for me to know?

_____ Do I have any questions about the book before I read it?

During Reading

_____ Am I understanding what I'm reading?

_____ What can I do if I don't understand this information?

_____ Why am I learning this?

_____ Is there something here similar to what I've read before?

_____ How does this information differ from what I know already?

_____ Why is this difficult or easy for me to understand?

_____ Is this interesting or enjoyable?

_____ Do I have any unanswered questions about the topic of this book?

_____ What new information am I learning?

_____ What information do I still need to learn?

After Reading

_____ Can I write a brief summary of the book?

_____ What did I learn in this book?

_____ Where can I go to learn more information about this topic?

_____ Did I confirm my initial purpose for reading this book?

_____ Is there anything else I'd like to know about this topic?

_____ Do I have any unanswered questions?

From *MORE Science Adventures with Children's Literature: Reading Comprehension and Inquiry-Based Science* by Anthony D. Fredericks. Westport, CT: Teacher Ideas Press. Copyright © 2008.

LUNAR LANDINGS

Would you like to get "up close and personal" with the surface of the moon? Would you like to know exactly where each of the manned moon expeditions landed on the moon—including the first one with Buzz Aldrin? Then check out the following Web site: http://moon.google.com/ Google Moon enables you to surf the moon's surface and check out the exact spots that the Apollo astronauts made their landings. Use the information on this site (as well as other sites) to complete the following:

Apollo 11

Landing date: _____

Personnel: _____

Time on lunar surface: _____

Interesting facts: _____

Apollo 12

Landing date: _____

Personnel: _____

Time on lunar surface: _____

Interesting facts: _____

Apollo 14

Landing date: _____

Personnel: _____

Time on lunar surface: _____

Interesting facts: _____

From *MORE Science Adventures with Children's Literature: Reading Comprehension and Inquiry-Based Science* by Anthony D. Fredericks. Westport, CT: Teacher Ideas Press. Copyright © 2008.

LUNAR LANDINGS (CONTINUED)

Apollo 15

    Landing date: _____

    Personnel: _____

    Time on lunar surface: _____

    Interesting facts: _____

Apollo 16

    Landing date: _____

    Personnel: _____

    Time on lunar surface: _____

    Interesting facts: _____

Apollo 17

    Landing date: _____

    Personnel: _____

    Time on lunar surface: _____

    Interesting facts: _____

From *MORE Science Adventures with Children's Literature: Reading Comprehension and Inquiry-Based Science* by Anthony D. Fredericks. Westport, CT: Teacher Ideas Press. Copyright © 2008.

PLOP PLOP

This (very messy) activity demonstrates how the moon's craters were created.

Materials:
- large baking pan
- spatula
- sifted all-purpose flour
- dried peas, marbles, golf balls

Directions:
1. Fill the baking pan with about ½ inch of all-purpose flour. Smooth the surface with the spatula. (Note: Because this activity will be very messy, it is suggested that you do it outdoors on a grassy area.)
2. Take three or four dried peas and drop them on the flour from different heights. Note the "craters" that are created on the surface of the flour.
3. Use the spatula to smooth the flour. Now drop three or four marbles (from different heights) onto the surface of the flour. Note the "craters."
4. Smooth the flour again, and drop three or four golf balls onto the surface. Once again, note the "craters."
5. Smooth the flour (you may need to add more flour) once again. Now drop two or more peas, two or more marbles, and two or more golf balls (all from different heights) onto the surface. What do you notice about the "craters" that form?

Description:

You noticed that the larger objects made larger craters (and scattered more flour in various directions) than did the smaller objects. The constant bombardment of asteroids on the moon's surface not only created craters but also pulverized the surface, creating a powdery dust very similar to the flour in this activity. In some places the moon dust may range from 3 feet to more than 60 feet in depth. (Imagine standing in a pile of flour that is 60 feet deep!)

From *MORE Science Adventures with Children's Literature: Reading Comprehension and Inquiry-Based Science* by Anthony D. Fredericks. Westport, CT: Teacher Ideas Press. Copyright © 2008.

LUNAR ECLIPSES

When you are walking on a sunny day, you probably notice that you have a shadow. The shadow results from the fact that you are between the sun and the ground; in other words, you are blocking some of the sunlight from reaching the ground.

The same thing happens in space, too. Earth casts a shadow in space, just as you do on earth. Whenever Earth is between the sun and some other object, a shadow is projected onto that object. For example, sometimes the moon passes through Earth's shadow. This does not happen very often; because the moon's orbit is tilted slightly, it is not usually lined up with the sun and Earth. However, when it does happen, a full or partial lunar eclipse occurs. During a lunar eclipse you can see the round shadow of Earth move across the face of the moon and slowly darken it.

Following is a chart of lunar eclipses due to occur in the next 10 years, the type of eclipse, and locations where they can best be seen from Earth.

Date	Type	Best Viewing Area
August 16, 2008	Partial	South America, Europe, Africa, Asia, Australia
December 31, 2009	Partial	Europe, Africa, Asia, Australia
June 26, 2010	Partial	east Asia, Australia, Pacific, western Americas
December 21, 2010	Total	east Asia, Australia, Pacific, Americas, Europe
June 15, 2011	Total	South America, Europe, Africa, Asia, Australia
December 10, 2011	Total	Europe, east Africa, Asia, Australia, Pacific, North America
June 4, 2012	Partial	Asia, Australia, Pacific, Americas
April 25, 2013	Partial	Europe, Africa, Asia, Australia
April 15, 2014	Total	Australia, Pacific, Americas
October 8, 2014	Total	Asia, Australia, Pacific, Americas
April 4, 2015	Total	Asia, Australia, Pacific, Americas
September 28, 2015	Total	east Pacific, Americas, Europe, Africa, west Asia
August 7, 2017	Partial	Europe, Africa, Asia, Australia
January 31, 2018	Total	Asia, Australia, Pacific, west North America
July 27, 2018	Total	South America, Europe, Africa, Asia, Australia

From *MORE Science Adventures with Children's Literature: Reading Comprehension and Inquiry-Based Science* by Anthony D. Fredericks. Westport, CT: Teacher Ideas Press. Copyright © 2008.

Nature in the Neighborhood

Gordon Morrison

Boston: Houghton Mifflin, 2004

SELECTED CITATIONS

- **2005 Outstanding Science Trade Book**—Children's Book Council/National Science Teachers Association

- "[T]his offering . . . serve[s] as a resource for nature study or community units and will encourage readers to observe and appreciate their own surroundings."—*School Library Journal*

SUMMARY

Swooping birds soar through the air, tiny critters scurry over the landscape, caterpillars slowly but beautifully transform themselves into butterflies, and toads soak up water in a makeshift puddle. This may seem like a scene from a rural landscape, but it takes place right inside an urban environment. Children will delight in all the discoveries that can be made right in their own backyards or right down the street from where they live. With this book they will gain newfound insights into life in their own neighborhood—a neighborhood teeming with critters and creatures that rival those found in any forest, glen, or meadow far away in the country. This book will spark some incredible discoveries (and rediscoveries) across the life sciences.

SUGGESTED GRADE LEVELS: 3–6

LESSON OBJECTIVES

Science Standards

- Content Standard A: Science as Inquiry

    Abilities necessary to do science inquiry (K–4, 5–8)

    Understanding about science inquiry (K–4, 5–8)

- Content Standard C: Life Science

    The characteristics of organisms (K–4)

    Life cycles of organisms (K–4)

    Organisms and environments (K–4)

    Regulation and behavior (5–8)

    Populations and ecosystems (5–8)

    Diversity and adaptations of organisms (5–8)

- Content Standard F: Science in Personal and Social Perspectives

    Characteristics and changes in populations (K–4)

    Populations, resources, and environments (5–8)

CRITICAL THINKING QUESTIONS

1. What was the most interesting part of this book?

2. How did the illustrations contribute to your enjoyment of this book?

3. What parts of this book are similar to the environment in which you live?

4. What are some animals in your location that are different from those described in this book?

5. Why do you think the author focused on "nature in the neighborhood?"

COMPREHENSION LESSON (ANTICIPATION GUIDE)

Setting the Stage

Distribute copies of the book to students. Invite students to look at the cover illustration and describe what they see. How does that illustration compare with what they might find in their own neighborhood?

Before Reading

Make copies of the Anticipation Guide and distribute them to students. Invite students to agree or disagree with each of the Anticipation Guide statements. They should mark their responses in the BEFORE column.

During Reading

Invite students to read the entire book (or to listen to it as a read-aloud). Invite students to look for (or listen for) confirmation of the Anticipation Guide statements.

After Reading

After students have completed the book, ask them to re-read the Anticipation Guide statements and decide which are correct and which are incorrect. They should mark their post-reading responses in the AFTER column. Allow time for students to confirm or verify their decisions by re-reading appropriate passages. Ask students to talk about changes between their pre-reading knowledge and their post-reading knowledge.

LITERATURE EXTENSIONS

Invite students to select one or more of the following activities:

1. Invite students to write to the National Wildlife Federation (8925 Leesburg Pike, Vienna, VA 22184) and ask for information on endangered wildlife species—particularly those that might inhabit urban or suburban neighborhoods. The NWF's Web site (www.nwf.org) is also an excellent resource for information on endangered species.

2. Invite a zoologist or biologist from a local college to visit your classroom and share information related to urban wildlife. Students may wish to prepare a set of questions beforehand (particularly related to e vents in the book) to be sent to the guest speaker beforehand.

3. Ask students to each take on the role of a single animal in the book. Encourage them to do any necessary library research on their designated animal. This would include the habits, behavior, habitat, and life cycle of a particular critter. Then ask them to each write a diary entry—as their selected animal might record it—on a day in the life of that species.

4. Invite students to each select a tree on the school grounds and to "adopt" that tree for the length of the school year. Photos may be taken of each tree, bark rubbings may be made, measurements may be taken (of girth, height, etc.), leaf pressings may be made, and observations of any "visiting" animals may be recorded. Encourage students to maintain a journal of their observations throughout the year. Some students may wish to develop an appropriate PowerPoint presentation on their selected trees.

5. Melt a chunk of suet (available from your local butcher or supermarket) over a double boiler. Allow it to cool and mix in a handful each of birdseed, cornmeal, and chopped nuts. Allow this to solidify and then scoop a portion into a 5-by-5-inch mesh bag (like an onion bag). Tie the top of the bag shut and hang it in a tree outside your classroom window. Invite students to note and record the number and types of birds that visit the feeder over a designated period of time (a week, a month).

6. Ask students to keep a journal of the activities, habits, travels, and motions of a single animal. Students should select a house pet or some other animal (class pet) that can be observed quite regularly throughout the day. Provide students with a "Field Journal," a simple notebook wildlife biologists frequently use to track the activities of one or more wild animals over an extended period of time.

7. Invite students to create an advertisement (written or oral) for their favorite animal or group of animals. Each student should describe the distinguishing features or characteristics that should be highlighted in the promotion of her or his animal. What data would get people excited about that particular species?

8. Ask students to create a booklet or Web page on "Incredible Animal Facts." Encourage them to conduct the necessary library or Internet research and assemble a collection of amazing facts (about neighborhood animals) that could be shared with other students. Here are a few facts to get them started:

    – The body temperature of butterflies must be at least 81°F before they can fly.

    – Frogs do not drink water—they absorb it through their skin.

    – A queen termite produces 11 million eggs every year for 15 years.

    – Flies have tiny balancing organs at the back of their bodies, which help them land upside down

9. Put different types of soil (humus, clay, garden soil) in each of several plastic drinking cups. Sprinkle birdseed on the surface of each one and place another plastic cup upside down over the top of the soil cups. Tape the cups together. Place these miniature "greenhouses" in a sunny location. Invite students to make prediction about which cup will show the most growth. Which one will show the least growth? What soil "ingredients" do plants need to grow and survive?

ANTICIPATION GUIDE

Look at the sentences on this page. The statements are numbered from 1 to 6. Read each sentence; if you think that what it says is right, print "Yes" on the line under the word BEFORE. If you think the sentence is wrong, print "No" on the line under the word BEFORE. Do the same thing for each sentence. Remember how to do this, because you will do it again after reading *Nature in the Neighborhood* (except you will write "Yes" or "No" on each line under the word AFTER).

BEFORE   AFTER

_____ _____   1. Weeds can be found growing in empty lots.

_____ _____   2. Monarch butterflies all fly to Mexico to spend the winter.

_____ _____   3. Birds can always be found in any neighborhood.

_____ _____   4. The down on some seeds is like a parachute.

_____ _____   5. Cattail plants grow very tall.

_____ _____   6. Toads and frogs are quite similar.

From *MORE Science Adventures with Children's Literature: Reading Comprehension and Inquiry-Based Science* by Anthony D. Fredericks. Westport, CT: Teacher Ideas Press. Copyright © 2008.

SEED TIME

Seeds need several things to begin growing. Here's how you can find out what they need.

Materials:

- 36 radish seeds
- 6 small sealable plastic bags
- 3 paper towels
- safety scissors
- water
- bottle of nail polish
- felt-tip marker

Directions:

1. Label each small bag with a number.
2. Cut each paper towel in half.
3. Moisten four of the pieces, leaving one dry (you will not need the sixth piece).
4. As directed below, place the towels in the bottoms of the bags.
5. Drop six radish seeds into each bag and then finish setting up each of the bags as follows:
   - Bag 1: moist paper towel (water, no light (put in a drawer or closet), room temperature
   - Bag 2: moist paper towel (water), light, room temperature
   - Bag 3: dry paper towel (no water), light, room temperature
   - Bag 4: no paper towel, water (seeds floating), light, room temperature
   - Bag 5: moist paper towel (water), no light, keep in refrigerator or freezer
   - Bag 6: moist paper towel (water), no light, room temperature, seeds covered by nail polish

Record the date and time you begin this activity and check each of the bags twice daily for any changes.

Description:

The seeds in Bag 1 and Bag 2 germinate (begin to grow). You may see some small difference in the seeds in Bag 4. The seeds in the other bags do not start growing.

Seeds need favorable temperature, enough moisture, and oxygen to germinate. Light is not needed for germination (most seeds germinate underground, where it is dark), but light is necessary later for growth. The seeds in Bag 6 can't get any air or moisture through the nail polish, so they don't germinate.

From *MORE Science Adventures with Children's Literature: Reading Comprehension and Inquiry-Based Science* by Anthony D. Fredericks. Westport, CT: Teacher Ideas Press. Copyright © 2008.

IN YOUR NEIGHBORHOOD

Imagine you are taking a walk in your neighborhood. Write a short story describing the nature (birds, plants, insects, trees, animals) you might discover in your neighborhood. Draw a picture to illustrate your story and write a caption for the picture.

Caption: _____

_____.

From *MORE Science Adventures with Children's Literature: Reading Comprehension and Inquiry-Based Science* by Anthony D. Fredericks. Westport, CT: Teacher Ideas Press. Copyright © 2008.

HIGHER AND HIGHER

In the book *Nature in the Neighborhood,* the author describes an old red oak tree that stands behind the school. You probably have trees in your neighborhood, too. But have you ever wondered how high those trees are? Well, here's an activity that will allow you to measure the height of any tree—without having to climb up into the branches.

Materials:

- 2 rulers
- length of string
- tape measure

Directions:

1. Go outside on a sunny day and locate a tree you would like to measure.
2. Stand a 12-inch ruler on the ground and measure the length of the ruler's shadow.
3. Take a length of string and measure the length of the tree's shadow.
4. Go back inside and use the formula below to compute the exact height of the tree.

$$\frac{\text{height of ruler}}{\text{length of ruler's shadow}} \times \frac{\text{height of tree}}{\text{length of tree's shadow}}$$

Example:

Height of ruler = 12 inches
Length of ruler's shadow = 24 inches
Length of tree's shadow = 720 inches

$$\frac{12}{24} \times \frac{x}{720}$$

24x = 8,640 (12 x 720)

x = 360 inches (30 feet)

The tree is 30 feet tall.

From *MORE Science Adventures with Children's Literature: Reading Comprehension and Inquiry-Based Science* by Anthony D. Fredericks. Westport, CT: Teacher Ideas Press. Copyright © 2008.

Following the Coast

Jim Arnosky

New York: HarperCollins, 2004

SELECTED CITATIONS

- **2005 Outstanding Science Trade Book**—Children's Book Council/National Science Teachers Association

- "[T]he reader is absolutely pulled into each fascinating page filled with beauty, adventure, and information."—*Children's Literature*

SUMMARY

Life teems in the salt marshes that outline the Atlantic seaboard. The sweep of grassy fields, the scurry of nutrias, the slither of water snakes, the dance of roseate spoonbills, and the multihued palette of an evening sunset all combine to identify this far-flung ecosystem as one of the most intriguing in the entire country. It's also one of the most unknown and thus an area ripe for exploration. This talented author and illustrator takes readers along on a voyage of discovery, one they will not soon forget.

SUGGESTED GRADE LEVELS: 2–5

LESSON OBJECTIVES

Science Standards

- Content Standard A: Science as Inquiry

    Abilities necessary to do science inquiry (K–4, 5–8)

• Content Standard C: Life Science

The characteristics of organisms (K–4)

Life cycles of organisms (K–4)

Organisms and environments (K–4)

Populations and ecosystems (5–8)

Diversity and adaptations of organisms (5–8)

• Content Standard F: Science in Personal and Social Perspectives

Characteristics and changes in populations (K–4)

Populations, resources, and environments (5–8)

CRITICAL THINKING QUESTIONS

1. How did the author influence you to explore a salt marsh ecosystem?

2. How could you locate a similar ecosystem near where you live?

3. How did the illustrations contribute to your enjoyment of this book?

4. What are two facts you learned that you didn't know before reading this book?

5. Are there any salt marsh animals that could thrive where you live?

COMPREHENSION LESSON (S.M.A.R.T.)

Setting the Stage

Provide enough copies of the book for all students (or use the book for a whole class read-aloud). Record the title of the book on the chalkboard and invite students to ask questions about the title or the contents of the book. Record all questions.

Before Reading

Based on the questions written on the chalkboard, invite students to make predictions about the content and plot of the book. Students can also decide on the questions they feel to be most appropriate for exploration. Invite students to read the book independently (or to listen to it as a read-aloud).

During Reading

Ask students to examine all the illustrations in the book and to pose additional questions during the reading process. Add these questions to those already on the chalkboard. Based on the list of questions recorded, ask students to generate additional predictions about the story line. Students may continue to read, searching for answers to some of their previously posed queries. As they find answers, the students may talk about them and attempt to arrive at agreed-upon responses.

After Reading

Upon completion of the book, students may discuss all recorded questions and answers provided in the book. Students (individually or in a group) should decide on appropriate answers. Questions that were not answered from the book may also be shared. Encourage students to refer back to the book to answer any lingering questions.

LITERATURE EXTENSIONS

Invite students to select one or more of the following activities:

1. Jim Arnosky has won many awards for his children's books. Invite students to sample some of his other books. Ask them to discuss some of the themes he emphasizes in his work. What is the major emphasis in Arnosky's work? How are his nature books different from the nature books of other writers? Why do you think he has won so many awards?

2. Swamps, marshes, and other wetland ecosystems are often misunderstood by the general public. Invite students to consult other books about wetland ecosystems. Ask them to assemble information into an informative brochure or PowerPoint presentation that could be used to educate the general public about wetland environments throughout the United States.

3. Invite students to imagine that they live next to a saltwater marsh and are writing to a friend to convince her or him to visit for several days. What features or attractions should be mentioned in the letter? Afterward, invite students to imagine they are in an urban environment and writing to a friend who lives near a saltwater marsh, inviting that person for a visit.

4. Encourage students to create a possible sequel to the book. Although the author and his wife ended their journey in Delaware, what would they have discovered if they had continued up the East Coast? Are there other saltwater marsh areas they could have visited? Invite students to continue the journey through a series of creative writing projects.

5. Invite students to prepare an advertisement or commercial promoting this book to friends or students in another class. What type of information should be included to "sell" the book to others? Should the advertisement/commercial be humorous or serious?

6. Ask students to create a guidebook to the flora and fauna found in a saltwater marsh or other wetlands area (one within a reasonable distance from the school). Encourage students to do the appropriate research (contacting experts, books, Internet, etc.) in assembling their data. Ask students to prepare the guidebook for your visitors to the wetlands area.

7. Invite students to create their own imaginative stories about an adventure they had one day in a wetlands environment. What creatures did they see? What plants did they encounter? What did they observe, and what did they learn? Later, students may wish to develop their stories into a skit or readers theatre production.

8. Ask students to rewrite part of the story from the perspective of one of the animals. For example, how would a marsh hawk view the actions of the other creatures? How would a water snake view the actions of the author and his wife?

9. Invite students to each select an animal from the book to study. Students can pretend that they are writing a newspaper birth announcement about the birth of their chosen animal. They will need to do some research to gather the appropriate information. Provide the birth announcement section of the daily newspaper for students to use as a model for writing their pieces. Decorate a bulletin board to look like a section of a newspaper and post the animal birth announcements on it. Students may wish to include illustrations of the new babies.

10. Invite students to collect objects from home that might serve as metaphors for a wetlands environment, for example:

   - **Sponge**—Wetlands absorb the runoff from streams and rivers.
   - **Coffee filter**—Wetlands filter impurities out of the water.
   - **Pillow**—Wetlands provide a resting place for migratory birds.
   - **Small baby cradle**—Wetlands provide a sheltering place for many types of baby animals.
   - **Calendar**—Wetland creatures come and go according to the seasons of the year.

S.M.A.R.T.

As you locate answers to your questions (while reading), place a checkmark in the appropriate box.

Title: *Following the Coast*

Write down questions you consider most appropriate for exploration.

Questions:	**Answered:**
1.	☐
2.	☐
3.	☐
4.	☐

Prediction:

Examine the illustrations and propose questions about them.

Illustrations Selected:

Questions:	**Answered:**
1.	☐
2.	☐
3.	☐
4.	☐

More Questions:

	Answered:
5.	☐
6.	☐

From *MORE Science Adventures with Children's Literature: Reading Comprehension and Inquiry-Based Science* by Anthony D. Fredericks. Westport, CT: Teacher Ideas Press. Copyright © 2008.

DAY TRIPPING

The author of *Following the Coast* traveled from Florida up the east coast of the United States to Delaware. Trace a map of the eastern United States in the box below. Use a colored pencil to draw a line from the Banana River in Florida to Bombay Hook in Delaware—a line that indicates all of the places the author and his wife traveled through during their journey. Consult the book and write in the names of the places they visited.

From *MORE Science Adventures with Children's Literature: Reading Comprehension and Inquiry-Based Science* by Anthony D. Fredericks. Westport, CT: Teacher Ideas Press. Copyright © 2008.

ANIMAL PARADE

The author of *Following the Coast* describes and illustrates many animals that he saw during his journey. Select any three animals from the book—one water animal, one land animal, and one flying animal—and discover as much information about each as you can. Compete each of the boxes below. Be sure to share your information with other students.

Water Animal

Name:	Interesting Information:
	1.
	2.
	3.
	4.

Land Animal

Name:	Interesting Information:
	1.
	2.
	3.
	4.

Flying Animal

Name:	Interesting Information:
	1.
	2.
	3.
	4.

From *MORE Science Adventures with Children's Literature: Reading Comprehension and Inquiry-Based Science* by Anthony D. Fredericks. Westport, CT: Teacher Ideas Press. Copyright © 2008.

ALMOST ALIKE, ALMOST DIFFERENT

In the book *Following the Coast*, the author and his wife spent their journey traveling through and along saltwater marshes up the East Coast of the United States. Did you know that there are also lots of freshwater marshes throughout the United States as well?

Consult some other library books and Web sites. What are some of the similarities between saltwater marshes and freshwater marshes? What are some of the differences?

Similarities	Differences

Which would you like to visit most—a saltwater marsh or a freshwater marsh?

Why?

From *MORE Science Adventures with Children's Literature: Reading Comprehension and Inquiry-Based Science* by Anthony D. Fredericks. Westport, CT: Teacher Ideas Press. Copyright © 2008.

Hidden Worlds

Stephen Kramer

Boston: Houghton Mifflin, 2001

SELECTED CITATIONS

- **2002 Outstanding Science Trade Book**—Children's Book Council/National Science Teachers Association

- "This book opens up a world of exciting and important information, sure to appeal to readers of all ages. Simply opening this book is guaranteed to educate even the most knowledgeable audience."—*Children's Literature*

SUMMARY

Take an incredible journey through the lens of Dennis Kunkel's microscope and into the world of some of the tiniest organisms on the planet. It's a world filled with monsters, thieves, acrobats, and polymorphic critters that will amaze even the most reluctant of learners. Here is a world that teems with undiscovered possibilities and terrific stories that would rival the best novelists. Spiced with remarkable photographs, this is a captivating and mesmerizing science book for any classroom.

SUGGESTED GRADE LEVELS: 4–6

LESSON OBJECTIVES

Science Standards

- Content Standard A: Science as Inquiry

  Abilities necessary to do science inquiry (K–4, 5–8)

  Understandings about science inquiry (K–4, 5–8)

• Content Standard C: Life Science

> The characteristics of organisms (K–4)
>
> Life cycles of organisms (K–4)
>
> Populations and ecosystems (5–8)
>
> Diversity and adaptations of organisms (5–8)

• Content Standard E: Science and Technology

> Abilities of technological design (K–4, 5–8)

• Content Standard G: History and Nature of Science

> Science as a human endeavor (K–4, 5–8)

CRITICAL THINKING QUESTIONS

1. Prior to reading this book, what were some of your thoughts or feelings about microorganisms?

2. Would you enjoy doing the work of Dennis Kunkel?

3. What one question would you like to ask Dennis Kunkel?

4. What was the single most amazing microorganism?

5. What subjects would you need to study to be a microbiologist?

COMPREHENSION LESSON (QUICK WRITE)

Setting the Stage

Before inviting students to read *Hidden Worlds,* show them the cover of the book. Point out the microphotograph on the cover along with the book's title.

Before Reading

After viewing the book's cover, ask students to write (in paragraph form) everything they know about microscopes or microorganisms. After a few minutes, ask students to revisit their respective paragraphs, inviting them to think of some questions about the topics generated by that paragraph. This step may be done in small groups or on an individual basis. Invite students to record their questions on separate sheets of paper.

Provide students with the titles of the chapters in the book, asking them to mark which questions on their respective lists they think will be answered in the book. Students may wish to assign chapter numbers to respective questions on their sheet. Provide opportunities for students to share their questions and their predictions.

During Reading

Invite students to read the book silently and to look for answers to their questions, if possible.

After Reading

After the reading, students may use any unanswered questions to stimulate group discussion or for independent research projects.

LITERATURE EXTENSIONS

Invite students to select one or more of the following activities:

1. Ask students to conduct an interview with a scientist in your local community. This may be a parent of one of your students. Students may wish to interview a science teacher at the middle school or high school or a professor at a nearby college or university. Perhaps a college student (home over a vacation or weekend) majoring in a scientific field might make a suitable candidate. Invite students to query selected individuals on their reasons for entering the field of science, what they enjoy most about it, and some of the discoveries they have made. Provide opportunities for students to share the results of their interviews with each other.

2. Bring in several different college catalogs. Show students how to find information (required courses, labs, credits, GPA, etc.) for various scientific fields. What would students need to take or do in order to graduate with a degree in microbiology, chemistry, thermonuclear physics, or any other scientific field? Are those requirements more difficult or more challenging than the requirements for other academic fields?

3. If possible, invite a science professor from the local college or university to visit your classroom and discuss some of the academic requirements of her or his field. What training is needed? What experience is essential? How is her or his training similar to (or different from) the training of Dennis Kunkel?

4. There are lots of incredible photographs in this book. Invite students to select the two or three that they find most fascinating. What makes those photos more interesting or dynamic than others? What is it about the subject(s) in those photos that makes them so intriguing? Why are some microorganisms more interesting than others? If students could just study one microorganism, which one would they choose?

5. Encourage students to write an imaginary letter to Dennis Kunkel asking him any questions that were not answered in the book *Hidden Worlds*. What else would they like to know about his job and the work that he does? Has he discovered anything new or interesting since the book has been written? Why does he continue in this field?

6. Many schools have loupes or hand lenses available to share with students. If possible, obtain some for your students and invite them to examine some of the common microorganisms in and around their homes (several examples are discussed in the book). Is it easy finding those microorganisms? Are some impossible to find?

7. Encourage students to create a "shape book." Invite them to cut a large circle from two sheets of oak tag. Students may wish to staple several sheets of blank paper between the two outlines to form a book. Ask them to each draw an illustration of a selected microorganism inside the circle (microscope lens) on the cover. On the blank pages they may record any information about that microorganism they locate in library resources or on the Internet. You may want to arrange these books in an attractive display in the classroom or library.

8. A small group of students may create a time line of some of the most important events in the history of microbiology. They may wish to start with the invention of the microscope and continue their time line up to the present day. What were some of the most significant historical events?

9. Invite students to check out some of the resources listed on page 54 of the book ("Further Reading"). Which of those books was most interesting? Which would be interesting to those who might want to go into microbiology as a career? Students may wish to check out other library resources published since *Hidden Worlds* came out and add new selections to this list.

QUICK-WRITE

Look at the cover of the book *Hidden Worlds: Looking Through a Scientist's Microscope*. Write (in paragraph form) everything you know about microscopic plants and animals:

_____

_____

_____

_____

_____

_____

_____

_____

Based on your paragraph above, what are some questions you have about microscopic organisms?

1.

2.

3.

4.

5.

6.

On the next page are the titles of the chapters and chapter sections in the book *Hidden Worlds: Looking Through a Scientist's Microsope*. Circle the questions on your list above that you think will be answered in these chapters (write the chapter number after each question). Remember that you are only making predictions, so there are no right or wrong responses.

From *MORE Science Adventures with Children's Literature: Reading Comprehension and Inquiry-Based Science* by Anthony D. Fredericks. Westport, CT: Teacher Ideas Press. Copyright © 2008.

QUICK-WRITE (CONTINUED)

1. Becoming a Scientist

2. Working as a Scientist
   Mt. St. Helens
   Muscle Cells
   Box Jellyfish
   Studying Unusual Life
   Working with Students

3. Magnifying Mosquitoes
   Loupe
   Light Microscopes
   Electron Microscopes

4. Seeing Hidden Worlds in Nature

5. Sharing Hidden Worlds

6. How to Become a Scientist

After completing the book, what are some of your unanswered questions (from your list above)?

A. _____

_____

_____

B. _____

_____

_____

C. _____

_____

_____

D. _____

_____

_____

MICROSCOPIC CRITTERS

Brine shrimp are microscopic creatures that you can observe with a microscope—just as Dennis Kunkel does with his.

Materials:

- brine shrimp eggs (from the pet store)
- kosher or noniodized salt
- 2-quart pot or other container
- water
- teaspoon
- medicine dropper
- hand lens or microscope

Directions:

1. Fill the pot with two quarts of water and allow it to sit for three days, stirring it occasionally. (Most city water has chlorine in it, which would kill the shrimp. By letting it "age" for a while, the chlorine gas can escape from the water.)
2. Dissolve five teaspoons of noniodized salt into the water.
3. Add ½ teaspoon of brine shrimp eggs to the salt water and place the pot in a warm spot.
4. Each day, use the medicine dropper to remove a few eggs from the water and observe them with a hand lens or microscope (you may wish to draw a series of illustrations in your journal to record the growth of your brine shrimp).

Description:

The brine shrimp eggs will hatch in about two days. They will continue to grow in the water until they reach their adult stage. You can watch this process over a period of many days.

The brine shrimp eggs you can buy at the pet store are dried so they can be stored for a long period of time. When these eggs are placed in salt water they begin to grow. Although they are very small, you can watch them grow for some time.

Note: Brine shrimp eggs are sold as food for aquarium fish.

From *MORE Science Adventures with Children's Literature: Reading Comprehension and Inquiry-Based Science* by Anthony D. Fredericks. Westport, CT: Teacher Ideas Press. Copyright © 2008.

JOB APPLICATION

Let's pretend that you want to apply for a job as a microscopist—the same type of work that Dennis Kunkel does. Use the form below to list your qualifications, abilities, and training (please feel free to use your imagination). What information from the book will help you complete the form below?

Name: _____

Address: _____

_____

Position applied for: _____

Work Experience: _____

_____

Training/Education: _____

_____

Special Qualifications: _____

_____

Awards/Certificates: _____

_____

References: _____

_____

From *MORE Science Adventures with Children's Literature: Reading Comprehension and Inquiry-Based Science* by Anthony D. Fredericks. Westport, CT: Teacher Ideas Press. Copyright © 2008.

LOOKING AT A MICROSCOPE

Below is an illustration of a microscope. Using library books as well as Web sites, label the various parts of a common microscope. See if you can identify and label six different parts of this microscope (*Hint:* There may be some clues in the book *Hidden Worlds*).

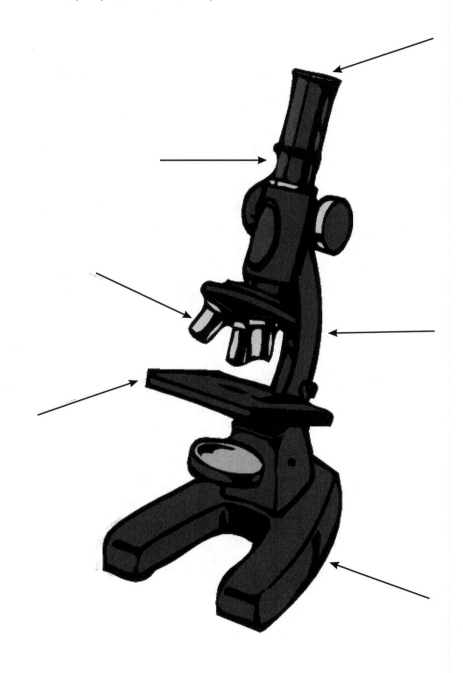

272   From *MORE Science Adventures with Children's Literature: Reading Comprehension and Inquiry-Based Science* by Anthony D. Fredericks. Westport, CT: Teacher Ideas Press. Copyright © 2008.

The Star People: A Lakota Story

S. D. Nelson

New York: Harry N. Abrams Publishers, 2003

SELECTED CITATIONS

- "A solid addition to collections of Native American tales and an enjoyable read-aloud."—*School Library Journal*

- "An exemplary offering."—*Kirkus Reviews*

SUMMARY

Sister Girl and Young Wolf wander away from their village and soon find themselves lost on the prairie. Suddenly, animals race by them as a fire sweeps across the land. They save themselves by jumping into a stream, but soon miss their parents. They find comfort (and their way) from the Star People overhead. The illustrations in this book draw upon traditional Lakota art, and the story celebrates a timeless Lakota/Sioux story.

SUGGESTED GRADE LEVELS: 2–4

LESSON OBJECTIVES

Science Standards

- Content Standard B: Physical Science

    Position and motion of objects (K–4)

- Content Standard D: Earth and Space Science

  Objects in the sky (K–4)

  Changes in Earth and sky (K–4)

- Content Standard G: History and Nature of Science

  Science as a human endeavor (K–4, 5–8)

CRITICAL THINKING QUESTIONS

1. Why do you think Sister Girl and Young Wolf first wandered out into the prairie?

2. How would the fire have started?

3. Young Wolf and Sister Girl always seem to be helping each other. Why?

4. What kinds of things do you see when you look up at the stars?

5. Have you ever been scared in your life?

6. How did Elk Tooth Woman help the children find their way back to the village?

COMPREHENSION LESSON (STORY PYRAMID)

Setting the Stage

Ask students to discuss a time in their lives when they were lost (at a shopping mall, in a park, on a vacation). Provide opportunities for students to share those events as well as their feelings about the events. Plan time to discuss ways to handle situations such as these.

Before Reading

Provide all students with copies of the Story Pyramid. Inform them that they will be completing this sheet upon conclusion of the book. Take a few minutes to go over the elements of the pyramid with students.

During Reading

Invite students to read the book. This may be done as a silent reading assignment or as part of a read-aloud session. Invite students to look for some of the details they will need to complete the pyramid after the reading is done.

After Reading

Upon completion of the book, ask students to fill in the appropriate information on the Story Pyramid. Students may wish to complete these on an individual basis or in pairs. Invite students to share their individual Story Pyramids with one another. A healthy discussion will no doubt ensue as students defend their choice of events and descriptive words to one another.

LITERATURE EXTENSIONS

Invite students to select one or more of the following activities:

1. Students can learn about the history and customs of the Lakota Indians by accessing the following Web sites:

   http://library.thinkquest.org/CR0212101/

   http://www.windows.ucar.edu/tour/link=/mythology/northamerican_culture.html

   http://www.carnegiemuseums.org/cmnh/exhib-its/north-south-east-west/lakota/index.html

   http://wintercounts.si.edu/

   After they have had an opportunity to learn about the Lakota/Sioux, encourage them to create a display or mobile of some of the information they have learned.

2. Invite students to write or illustrate an event their lives in which they were away from their parents for a significant amount of time. Establish a time during which students can share these experiences as well as the attendant feelings. Plan time to discuss how their feelings may or may not have been similar to those expressed by the two characters in the book.

3. Ask students to create a bulletin board display of the various constellations illustrated in this book. They may wish to use a star map to identify constellations that the author/illustrator depicted in the illustrations.

4. If possible, borrow some costumes from the local high school or community little theater. Invite students to create an original skit about a day in the life of a Lakota Indian boy or girl. What activities, games, or chores would that individual participate in during the course of a typical day?

5. In the Author's Note in the back of the book, he talks about the significance of Cloud People and Star People. After sharing this information with students, invite them to go outside and locate imaginary Cloud People in the clouds overhead. They may wish to locate imaginary Star People at night when they are home. Invite students to create illustrations of the "people" they see in the clouds or stars.

6. As an extension of the activity above, invite students to each select one of the illustrations and create an imaginary story about that "person" or those "people." Ask students to invent their own legend that incorporates that "individual" or "individuals" into the plot of the story.

7. Encourage students to pretend that they are newspaper reporters assigned to cover the events depicted in this book. Which facts or details would they include in a TV broadcast? Which ones would be appropriate for newspaper articles? Invite students to defend their choices.

8. Invite students to interview their parents, grandparents, or relatives about family stories, folktales, or legends they learned as children. If some families have recently immigrated to this country, you may wish to invite children's relatives to share stories and legends from their countries of origin.

9. Ask students to search through the school library and assemble a collection of literature focused on Native American legends. Students may wish to create a special display in the library or put together an annotated bibliography of books to be shared with other classes throughout the school.

STORY PYRAMID

Line 1: Name of the main character

Line 2: Two words describing the main character

Line 3: Three words describing the setting

Line 4: Four words stating the problem

Line 5: Five words describing the main event.

Line 6: Six words describing a second main event.

Line 7: Seven words describing a third main event.

Line 8: Eight words stating the solution to the problem.

1._____

2._____ _____

3._____ _____ _____

4._____ _____ _____ _____

5._____ _____ _____ _____ _____

6._____ _____ _____ _____ _____ _____

7._____ _____ _____ _____ _____ _____ _____

8._____ _____ _____ _____ _____ _____ _____ _____

From *MORE Science Adventures with Children's Literature: Reading Comprehension and Inquiry-Based Science* by Anthony D. Fredericks. Westport, CT: Teacher Ideas Press. Copyright © 2008.

TWINKLE, TWINKLE LITTLE STAR

One question many people ask is, "Why can't I see the stars in the daytime?" Another question is, "Do stars disappear during the day?" The following activity will help you answer those questions.

Materials:

- 3-by-5-inch index card
- paper punch
- 2 sheets of blank paper
- flashlight
- cellophane tape

Directions:

1. Use the paper punch to punch five to seven holes randomly on the index card.
2. Tape the index card to the middle of one sheet of paper.
3. Tape the other sheet of paper on top of the first (so that the index card is "sandwiched" between the two sheets of paper).
4. Hold your paper "sandwich" in front of you. Turn on the flashlight and aim it at the front of the "sandwich" (at the spot where the index card is positioned).
5. Now take the flashlight and hold it behind the paper "sandwich," aiming it at the spot where the index card is.

Description:

When you hold the flashlight at the front of the paper "sandwich," you aren't able to see the holes in the index card. This is because the light is bright and is coming from the same direction your eyes are looking from. This is similar to daylight hours, when the stars are in the sky but the brilliant light of the sun is coming from behind you. As a result, you can't see the stars.

When you place the flashlight behind the paper "sandwich," the light comes through the holes in the index card, making them easy to see. This is similar to what happens at night. The stars give off their own light, and that light is not influenced by the light from the sun (which has set).

So, stars are always there—it's just that we can't see them during the daylight hours.

From *MORE Science Adventures with Children's Literature: Reading Comprehension and Inquiry-Based Science* by Anthony D. Fredericks. Westport, CT: Teacher Ideas Press. Copyright © 2008.

STAR LEGENDS

There are many legends and folktales about the stars. Listed below are several books that have star legends in them. Seek them out in your school library or at your local public library. Talk with the librarian and ask for other suggested books containing star legends. After you have read a few, complete the box at the bottom.

Stories from the Stars: Greek Myths of the Zodiak by Juliet Sharman Burke (New York: Abbeville Press, 1996).

All the Stars in the Skies: Native Stories from the Heavens by C. J. Taylor (Seattle, WA: Tundra Books, 2006).

The Light of Stars by Phyllis Glowatsky and Karen J. Stringer (Charleston, SC: Coastal Publishing, 2003).

Starry Tales by Geraldine McCaughrean (New York: McElderry Books, 2001).

What are some of the similarities in legends and folktales about stars?

THE BIG DIPPER AND THE NORTH STAR

One of the most well-known constellations is the Big Dipper. Why is it called the Big Dipper? Simply because it looks like a giant dipper or ladle for water. Here's how you can locate this constellation:

- On a cloudless, moonless night away from the bright lights of a city, face north (use a compass) and look up.
- You'll see a pattern of seven stars (see the illustration), four of which form the "bowl" of the Big Dipper and three of which form the "handle."
- Once you've sighted the Big Dipper, draw an imaginary line along the two stars on the outer end of its bowl.
- That line will take you to a star on the handle end of the Little Dipper constellation.

The star on the handle end of the Little Dipper is one of the most famous in the sky: the North Star, or Polaris. For centuries sailors have used the North Star to guide them across endless expanses of ocean. The North Star and the Big Dipper were also important in helping large numbers of black slaves make their way to the free northern states and Canada in the years before the Civil War.

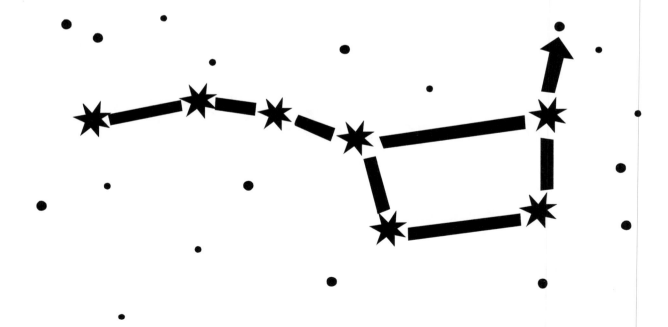

 From *MORE Science Adventures with Children's Literature: Reading Comprehension and Inquiry-Based Science* by Anthony D. Fredericks. Westport, CT: Teacher Ideas Press. Copyright © 2008.

Guts: Our Digestive System
Seymour Simon
New York: HarperCollins, 2005

SELECTED CITATIONS

- **2006 Outstanding Science Trade Book**—Children's Book Council/National Science Teachers Association

- "Guts has a lot going for it. In addition to its charmingly pithy title, it's decorated with any number of computer-enhanced Technicolor photographs of innards."—*Kirkus Reviews*

SUMMARY

Here's an inside look at how the human digestive system works. From the teeth that grind the food all the way down and out the other end, students are given a firsthand look at the parts and processes of digestion. With his usual flair for up-close-and-personal facts and information, Simon provides readers with accurate data and lots of "food for thought" (pardon the pun) regarding this all-important body system. Students will have a hard time putting this book down.

SUGGESTED GRADE LEVELS: 3–5

LESSON OBJECTIVES

Science Standards

- Content Standard C: Life Science

     The characteristics of organisms (K–4)

     Regulation and behavior (5–8)

- Content Standard F: Science in Personal and Social Perspectives

     Personal health (K–4, 5–8)

CRITICAL THINKING QUESTIONS

1. What part of the human digestive system was most interesting?

2. What did you learn about your guts that you didn't know before?

3. Why is the digestive system considered to be a major body system?

4. What are some ways in which we can take care of our digestive systems?

5. If your digestive system could write a letter to you, what would it say?

COMPREHENSION LESSON (CHAPTER SLAM)

Setting the Stage

Invite students to list everything they know about "guts" or the human digestive system. Students may wish to do this individually or as members of small groups.

Before Reading

Ask students to group all the items on their lists into various categories (students select the category titles or designations). After students have assigned a name to each group of items, ask them to arrange the categories as though they were a table of contents for a book. Again, this can be done on an individual basis or in small groups.

Invite students to write a "book" about the topic of "guts" or "the human digestive system" using the categories they selected as chapter titles. Encourage them to write as much about each topic as they can, summarizing what each section is about. If students get stuck, allow them to make up what they don't know.

During Reading

Invite students to read the book (or listen to a read-aloud). Encourage them to listen for specific information that may (or may not) be compatible with the pre-reading categories they selected earlier.

After Reading

After students have finished reading *Guts,* invite them to write another "book" and compare it (orally) with the one generated at the beginning of the lesson. Students will undoubtedly discover that some of their previous perceptions about the human digestive system have changed.

LITERATURE EXTENSIONS

Invite students to select one or more of the following activities:

1. Students may wish to assemble a book of "Amazing Facts About the Digestive System." Using library resources, appropriate Web sites, and/or conversations with their family doctors, students can gather several interesting and incredible facts about the digestive system. These may include the following:

   – The average person eats three pounds of food each day.

   – The average male will eat about 50 tons of food during his lifetime.

   – The human mouth produces one to three pints of saliva every day.

   – There are more than 400 different species of bacteria in your colon.

   – The intestines of an adult horse are 89 feet long.

2. Ask students to each draw an oversized illustration of a human stomach on a sheet of poster board or oak tag. Provide them with scissors and several old magazines. Ask them to cut out pictures of the various types of food they have consumed in the past 24 hours and to glue each picture inside the illustration of the stomach. Afterward, post these on one wall of the classroom and discuss the variety and amount of food consumed by the entire class in the past 24 hours.

3. Invite students to create a series of true or false questions about their digestive systems. Print these statements on sheets of paper and duplicate them. Distribute one sheet each day and invite students to see how much they know about the human digestive system. When their sheets are completed, individuals can stand and explain each of the statements to the other students.

4. Ask students to interview their parents or other adults about various stomach ailments or difficulties they have experienced. Which of the problems seems to be the most prevalent? Which of the problems requires something more than an over-the-counter medication? Which of the problems requires regular visits to the doctor?

5. Invite students to interview friends, family, and other acquaintances, asking them for a list of single adjectives that could be used to describe the human digestive system in general or the stomach specifically. After students have gathered an adequate sampling of adjectives, invite them to sort the adjectives (printed on individual index cards) into several categories (e.g., adjectives related to size, adjectives related to discomfort, adjectives related to food). Provide students with an opportunity to decide on the categories they would like to use.

6. Ask the children to each imagine that she or he is a specific organ related to the human digestive system (e.g., stomach, small intestine, kidney, etc.). What would that organ like to say to the other organs in the body? What kinds of interactions does that organ have with other organs? How does it like its "daily job"?

7. Show students a tube of toothpaste. With the cap screwed on tight, use your fingers to squeeze the tube in different places. Tell students that this is an example of how the sphincter muscle holds food in the stomach until the duodenum is ready to receive it. Next take the cap off the toothpaste tube and squeeze the tube over a small paper cup. Tell students that this is an example of what happens when the sphincter muscle relaxes and opens up, allowing food to pass into the duodenum.

8. Ask students to write the word "stomach" vertically down the left side of a sheet of paper. Encourage them to come up with words, phrases describing attributes of the stomach, each starting with a letter in the word "stomach." Here's an example to get you started:

   S—shaped like a comma

   T—

   O—

   M—mushy, mushy stuff

   A—

   C—contains lots of acid

   H—

9. Invite students (in small groups) to create a song about the human digestive system. Using the tune to a popular song, students may create their own personal lyrics.

CHAPTER SLAM

Make a list of all the words you know that pertain to the human digestive system:

_____ _____ _____ _____ _____

_____ _____ _____ _____ _____

_____ _____ _____ _____ _____

Now organize those words into various categories. Create a name or title for each category.

Category 1 Name:
Words:

Category 2 Name:
Words:

Category 3 Name:
Words:

Using the category names above as chapter titles, write a "book" about the human digestive system. If you get stuck, you can make up what you don't know. You'll be able to revise your "book" after reading *Guts*.

From *MORE Science Adventures with Children's Literature: Reading Comprehension and Inquiry-Based Science* by Anthony D. Fredericks. Westport, CT: Teacher Ideas Press. Copyright © 2008.

STOMACH THIS

This activity will help you learn about the digestive process in your stomach.

Materials:

- 3 small clear plastic cups
- whole milk
- tablespoon
- water
- plastic wrap
- rubber bands
- lemon juice or vinegar
- meat tenderizer

Directions:

1. Pour three tablespoons of milk into each of three plastic cups.
2. In the first cup put two tablespoons of water. Cover the cup with a sheet of plastic wrap, using a rubber band to hold the wrap in place.
3. In the second cup put two tablespoons of a weak acid such as lemon juice or vinegar and cover as above.
4. In the third cup put two tablespoons of an enzyme such as meat tenderizer and cover as above.
5. Wait for one or two hours

Description:

After waiting for one or two hours, observe the changes that occur in each cup. The changes that occur in the second and third cup are similar to the digestive process that takes place in your stomach every day. After you eat some food, the acids and enzymes in your stomach begin to work on that food to break it down so that its nutrients can be absorbed by the body as it passes through the rest of the digestive track. Water alone has very little effect on the breakdown of food.

 From *MORE Science Adventures with Children's Literature: Reading Comprehension and Inquiry-Based Science* by Anthony D. Fredericks. Westport, CT: Teacher Ideas Press. Copyright © 2008.

DIGESTIVE DISEASES

There are several diseases that can affect the human digestive system. Listed below are a few of the more common ones. Using a dictionary, encyclopedia, appropriate Web sites, or information from your family doctor, provide a definition or explanation for each of the listed diseases.

GERD:

Acid Reflux:

Celiac Disease:

Ulcers:

Constipation:

Irritable Bowel Syndrome:

Gallstones:

Stomach Cancer:

From *MORE Science Adventures with Children's Literature: Reading Comprehension and Inquiry-Based Science* by Anthony D. Fredericks. Westport, CT: Teacher Ideas Press. Copyright © 2008.

STOMACH DIARY

Pretend that your stomach has the ability to write. Select one day of the past week. For each of the time slots listed below, have your stomach write a diary entry. Your stomach may wish to describe different foods that came down the esophagus, the actions it took on various foods, problems it encountered, challenges it met, or any other possible action during the course of that day. You may wish to compare your stomach's diary with the stomach diaries of some of your classmates.

A.M.

7:00–8:00:

8:00–9:00:

9:00–10:00:

10:00–11:00:

11:00–12:00:

P.M.

12:00–1:00:

1:00–2:00:

2:00–3:00:

3:00–4:00:

4:00–5:00:

5:00–6:00:

6:00–7:00:

7:00–8:00:

8:00–9:00:

9:00–10:00:

From *MORE Science Adventures with Children's Literature: Reading Comprehension and Inquiry-Based Science* by Anthony D. Fredericks. Westport, CT: Teacher Ideas Press. Copyright © 2008.

Forces of Nature
Catherine O'Neill Grace
Washington, DC: National Geographic, 2004

SELECTED CITATIONS

- **2005 Outstanding Science Trade Book**—Children's Book Council/National Science Teachers Association

- "Sure to be gobbled up by anyone who can't resist awestruck immersion into the destructive power of nature, or who enjoys watching passionately curious scientists learn more about our world."—*Children's Literature*

SUMMARY

With jaw-dropping photographs and mesmerizing text, this book will open students' eyes (very wide, indeed) to the power and force of three natural disasters—volcanoes, earthquakes, and tornadoes. Students will be enthralled by this dynamic book, filled to overflowing with incredible statistics, stunning real-life disasters, and amazing stories. There's much to learn in the pages of this book—one students will return to again and again.

SUGGESTED GRADE LEVELS: 4–6

LESSON OBJECTIVES

Science Standards

- Content Standard A: Science as Inquiry

  Abilities necessary to do science inquiry (K–4, 5–8)

  Understandings about science inquiry (K–4, 5–8)

- Content Standard B: Physical Science

    Position and motion of objects (K–4)

    Motions and forces (5–8)

    Transfer of energy (5–8)

- Content Standard D: Earth and Space Science

    Structure of the Earth system (5–8)

- Content Standard E: Science and Technology

    Understanding about science and technology (K–4, 5–8)

- Content Standard F: Science in Personal and Social Perspectives

    Natural hazards (5–8)

    Risks and benefits (5–8)

- Content Standard G: History and Nature of Science

    Science as a human endeavor (K–4, 5–8)

CRITICAL THINKING QUESTIONS

1. What was the most amazing thing you learned in this book?

2. If you could study just one natural disaster, what would it be? Why?

3. Which of the three natural disasters in this book do you think is most dangerous?

4. What are some ways people can prepare for natural disasters?

5. Why do natural disasters fascinate humans?

COMPREHENSION LESSON (CONCEPT CARDS)

Setting the Stage

Invite students to share what they know about volcanoes, earthquakes, and tornadoes. Where did they get their information? How accurate is their information? What uncertainties do they have about the topic?

Duplicate the Concept Cards on sheets of card stock (65lb. paper). Cut the cards apart into four to six sets of 25 cards each. Place each set of cards inside a zipper-close sandwich bag.

Before Reading

Divide the class into four to six small groups. Provide each group with a set of Concept Cards. Invite each group to arrange the cards into several categories. Inform students that there are no right or wrong answers for this activity. There is no set numbers of categories, nor is there a set number of words within a category. That is entirely up to each individual group. After allowing sufficient time, invite the groups to describe their various categories and some of the words they placed within each category (there are often significant differences).

During Reading

After students have arranged their cards into categories and shared the words in each category, invite them to read the book. Encourage students to look for the words they saw on the Concept Cards.

After Reading

Invite students to return to their Concept Cards and rearrange them according to information learned in the book. What new categories do they need to create? What words need to be shifted from one category to another? Are there any new words that could be added to a category? Allow time for students to discuss the changes they have made.

LITERATURE EXTENSIONS

Invite students to select one or more of the following activities:

1. Students may visit a Web site that has the "Top 101 Frequently Asked Questions" about volcanoes, http://volcano.und.edu/vwdocs/ask_a.html, which is a list of questions asked by students across the country, answered by some of the word's leading volcanologists. Ask students to review the listed question and determine whether they have a volcano question that is not represented on the list.

2. Students may create a model of the Soufriere Hills volcano on Montserrat. Using photographs and illustrations from the book, encourage them (individually or in small groups) to create several replicas of the volcano using the following recipe:

    > 1 cup flour
    >
    > ½ cup salt
    >
    > ⅓ cup water
    >
    > Mix the flour and salt. Add the water, a little at a time. Squeeze the dough until it is smooth. Form it into a volcanic shape (similar to the Soufriere Hills volcano). Let it air dry for 3 or 4 days or bake it at 225°F for about 60 minutes. Paint it with tempera paints. (Note: This recipe is sufficient for one "volcano." Adjust it according to the number of volcanoes students wish to construct.)

3. Invite students to blow up several small balloons. Mix equal parts of liquid starch and water together until the starch is dissolved. Then soak newspaper strips (two inches wide by eight inches long) in the mixture and layer them all over the balloon. When the paper has dried, students may use tempera paints to create the continents and oceans of the world. Have them indicate (with stickers or paint) (1) the locations of major volcanoes around the world and/or (2) the lines for some of the major tectonic plates. These globes should be appropriately displayed in the classroom or library.

4. Obtain copies of several different telephone books. Invite students to browse through the yellow pages of a telephone book and locate items or services that might be needed in the event of a local volcanic eruption, earthquake, or tornado (e.g., telephone service, carpet cleaning, home repair). Students may wish to create their own "Disaster Yellow Pages," listing services that are not normally found in most municipal phone books (e.g., lava removal, tectonic plate repair, air purification).

5. Invite students to each "adopt" a volcano from somewhere in the world. Each student must provide a biography of her or his volcano, including the height and activity of the adoptee, recent rumblings, and other vital information and statistics. Provide regular opportunities for students to share their adoptees with other members of the class.

6. Obtain two different colors of modeling clay from a hobby store. Flatten each into a four-inch square. Place the squares side by side on a smooth surface that has been lightly oiled with vegetable oil or olive oil. Ask one student to place his or her hands on the outer edges of the squares and attempt to push them together. Encourage other students to note what happens to the clay as it is slowly pushed together. Reform the squares and repeat the demonstration, asking another student to set the squares side by side. Invite the student to place one hand on one square and the hand on the other and then attempt to move them in opposite directions. Inform students that these two actions are similar to what happens to Earth's surface during an earthquake.

7. Invite students to post an oversized U.S. map on one wall of the classroom. Ask them to record on the map the major earthquakes that have struck the United States in the past 100 years. Students may also wish to post a world map on the wall and indicate (with index cards) the major earthquakes from around the world that have occurred in the past 100 years. Which country has suffered the most earthquakes in the past century?

8. The following Web site provides viewers with eyewitness accounts of the earthquake that struck Turkey in August 1999: http://www.turkeyresearch.com/earthquake/. Children who lived through the earthquake have provided descriptions of it through photographs, writings, drawings, and paintings, allowing visitors to the site to experience the tragedy of this great earthquake. After students have had an opportunity to view this site, take time to discuss the implications of an earthquake on the lives of children. Do children suffer more in an earthquake? Do children experience more stress? Students may wish to record their thoughts in personal or whole-class journals.

9. After students have investigated the nature of tornadoes, invite them to write an informational brochure or newsletter specifically for children on what to do in the event of a tornado. What information should they include? How should they write it so that young children will understand it? What should children know about tornadoes so that they are prepared in case one strikes when no adults are available to help them?

10. Invite a local meteorologist to visit your class and discuss the generation of tornadoes. What conditions are necessary for a tornado to begin? What sustains a tornado? How fast does a tornado travel over the ground? How does the information in the "Tornado" chapter of the book compare to the information shared by the meteorologist?

CONCEPT CARDS

risky	steam	plate	mantle	pumice
lava	gases	flow	pressure	crust
energy	shock waves	fault	magnitude	collapse
warning	force	powerful	wind	funnel
damage	circular	twister	shelter	storm

From *MORE Science Adventures with Children's Literature: Reading Comprehension and Inquiry-Based Science* by Anthony D. Fredericks. Westport, CT: Teacher Ideas Press. Copyright © 2008.

BLOW YOUR TOP

With the assistance of an adult, you will be able to create your own chemical volcano in the following activity.

Materials:

- piece of cardboard
- scissors
- cellophane tape
- empty baby food jar
- small spoon
- cookie sheet
- hydrogen peroxide (available at the drug store)
- quick-rising yeast (available at the grocery store)

Directions:

1. Cut a piece of cardboard into the shape of a cone (this cone should be able to fit over the top of the baby food jar). Tape the cone together. The cone should have a small hole in the top

2. Place the jar on a cookie sheet.

3. (NOTE: The following steps need to be done very rapidly.) Hold the cone in one hand.

4. With the other hand, pour ½ cup of hydrogen peroxide into the jar.

5. Follow that quickly with ½ teaspoon of quick-rising yeast.

6. Stir the mixture thoroughly (and quickly), then place the cone over the jar. (You may need to stir the mixture again to continue the "eruption.")

Description:

The mixture of yeast and hydrogen peroxide results in a lot of foam, some steam, and a little hissing. This chemical reaction also will produce some degree of heat (you will be able to feel the heat on the sides of the jar). This is an example of an exothermic chemical reaction, one that generates heat. This reaction is similar to the heat an erupting volcano generates.

 From *MORE Science Adventures with Children's Literature: Reading Comprehension and Inquiry-Based Science* by Anthony D. Fredericks. Westport, CT: Teacher Ideas Press. Copyright © 2008.

RECORDS

Conduct some library research or a search of Web sites and complete the chart below.

Volcanoes	Earthquakes	Tornadoes
Tallest:	Most severe:	Largest recorded:
Shortest:	Most recent:	Most dangerous year:
Oldest active:	Greatest loss of life:	Greatest wind speed:
Most active:	Oldest recorded:	Greatest loss of life:
Most active in United States:	Greatest loss of property:	Most prone state:
Most lava:	Largest in United States:	Heaviest object carried:
Most violent eruption:	Highest magnitude:	Most dangerous U.S. city:

From MORE Science Adventures with Children's Literature: Reading Comprehension and Inquiry-Based Science by Anthony D. Fredericks. Westport, CT: Teacher Ideas Press. Copyright © 2008.

CHECK THEM OUT

Below are some selected Web sites on tornadoes. You might want to check them out.

- Which one is most informative?

- Which one is the most interesting?

- Which one is geared mostly for adults?

- Which one is geared primarily for kids?

- Which one did you enjoy the most?

http://www.usatoday.com/weather/resources/2006–04–03–tornado-basics_x.htm

http://www.photolib.noaa.gov/nssl/tornado1.html

http://wywy.essortment.com/informationont_rmgu.htm

http://www.spc.noaa.gov/faq/tornado/

http://skydiary.com/kids/tornadoes.html

http://www.wildwildweather.com/twisters.htm

http://www.fema.gov/hazard/tornado/index.shtm

http://www.redcross.org/services/disaster/0,1082,0_591_,00.html

From *MORE Science Adventures with Children's Literature: Reading Comprehension and Inquiry-Based Science* by Anthony D. Fredericks. Westport, CT: Teacher Ideas Press. Copyright © 2008.

Red Eyes or Blue Feathers:
A Book About Animal Colors

Patricia M. Stockland

Minneapolis, MN: Picture Window Books, 2005

SELECTED CITATIONS

- **2006 Outstanding Science Trade Book**—Children's Book Council/National Science Teachers Association

- "A magical and colorful journey that builds bridges between science and art. A 'must' for any classroom!"—Kristen P., teacher

SUMMARY

For most animals, life is simply a matter of survival. Many animals are able to survive through a process of adaptation. One of the most common forms of adaptation is color. An animal's color may help it hide from its enemies. Color is how many animals are able to locate a potential mate. And color is a form of communication for several different species. This colorful book describes in words and illustrations a diverse group of creatures and the ways in which color is an essential element in their ability to survive. Engaging text and delightful illustrations combine to create a book that will initiate many questions (as well as investigations of those questions).

SUGGESTED GRADE LEVELS: 2–4

LESSON OBJECTIVES

Science Standards

• Content Standard C: Life Science

> The characteristics of organisms (K–4)
>
> Organisms and environments (K–4)
>
> Reproduction and heredity (5–8)
>
> Populations and ecosystems (5–8)
>
> Diversity and adaptations of organisms (5–8)

CRITICAL THINKING QUESTIONS

1. Which creature in this book was most unusual; most amazing?

2. Which of the animals would you like to see "in person"?

3. What other animals could have been included in this book?

4. How have you used camouflage to hide from someone?

5. In what kind of environment do most camouflaged animals live? Why?

COMPREHENSION LESSON (METACOGNITIVE QUESTIONS)

Setting the Stage

Provide a copy of the book for each student. Record the title of the book on the chalkboard and invite the class to ask questions about the title or the illustration on the cover.

Before Reading

Provide each student with a copy of the Metacognitive Questions project page. Take a few minutes to discuss the questions and let students know that they will be looking for answers to these questions as they are reading (or listening to) the book.

During Reading

Ask students to begin reading (or listening to) the book. They may wish to stop every so often and fill in an answer to one or more of the questions on the sheet. It is important for students to know that there are no right or wrong responses to these questions—rather, these are questions that accomplished readers ask themselves all the time as they are reading.

After Reading

Upon completion of the book, allow time for students to share and discuss their responses to some of the Metacognitive Questions. Invite students to note any commonalities in their responses. Were any questions challenging to answer? Did any questions not have an answer at all? Which questions were the easiest to answer?

LITERATURE EXTENSIONS

Invite students to select one or more of the following activities:

1. Invite students to investigate some of the animals that live in the local environment. Ask them to consider birds, fish, mammals, reptiles, amphibians, and insects. Encourage them to collect a list of the various animals and to divide the creatures by their major colors. For example, how many animals have red as the predominant color? How many are entirely green? How many have at least three primary colors? What color seems to be the most prevalent?

2. Create a "Word Wall" in the classroom or library. Invite students to select some of their favorite phrases, terms, and color descriptions from the book to post on the wall. Encourage students to be aware of other color descriptions in the books they read or listen to that could be added to the word wall.

3. Invite students to create some colors that may not have been included in the book. Using the same language as the author, invite students to create their own original colors for animals. They may wish to start with animals in their local community, then move on to creatures in their geographical region of the country, and then to critters that are indigenous to the entire country. What new colors can they create for animals that they may be familiar with or come into contact with on a regular basis?

4. Encourage students to look at various colors in nature. Have them bring in various plants and pictures of plants that exhibit the same colors as those depicted in the book. Discuss with students some of the similarities between plant colors and animal colors. Are plants more colorful than animals, or vice versa? How do colors help plants survive?

5. Ask students to participate in a friendly competition. Divide the class into two groups. Tell one group that its task is to collect a list of camouflaged animals. Tell the other group that its task is to assemble a list of animals that are not camouflaged. Suggest a time limit and see which group can come up with the longest list. What would students predict as the longest list (before beginning the competition)?

6. Have students do a little investigation in books or Internet sites. Which color is most represented in nature? Students may wish to construct two lists—a plant list and an animal list. Invite them to rank order colors on each list according to the number of species that exhibit each color. Students may predict that "green" is the most prevalent color for plants, but what would be the next most common color? They may predict

that brown is the most common for animals, but what is Color 2? Make sure students can substantiate their lists with appropriate resource materials.

7. Divide students into various groups. Invite each group to make a collage of all the colors of nature that it can find in old magazine, brochures, periodicals, and other printed matter. Which collage has the greatest variety of colors?

8. Repeat the activity above, but this time, invite students to create a collage according to the nature colors found in a specific country. How many colors would be found in Australia? How many nature colors would be found in Nigeria? What nature colors are represented in the country of Uruguay?

9. Invite students to create an advertisement for this book. What could they say that would attract more people to read this book? Students may wish to create posters or three-dimensional exhibits for display throughout the library or school.

METACOGNITIVE QUESTIONS

Good readers are always asking themselves questions as they read. The questions that you ask yourself while you read are called "metacognitive questions." These are some of the things that a good reader thinks about during all kinds of reading. There is no right or wrong way to answer these questions simply because every reader will respond differently to a book or story.

While reading (or listening to) the book *Red Eyes or Blue Feathers: A Book About Animal Colors,* write down answers for as many of these questions as you can.

1. Why would this information be important for me to know?

2. Is this material similar to anything I've read about previously?

3. Does this information give me any clues as to what may happen later in the book?

4. How does this information differ from other things I know?

5. Why is this difficult for me to understand?

6. Do I need additional information to help me understand this topic?

7. Can I write a summary of this part of the story?

8. What do I know so far?

9. What did the author do to make me think this way?

10. Am I satisfied with this story?

From *MORE Science Adventures with Children's Literature: Reading Comprehension and Inquiry-Based Science* by Anthony D. Fredericks. Westport, CT: Teacher Ideas Press. Copyright © 2008.

CAN'T SEE ME!

In order to survive, smaller animals sometimes need to hide from larger ones. One way that certain animals avoid being seen, and protect themselves from being eaten, is to use protective coloring, or camouflage. These animals match their body colors to the colors in their environment so that they blend in and almost disappear.

Materials:

- 100 green and 100 red toothpicks (from a party store or grocery store)
- watch of stopwatch
- a helper
- journal/notebook

Directions:

1. Ask a friend to mix up all 200 toothpicks and spread them out over a certain area of grass (your front lawn or a section of a park, for example). The area should be about 25 yards square.

2. Ask your friend to time you for one minute, two minutes, and five minutes. See how many toothpicks you can find in each of those time frames.

3. Put the found toothpicks aside in bunches after each time period.

4. Count the red and green toothpicks found in each of the three time periods. Record the exact number in a journal or notebook.

Description:

In each of the time frames, you probably noticed that you were finding and picking up more red toothpicks than green toothpicks. Because the green toothpicks were closer to the color of the green grass than the red ones were, the green ones were harder to see and find. Animals that are able to blend into their environment have a better chance for survival than those who have colors that make them easy to see. The ability of animals to match the colors of their surroundings helps them to protect themselves. For example, green lizards are able to hide better in an area with lots of green plants than red or yellow lizards would be.

From *MORE Science Adventures with Children's Literature: Reading Comprehension and Inquiry-Based Science* by Anthony D. Fredericks. Westport, CT: Teacher Ideas Press. Copyright © 2008.

INTERESTING FACTS

Here are some interesting facts about animals that are able to camouflage themselves because their color or shape helps them look like something else in their environment. Rank order (from "Most Interesting" to "Least Interesting") these facts in the box at the bottom of the sheet. Take time to share your list—and the reasons why you put items in the order you did—with other students in the class.

- If a chameleon is angry, its skin color changes to black.
- Some species of leaf insects can change their color—becoming light in the daytime and dark at night.
- The pipefish looks like a strand of seaweed. It spends its entire life standing on its head.
- The casque-headed frog looks exactly like a small pile of dead leaves.
- The orchid praying mantis is colored a delicate shell-pink—just like the rhododendron flower on which it lives.
- A sea dragon looks just like a piece of floating seaweed.
- The flying gecko looks just like the bark of the tree on which it lives.
- The walking stick insect can stay motionless for several hours.
- The ptarmigan bird can change the color of its feathers according to the season.

Most Interesting

↓

↓

↓

↓

↓

↓

↓

↓

Least Interesting

WORLD'S GREATEST BIRD FOOD

NOTE: This activity requires adult assistance. Do not do this on your own.

This fantastic recipe will have birds flocking to your house all year long.

Materials:

- plastic cups (short, wide, and small)
- plastic plates
- epoxy glue
- suet (from a local butcher or grocery store)
- large frying pan
- 1 cup each of chunky peanut butter, chopped nuts, sunflower seeds, and corn-meal
- 1 tablespoon of crushed eggshells
- mixing bowl

Directions:

1. Glue two or three small plastic cups each to the middle of two or three plastic plates. Set aside.
2. With the help of an adult, cut the suet into small pieces and melt it slowly in a large frying pan (*be very, very careful of splatters—hot fat can cause serious burns*).
3. Measure one cup of the melted fat.
4. Let the melted fat cool until it becomes solid. Then reheat it again and allow the liquid fat to cool off once more.
5. Thoroughly mix all of the other ingredients into the soft suet.
6. Spoon the mixture into the small plastic cups and put the cup/plate assembly into the refrigerator.
7. When the mixture is firm, set the plates outside in a protected area.

Description:

This bird food is an excellent mix for all types of birds—particularly during the winter months. The suet provides the birds with necessary fat in order to keep warm when it is cold outside. Make sure other animals (pet dog, pet cat, other animals in the neighborhood) do not have access to this food—it could make them sick if they eat too much.

 From *MORE Science Adventures with Children's Literature: Reading Comprehension and Inquiry-Based Science* by Anthony D. Fredericks. Westport, CT: Teacher Ideas Press. Copyright © 2008.

G Is for Galaxy:
An Out of This World Alphabet

Janis Campbell and Cathy Collison

Chelsea, MI: Sleeping Bear Press, 2005

SELECTED CITATIONS

- "This is one alphabet book that will keep readers coming back."—*Children's Literature*

- "With inviting rhymes, *G Is for Galaxy* guides us through the alphabet, from A to 'Z is for Zodiac,' providing lots of fascinating information about the planets and stars along the way."—barnesandnoble.com

SUMMARY

Each letter of the alphabet stands for a specific feature, condition, or concept related to the study of our universe. Using a simple poem (for young readers) in concert with expository information (for older readers), the authors have effectively captured the beauty, wonder, and amazing discoveries that have been made over the centuries. This is the ideal book for aspiring astronomers as well as educators seeking interesting and engaging descriptions of space. This is a reference tool students will be turning to time after time.

SUGGESTED GRADE LEVELS: 3–6

LESSON OBJECTIVES

Science Standards

- Content Standard B: Physical Science

    Position and motion of objects (K–4)

    Motions and forces (5–8)

- Content Standard D: Earth and Space Science

  Objects in the sky (K–4)

  Changes in Earth and sky (K–4)

  Earth in the solar system (5–8)

- Content Standard E: Science and Technology

  Understanding about science and technology (K–4, 5–8)

- Content Standard G: History and Nature of Science

  Science as a human endeavor (K–4, 5–8)

CRITICAL THINKING QUESTIONS

1. What was the most unusual fact in this book?

2. What information did the authors leave out of the book?

3. If you were asked to include something in this book, what would it be?

4. How has this book affected your interest in space exploration?

5. How interesting would it be to become an astronaut?

COMPREHENSION LESSON (DIVERGENT QUESTIONS)

Setting the Stage

Duplicate the Divergent Question project page for the book *G Is for Galaxy* and distribute the sheets to students.

Before Reading

Prior to reading the book (either individually or as part of a series of read-aloud sessions), invite students to review the questions on the Divergent Questions sheet. Inform students that you are not looking for right answers at this point, but are merely tapping into their background knowledge about space. After allowing sufficient discussion about the questions (and their responses), inform students that they should look for potential answers to the questions as they read the book.

During Reading

Each day students can read several sections of the book. They may wish to keep track of selected Divergent Questions (and the possible responses) on a separate sheet of paper.

After Reading

After students have finished reading the book, take time to review the Divergent Questions again. Make note of those questions for which students changed or altered their responses as a result of information learned in the book. What new information did they learn? Why did they change their initial responses? What might be some additional Divergent Questions the class could add to its list? Which question(s) caused them to think the most?

LITERATURE EXTENSIONS

Invite students to select one or more of the following activities:

1. Invite students to each make a travel brochure about a planet, moon, or star to interest people in visiting that celestial body. Students may use library resources or the Internet to complete their information. You may wish to set up an imaginary "Planetary Travel Agency" to display the brochures for other classes.

2. Depending on where you are located, invite a college professor specializing in space exploration to visit the class. Encourage students to brainstorm some questions they would like to ask the visitor.

3. Invite students to each select and research one of the world's space pioneers, to learn about his or her background, contributions, successes, failures, motivations, and any other pertinent data. Following the research, invite students to take on the role of their selected pioneer and share his or her views on the importance of the space program and its future. Space pioneers include (but are not limited to) the following:

Edward (Buzz) Aldrin Jr.	Virgil Grissom
Willaim A. Anders	Johannes Kepler
Neil Armstrong	James A. Lovell
Guton S. Bluford	Sharon (Christa) MacAuliffe
Frank Borman	Sir Isaac Newton
Scott Carpenter	Sally K. Ride
Michael Collins	Alan B. Shepard
Gordon Cooper	Wally Schirra
Robert L. Crippen	Valentina Tereshkova
Yuri Gagarin	Edward J. White
John Glenn	Wernher von Braun
Robert H. Goddard	James W. Young

4. Ask students to create a space time line. As students read about advances in space exploration, invite them to add selected events (e.g., manned space missions, unmanned space exploration missions, space shuttles, etc.) to the time line. For each event, students should include the name of the mission, the dates, the astronauts/cosmonauts (if appropriate), the main purpose(s) of the mission, and its most significant contributions. Invite students to illustrate each of the events they highlight.

5. Encourage students to draw illustrations of themselves as space shuttle crew members. Invite them to each write a letter to her or his family back on Earth. They may wish to tell the family what it feels like on the shuttle as well as what they do.

6. After students have had an opportunity to read this book, invite selected groups to compile a list of the "Top Ten" space facts. They can base their selection of facts on those that are (1) most interesting, (2) most unusual, (3) most amazing, or (4) most incredible, or other criteria as they choose. These lists may be organized into a larger book for display in the classroom.

7. Invite students to discuss which of the planets would be the most interesting to explore. Which planet would be the least interesting to explore? Encourage students to provide reasons and rationale for their opinions.

8. Ask students to work in small groups to create a scrapbook of articles and clippings about space exploration. These articles can be obtained from the local newspaper, news magazines, line Web sites (e.g., *USA Today*), or scientific periodicals (e.g., *Discover Magazine*). Invite students to discuss how the scrapbook could become an important feature of their space exploration studies.

9. Invite students to hold a mini-debate in which they discuss the following issue: Should funding for space exploration and colonization be continued when money is so badly needed to solve social problems such as hunger, crime, and diseases on Earth?

10. Divide students into three small groups. Provide each group with a raisin, an orange, and an inflated beach ball. Invite each group to designate the order of these three items so that they represent the relative sizes of the earth, sun, and moon. Invite groups to share their deliberations with the class.

11. Students may enjoy conducting some library or Internet research to determine the origin of the names of the planets. For whom were the planets named? Who is responsible for naming the planets? Are there any similarities in the names of the planets? If a new planet were to be discovered in our solar system, how would it be named?

DIVERGENT QUESTIONS

1. List all the words you can think of to describe the solar system.

2. List as many celestial bodies as you can.

3. How would someone standing on the moon view the various plants?

4. What would space exploration mean from the viewpoint of someone standing on Mars?

5. How would your grandparents describe the solar system?

6. How would you feel if you were standing on Jupiter?

7. What would Galileo do with all the new space technology?

8. You are an astronomer. Describe your feelings about Pluto.

9. How is Neptune like Uranus?

10. I only know about Earth's moon. Explain some other moons to me.

11. What ideas from this book are like ideas you've read about in other "galaxy" books?

12. What planet is most like Earth?

13. What would happen if there were more planets?

14. Suppose a large meteor struck Earth. What would happen?

15. Imagine if the conditions on Mars and those on Earth were reversed. What would happen?

FANTASTIC FACTS

Use a variety of resource materials in your classroom, school library, public library, or home (e.g., Internet) to locate two or three "Fantastic Facts" for each of the eight planets and Pluto. Several have already been provided for you.

Mercury

    1.   A year on Mercury is only 88 days long.

    2.

    3.

Venus

    1.   The surface temperature on Venus reaches 870°F.

    2.

    3.

Earth

    1.

    2.

    3.

Mars

    1.   Olympus Mons is the highest volcano in the solar system—17 miles high.

    2.

    3.

Jupiter

    1.   Jupiter is more than twice as heavy as all the other planets of the solar system combined.

    2.

    3.

From *MORE Science Adventures with Children's Literature: Reading Comprehension and Inquiry-Based Science* by Anthony D. Fredericks. Westport, CT: Teacher Ideas Press. Copyright © 2008.

FANTASTIC FACTS (CONTINUED)

Saturn

    1.   A year on Saturn is 29.5 Earth years long.

    2.

    3.

Uranus

    1.   The original name for this planet was "Herschel."

    2.

    3.

Neptune

    1.   This planet was named for the Roman god of the sea.

    2.

    3.

Pluto

    1.   This is the only (former) planet to have been discovered by an American.

    2.

    3.

STAR PARTY

Do the stars move in the sky? Or do you? Here's how you can find out.

Materials:

- sheet of clear acetate (or a transparency master)—available at any office supply store
- four permanent felt-tip markers (black, red, green, blue)
- cellophane tape
- masking tape

Directions:

1. Locate a windowpane in your house, one that has a clear line of sight to the sky (no trees or other objects in the way).

2. Stand close to the window and tape the sheet of acetate to the glass slightly above the level of your eyes.

3. Stand back about one foot and place a strip of masking tape on the floor.

4. On a clear (preferably moonless) night when several stars are clearly visible, stand with your toes on the strip of masking tape. Look out the window through the sheet of acetate taped to the glass.

5. Locate several prominent stars. Use the black marker to mark the location of six or seven of those stars directly on the sheet of acetate (make solid dots). Write the time and date at the bottom of the sheet.

6. One week later, stand at the same place (with your toes on the masking tape) at the same time. Note the position of the same stars and mark each one on the acetate with the red marker. Write the date on the sheet.

7. One week later, stand at the same place (with your toes on the masking tape) at the same time. Note the position of the same stars and mark each one on the acetate with the green marker. Write the date on the sheet.

8. One week later, stand at the same place (with your toes on the masking tape) at the same time. Note the position of the same stars and mark each one on the acetate with the blue marker. Write the date on the sheet.

From *MORE Science Adventures with Children's Literature: Reading Comprehension and Inquiry-Based Science* by Anthony D. Fredericks. Westport, CT: Teacher Ideas Press. Copyright © 2008.

STAR PARTY (CONTINUED)

Description:

You will note that the marks you placed on the sheet of acetate are different for each week, even though you were using the same stars each time. You may think this means that the stars have moved in the sky. Actually, the stars have remained in stationary positions in the sky; it is Earth that has moved. As Earth orbits the sun, it changes its position in the sky relative to the stars. So, each week Earth moves a little farther in its path, while the stars remain "fixed" in their positions.

Fantastic Fact: In one week, Earth travels more than 9 million miles in its orbit; in four weeks it will have traveled more than 36 million miles.

From *MORE Science Adventures with Children's Literature: Reading Comprehension and Inquiry-Based Science* by Anthony D. Fredericks. Westport, CT: Teacher Ideas Press. Copyright © 2008.

ROUND AND ROUND

This activity will help you appreciate the relative size of the sun.

Materials:

- 3-foot long piece of string
- measuring tape
- quarter

Directions:

1. Go to a backyard, park, or playground.
2. Form the string into a circle on the ground. The circle of string should be nine feet in diameter (the distance from edge to edge through the middle of the circle). This circle represents the sun.
3. Place the quarter on the ground along one edge of the string circle. The quarter represents Earth.

Description:

The equatorial diameter of the sun is 864,988 miles. The equatorial diameter of Earth is approximately 8,000 miles. That means that the diameter of the sun is about 108 times greater than the diameter of the earth.

The string circle represents the sun, and the quarter (which is about one inch in diameter) represents Earth. As you look at the model you have created, you can begin to understand how much bigger the sun is than our own planet as well as every other planet in the solar system.

From *MORE Science Adventures with Children's Literature: Reading Comprehension and Inquiry-Based Science* by Anthony D. Fredericks. Westport, CT: Teacher Ideas Press. Copyright © 2008.

Flotsam
David Wiesner
New York: Clarion Books, 2006

SELECTED CITATIONS

- **2007 Caldecott Medal**—*American Library Association*

- **2006 Best Children's Book Award**—*Child Magazine*

SUMMARY

This is an exceptional, wordless picture book that stimulates the imagination and provides magical ways of looking at the world—especially an incredible oceanic world. In this tale, a boy discovers an old-fashioned camera with its film intact. A trip to the photo store produces unbelievable snapshots: an octopus in an armchair; tiny, green alien tourists observing sea horses; and oversized sea stars. In addition, there are portraits of children—each holding another child's photo. After snapping his own photo, the boy returns the camera to the sea, where its journey begins anew.

SUGGESTED GRADE LEVELS: 1–6

LESSON OBJECTIVES

Science Standards

- Content Standard A: Science as Inquiry

    Understandings about science inquiry (K–4, 5–8)

- Content Standard B: Physical Science

  Properties of objects and materials (K–4)

  Motions and forces (5–8)

- Content Standard C: Life Science

  Organisms and environments (K–4)

- Content Standard E: Science and Technology

  Abilities of technological design (K–4)

  Abilities to distinguish between natural objects and objects made by @SubUlist = humans (K–4)

- Content Standard G: History and Nature of Science

  Science as a human endeavor (K–4, 5–8)

CRITICAL THINKING QUESTIONS

1. Which of the illustrations did you find most creative? Why?

2. How is this book similar to other David Wiesner books?

3. Why did Wiesner place this story at the seashore?

4. What did you enjoy most about the conclusion to this story?

5. Why do you think Wiesner decided to make this a wordless picture book?

COMPREHENSION LESSON (PICTURE PERFECT)

Setting the Stage

Invite students to briefly discuss some of the things they would discover if they visited the ocean. What types of things would be happening there? What types of animals would be living there?

Before Reading

Use a piece of paper to cover over the words on the cover of this book. Then create a transparency of the cover illustration. Project the transparency for the entire class. Divide the class into several groups. Invite members of each group to generate three to five questions about the illustration. Afterward, ask each group to exchange its list of questions with another group. Then invite each group to write a story that has answers to the other group's questions embedded in the story (one member of each group records the story that is contributed by all the other members of the group). After sufficient time, invite the groups to share their completed stories with each other.

During Reading

Invite students to go through the book (*Note:* This is a wordless picture book, so there is no reading involved). Ask them to pay attention to the details and information shared in each of the illustrations.

After Reading

Invite the groups to each return to its original "Picture Perfect" story and edit it in light of the information gathered from the book. What changes will the groups need to make in a second or third draft?

LITERATURE EXTENSIONS

Invite students to select one or more of the following activities:

1. Invite students to discuss why the author/illustrator decided to make this a wordless picture book. Is the story more powerful because he decided to use just illustrations instead of words? Would words have diminished the "power" of the story? Is this a stronger story because of the absence of words? What was the author/illustrator thinking about when he decided to do the book in this format?

2. Divide students into several groups. Invite each group to develop and create captions for the illustrations in a designated section of the book. Provide opportunities for the groups to work together so that there is consistency and flow to the entire story.

3. As an extension of the activity above, ask students if there could be multiple interpretations of one or more of the illustrations in this book. Is it possible that two different people might interpret a single illustration differently? What might be the consequences for the overall theme or plot of the story? Does the author/illustrator want all readers to interpret the story in the same way?

4. Invite students to examine other books by David Wiesner. Work with the school librarian to assemble a representative collection of his books. What themes does he use in many of his books? Why do students think he tends to concentrate on wordless (or nearly wordless) picture books? Is there an underlying message in his work?

5. Ask students to set up and conduct an imaginary interview with David Wiesner. Ask the art teacher or librarian to take on the role of Mr. Wiesner and to respond to previously prepared questions from your students. What would they like to know about his life? His artistic training? The types of children's books he writes/illustrates? Why does he do what he does (in his books)?

6. Invite students to investigate the history of and criteria for the Caldecott Medal. Whom is it named after? What is it given for? What are some recent winners and honor books of the Caldecott? You may wish to have the school librarian share some background information about this prestigious award in children's literature.

7. Ask students to write an imaginary letter of appreciation to Mr. Wiesner about *Flotsam*. What would they like to share with him? How much did they enjoy the book? Was there anything confusing or unusual about the book or the story? How did they feel when they completed the book?

8. Invite students to work with the school librarian to assemble a collection of wordless picture books. Do some authors specialize in wordless picture books? If so, who are they? Are wordless picture books only for students who have not yet learned how to read? Can they be used with older students, too? How?

9. Several marine creatures featured in this book, including the hermit crab, fiddler crab, barnacle, rockfish, octopus, lantern fish, sea turtle, sea star, sea horse, whale, sea anemone, squid, bass, and coral. Assign one or more of these creatures to each of several student groups. Invite the groups to conduct research (in other books or through Web sites) to locate appropriate background information on their designated animal(s). Provide opportunities for students to share the results of their research with each other.

10. Oceans cover nearly 70 percent of the earth's surface and contain nearly 97 percent of the planet's entire water supply. Invite students to investigate each of the five major oceans of the world. They may wish to collect a series of fascinating facts or interesting data for each of the major oceans. Here's some information to get them started:

   Pacific Ocean

   – It is twice as large as the second largest ocean, the Atlantic.

   – It reaches almost halfway around the world at its largest point.

   Atlantic Ocean

   – It contains some of the world's richest fishing grounds.

   – It is 5,965 miles across at its widest point.

   Indian Ocean

   – It has an average depth of 13,002 feet.

   – It contains the saltiest sea (the Red Sea) and the warmest gulf (the Persian Gulf).

   Antarctic Ocean

   – It's the fourth largest ocean.

   – It covers and area of 13,500,000 square miles.

   Arctic Ocean

   – It's the shallowest of the world's oceans.

   – It has a maximum depth of 17,880 feet.

PICTURE PERFECT

Write three to five questions about the illustration:

1.

2.

3.

4.

5.

Write a story that contains answers to the questions above:

From *MORE Science Adventures with Children's Literature: Reading Comprehension and Inquiry-Based Science*
by Anthony D. Fredericks. Westport, CT: Teacher Ideas Press. Copyright © 2008.

PRINT-O-FISH

Here's a great activity that will help you learn about fish physiology. This is actually a Japanese art form that has been practiced for many, many years.

Materials:

- 1 whole fish (this can be obtained from the seafood department of most supermarkets)
- newspaper
- paper towels
- newsprint (available from any art store or hobby store)
- water-soluble paint (liquid tempera paint and artist's acrylic paint are both available from hobby, craft, or art stores)
- artist's paint brushes
- masking tape

Directions:

1. Wash the fish thoroughly with soap and water to remove any mucus.
2. Lay the fish on a sheet of newspaper. Paint one side of the fish with the paint (any color will do). If necessary, thin the paint with a few drops of water. Stroke the fish from tail to head (this allows paint to catch under the edges of scales and spines and will improve the print, especially if you use a thin coat of paint.
3. Paint the fins and tail last, since they tend to dry out quickly. Do not paint the eye.
4. If the newspaper under your fish becomes wet with ink during the painting process, move the fish to a clean sheet of newspaper before printing. Otherwise, your print will pick up leftover splotches of color.
5. Carefully and slowly lay a sheet of newsprint over the fish. Taking care not to move the paper, use your hands and fingers to gently press the paper over the fish. Press the paper gently over the fins and tail. Be careful not to wrinkle the paper or you will get a blurred or double image.
6. Slowly and carefully peel the paper off. Paint in the eye with a small brush. Tape the print to a wall and allow it to dry.

From *MORE Science Adventures with Children's Literature: Reading Comprehension and Inquiry-Based Science* by Anthony D. Fredericks. Westport, CT: Teacher Ideas Press. Copyright © 2008.

PRINT-O-FISH (CONTINUED)

Description:

You have created a fish print that you can display in your room or classroom. This is a traditional Japanese practice called *gyotaku* (pronounced ghio-ta-koo). It comes from two Japanese words (gyo = fish, take = rubbing). This is one way Japanese people record their catches, and it has evolved into an art form throughout the world.

You may want to experiment with different types of paper for this activity. Thinner paper (tissue paper, rice paper) will provide a print that shows more details of the fish, but it tends to wrinkle more easily when wet. Thicker paper (construction paper) is easier to handle but does not provide a detailed print.

Note: You may need to practice this activity several times to get the technique down. Be patient, and you will discover that the more you practice, the more intricate your fish prints will become.

AQUARIUM VISIT

You may live near the ocean, or you may live far away from the ocean. Either way, a visit to an aquarium can be a magical experience. If you can't visit an aquarium in person, you can always visit one via the Internet. Here are some great Internet sites you may wish to check out.

Aquarium Center—Iowa State Fairgrounds: www.iowaaquarium.org

John Shedd Aquarium: www.sheddnet.org

Monterey Bay Aquarium: www.mbayaq.org

National Aquarium in Baltimore: http://aqua.org

New England Aquarium: www.neaq.org

Oregon Coast Aquarium: www.aquarium.org

The Seattle Aquarium: http://seattleaquarium.org

Tennessee Aquarium: www.tennis.org

From *MORE Science Adventures with Children's Literature: Reading Comprehension and Inquiry-Based Science* by Anthony D. Fredericks. Westport, CT: Teacher Ideas Press. Copyright © 2008.

WRITE ON

Select a single page from *Flotsam* that has multiple illustrations. For each illustration on the page write a caption.

Illustration 1:	Caption:

Illustration 2:	Caption:

Illustration 3:	Caption:

Illustration 4:	Caption:

Illustration 5:	Caption:

Illustration 6:	Caption:

From *MORE Science Adventures with Children's Literature: Reading Comprehension and Inquiry-Based Science* by Anthony D. Fredericks. Westport, CT: Teacher Ideas Press. Copyright © 2008.

Plantzilla

Jerdine Nolen

San Diego, CA: Silver Whistle, 2002

SELECTED CITATIONS

- "Employing the same tenderness and fanciful sense of wonder that characterized her [previous books], Nolen delivers another picture book with a far-out premise and plenty of heart."—*Publishers Weekly*

- "This humorous story may be shared with a group but will be best savored by individual readers who will have fun absorbing the wildly imaginative illustrations close up."—*School Library Journal*

SUMMARY

Kids will never look at plants the same way after reading this riotous and fanciful book about a class plant that takes on a life (and personality) all its own. This book would be a delightful and engaging introduction to any science unit on plant growth—especially because it looks at plant life from a totally wacky perspective. There is lots to discuss, lots to enjoy, and lots to savor in this humorous, dynamic, and creative story. Get this book and listen to all the laughter.

SUGGESTED GRADE LEVELS: 3–5

LESSON OBJECTIVES

Science Standards

• Content Standard C: Life Science

> The characteristics of organisms (K–4)
>
> Life cycles of organisms (K–4)
>
> Diversity and adaptations of organisms (5–8)

CRITICAL THINKING QUESTIONS

1. Does Plantzilla remind you of any plant in your house?

2. What did you enjoy most about Plantzilla?

3. How do you think your family would react to Plantzilla?

4. What are the three major differences between Plantzilla and other plants?

5. How did the illustrations contribute to your enjoyment of this story?

COMPREHENSION LESSON (IMAGE MAKERS)

Setting the Stage

Show students the cover of the book. Point out the title and the cover illustration. Invite students to make some predictions about the theme of the book.

Before Reading

Lead students through a mental imagery activity. Invite them to close their eyes while you read the story on the project page. Tell them that they should be creating a "movie" in their heads—pictures of the various scenes that you are describing for them. After sharing the story with students, ask them to open their eyes and describe some of the "mind pictures" they created in their heads. Invite them (as appropriate) to draw illustrations of their individual "mind pictures."

During Reading

Ask students to read the book independently. Or, you may elect to share it with them as a read-aloud.

After Reading

Upon completion of the reading, invite students to orally compare the "mind pictures" they had before they read the book with the new pictures they have (in their heads) now that they have completed the book. What similarities are there? What major differences? Let them know that the object is not to exactly match their "mind pictures" with the illustrations or theme of the book. Rather, it's more important to take the time to build some pictures in their heads before they read.

LITERATURE EXTENSIONS

Invite students to select one or more of the following activities:

1. Ask students to investigate the topic "Carnivorous Plants." What can they find in the resources of the school library? What can they learn about these plants on the Internet? Ask students to create an informative brochure or PowerPoint presentation about carnivorous plants.

2. As students search the Internet for information on carnivorous plants, they will discover several commercial nurseries that specialize in selling carnivorous plants. You can also buy carnivorous plants at many garden centers or local nurseries. If possible, obtain one of more of these plants and grow them in your classroom or library (be sure to find out the proper growing techniques from the nursery or from the Internet). Invite students to maintain a journal of each plant grown—rate of growth, nutrient supplied, amount of water, insects eaten, etc.

3. Students may wish to try growing pineapples in the classroom. Obtain a full pineapple from the grocery store. Cut off the crown of the pineapple (the top part with the green leaves), leaving about one to two inches of fruit attached. Dry the top for 36 hours and root it in a large container of potting soil. Keep the soil evenly moist (but not too wet) and place the container in a warm location (about 72°F is ideal). Invite students to give the plant a name and to create some inventive and imaginative stories about the plant as they are watching its growth process ("Pineapple Pete: The World's Most Dangerous Plant").

4. Cut a plain bagel in half. Wet the surface of each half and sprinkle some grass seed on it. Place the bagels in a sunny location and keep the surface damp (not drenched). Record the growth of any grass over a period of several weeks. (Students may want to experiment with different varieties of grass seed.) After several "bagel lawns" have been established, ask students to imagine that each lawn is a living individual. Ask students to write letters from those "bagel lawn individuals" to people in the school. What would they say to the principal? What would they say to the school secretary? What would they want to say to the entire student body?

5. Provide the class with the following materials: three bean plants (of equal size), petroleum jelly, drawing paper, and a ruler. Invite students to draw illustrations of the three plants ("Plant A," "Plant B," and "Plant C") and measure the heights of each. This information should be recorded in appropriate journals. Invite students to rub petroleum jelly on the top side of the leaves of Plant A and on the underside of the leaves of Plant B (Plant C will be the control). Ask students to predict what will happen to each of the

plants. Ask them to record the height of each plant (plants should be watered normally) every other day. (Plant B will show the least growth, because in the process of photosynthesis air enters the plant through the underside of the leaves.) You may wish to compare the growth (or nongrowth) of these plants with the plant in *Plantzilla*.

6. Invite students to imagine that they are each a specific species of plant. What species would they select, and why? Afterward, ask them to each write a story about their lives as though they were actually those plants. How would a sunflower describe her life? What would a cabbage say about his life in the garden? What kinds of adventures would each of the plants get into?

7. Contact a local gardening club and ask if someone could visit your class to share gardening tips and ideas. What basic gardening information should everyone know? What are some typical gardening challenges? What are some appropriate plants to begin growing at home?

8. Take some time to discuss the layout of the book—particularly the illustrations and accompanying letters. Why was the book designed in this manner? How did it contribute to your enjoyment of the story? Would the story have been different if the book had been set up like a regular children's book (e.g., straight narration)?

9. Invite students to alter the end of the story. What might be a different way of ending the story? How many different endings can you create for this book? What might be the most imaginative ending? What might be the most logical ending?

IMAGE MAKERS

Your teacher will be reading the following story to you before you read the book *Plantzilla*. Close your eyes and listen carefully. After hearing the story, you will draw an illustration of what you "saw" inside your head.

Close your eyes. Create a picture in your mind of a very large plant . . . a very large plant inside a pot. Imagine that you are standing off to the side of the very large plant. You are watching the plant. As you are looking at the plant you notice that it begins to move. The branches of the plant begin to wave. The leaves of the plant start to move back and forth. And then, the plant begins to move its branches toward you. The plant is moving in your direction. You notice that there is a mouth inside one of the flowers of the plant. The mouth begins to open and close. There are teeth inside the mouth. The plant is moving in your direction, but you can't get away. The plant is getting larger and larger and larger and . . . . You can't escape. The plant is moving closer, but you cannot run away. You realize that the plant is a living creature. And, the creature only wants one thing—YOU! It's getting closer and closer and closer and . . . .

Now, open your eyes.

Draw an illustration of the scene you created in your head in the box below:

From *MORE Science Adventures with Children's Literature: Reading Comprehension and Inquiry-Based Science* by Anthony D. Fredericks. Westport, CT: Teacher Ideas Press. Copyright © 2008.

GROWING YOUR NAME

How would you like to grow your own name? Here's how:

Materials:

- aluminum pie pan
- soil
- radish seeds
- toothpick
- water

Directions:

1. Fill an aluminum pie pan with soil (bagged soil from your local garden center is best).
2. Smooth it over with your hand so that the soil is level and moisten it with water.
3. Using a toothpick, trace your name into the surface of the soil.
4. Open a packet of radish seeds and carefully plant the seeds in the grooves you made for the letters of your name. (Be sure to follow the directions for proper planting depth and distance between seeds given on the seed packet.)
5. Cover the seeds with soil, place the pan in a sunny location, and water it occasionally.

Description:

After a few days, the radishes will sprout in the shape of your name. Later you may want to write your name in plants again, using different varieties of seeds such as grass, mung bean, and flower.

From *MORE Science Adventures with Children's Literature: Reading Comprehension and Inquiry-Based Science* by Anthony D. Fredericks. Westport, CT: Teacher Ideas Press. Copyright © 2008.

TO THE LIGHT!

Plants will always grow toward a light source. Here's a fascinating experiment that proves it.

Materials:

- small potted plant with a strong root system
- 2 large sponges
- several large rubber bands
- string
- hook
- water

Directions:

1. Carefully remove the plant from its pot (try to leave as much soil around the roots as possible).
2. Wet the two sponges, wrap them around the root system, and bind them together with several large rubber bands.
3. Turn the plant upside down (roots upward) and tie a length of string to the rubber bands.
4. Hang the plant from a hook in the ceiling near a sunny window. Check the plant occasionally and keep the sponges watered.

Description:

After a few days, the stem and top of the plant will turn and begin to grow upward toward the light. That's because all green plant life needs light to grow. Through a process known as *phototropism,* plants grow in whichever direction the light is. In your experiment, the plant grew toward the sunlight, even though it was hanging upside down. Also, a plant's roots will always grow downward, trying to reach the necessary nutrients in the soil.

 From *MORE Science Adventures with Children's Literature: Reading Comprehension and Inquiry-Based Science* by Anthony D. Fredericks. Westport, CT: Teacher Ideas Press. Copyright © 2008.

MY OWN BACKYARD

Did you know that your backyard can qualify as Certified Wildlife Habitat—a place where plants and animals are protected?

The National Wildlife Federation sponsors the Wildlife Habitat program. The Web site www.nwf.org/backyard will provide you with information about establishing your backyard as a wildlife preserve. As a Certified Wildlife Habitat your backyard will

- attract a wide variety of wildlife, from insects to mammals;
- become more attractive through the use of various plants;
- help support wildlife all year long;
- benefit the local environment with appropriate plants; and
- help expand your gardening knowledge.

There is a fee involved to get your backyard certified. However, once you are certified you'll receive an informational newsletter four times a year. You'll also be able to order a special sign that you can post in your yard. And you'll also become a member of the National Wildlife Federation.

Check it out!

From *MORE Science Adventures with Children's Literature: Reading Comprehension and Inquiry-Based Science* by Anthony D. Fredericks. Westport, CT: Teacher Ideas Press. Copyright © 2008.

Diary of a Worm

Doreen Cronin

New York: HarperCollins, 2003

SELECTED CITATIONS

- "Cronin's beguiling journal entries by a worm who can write are as witty and original as the missives from her popular cows who can type (*Click, Clack, Moo: Cows That Type*)."—*Publishers Weekly*

- "Each turn of the page will bring fresh waves of giggles as a young worm records one misadventure after another."—*Kirkus Reviews*

SUMMARY

What a great book to introduce students to the fascinating (and most humorous) world of worms. Kids will be rolling in the aisles (so will you) when they read (or listen to) this intriguing and very creative tale about one worm's trials and tribulations over a span of several months. The humor is everywhere, and the scientific insights are cleverly hidden among the joy and laughter. This is definitely a "must-have" book for any study of invertebrates, soil, or ecosystems. Run (don't walk) and get a copy of this book for your classroom (and personal) library.

SUGGESTED GRADE LEVELS: 1–4

LESSON OBJECTIVES

Science Standards

- Content Standard C: Life Science

    The characteristics of organisms (K–4)

    Organisms and environments (K–4)

CRITICAL THINKING QUESTIONS

1. What was the funniest part of this story?

2. If you could ask the worm in the story one question, what would it be?

3. Is the worm's life anything like your life?

4. If your pet (cat, dog, hamster) could write a diary, what do you this she or he would say?

5. What other "adventures" do you think the worm will get into?

COMPREHENSION LESSON (WHAT IF)

Setting the Stage

Before distributing copies of the book to students (or reading it aloud to the class), share the title and the cover illustration. Invite students to make predictions about the story. What will it be about? Who will be in it? How will it turn out?

Before Reading

Engage students in a What If activity. Ask them to imagine being an earthworm. What would they do all day? What would they eat? What would they notice? Stir the pot a little by providing students with a copy of the What If project page and invite them to respond to the questions (in writing or aloud).

During Reading

Provide a copy of the book for each student. Ask students to read the book silently on their own (or it can be used as a class read-aloud).

After Reading

Encourage students to talk about the humor in this book. What does the author/illustrator do to make this a funny book? How did the illustrations contribute to the humor? Did anything happen that you didn't expect? You may want to follow the reading by asking students some of the same questions you did in the "Before Reading" stage. Invite students to share reasons for any changes in their responses.

LITERATURE EXTENSIONS

Invite students to select one or more of the following activities:

1. This story lends itself to an adaptation as a readers theatre script. Using the examples in Part III of this book, invite students to create a script using the characters and events depicted in the book. Be sure students have an opportunity to present their script to students in another class.

2. Why are earthworms so important to farmers? Invite students to consult a number of resources (library books, Web sites, local farmers) about the value of earthworms to the farming community. What would be the consequences if all the earthworms were eliminated? Why should the average person be concerned about earthworms?

3. Place one student in the front of the classroom and designate her or him as the primary character in this book (she or he will take on the role of this central character). Invite other students to interview the worm character with questions about its life, the specific events of the story, and some of its thoughts (the "worm" must answer in character). As warranted, provide opportunities for other students to take on the role of the "worm."

4. If possible, obtain a dozen worms from your local bait shop, sporting goods store, or pet store. (In my area, I can get a container of one dozen worms for about $1.95.) Provide each of several groups with some of the worms (placed on desks covered with newsprint). Invite students to observe the worms and note their habits and behaviors. What do they see? What do the worms do that they did not expect?

5. How are worms similar to or different from other animals? Invite students to consult library and Internet resources and create a list of three things that worms do that are similar to the actions of one or more other animals. Also, ask them to create another list that has three things that worms do that no other animal can do. You may wish to post these lists in the classroom.

6. Invite students to investigate the various species of worms found throughout the world. How many different species are there? What is distinctive about each species? Which country (or continent) has the most species of worms? Which country (or continent) has the fewest species of worms?

7. Students may wish to create a list of "world records" for worms. Here are a few facts to get them started:

   – A species of earthworm that lives in Australia often grows to lengths of 9 feet or more.
   – The longest earthworm ever found was in South Africa. It was 22 feet long.
   – There can be more than a million earthworms in one acre of land.
   – Worms can grow new tails (if they're cut off), but not new heads.
   – Worms can eat their weight each day.

8. Encourage students to create a shape book. Invite them to cut out an outline of a worm from two sheets of oak tag. Students may wish to staple several blank sheets of paper between the two outlines to form a book and then record significant facts, features, or characteristics about worms. These books can be arranged into an attractive display in the classroom or library.

9. Divide the class into two groups. Assign one group the task of writing a prequel to the story and the other group the task of writing a sequel. Encourage students to discuss the various kinds of situations, events, or adventures the main character could have in both a prequel and sequel.

WHAT IF

Respond to each of the following "What If" questions. Keep in mind that there are no right or wrong responses to these questions—anything is possible.

What if you lived underground?

What if you turned into an earthworm?

What if (as an earthworm) you had to eat dirt all day?

What if (as an earthworm) someone tried to step on you?

What if (as an earthworm) you were attacked by a bird?

What if (as an earthworm) you had a conversation with a spider?

What if (as an earthworm) you could live anywhere you wanted?

From *MORE Science Adventures with Children's Literature: Reading Comprehension and Inquiry-Based Science* by Anthony D. Fredericks. Westport, CT: Teacher Ideas Press. Copyright © 2008.

HOUSES AND HOMES

Where do animals live? What kind of dwelling places do they call home? Let's take a look around.

Materials:

- notebook
- pen or pencil
- camera

Directions:

1. With an older friend or adult, take a walk around your town or neighborhood.
2. Look for places where animals live—nests, burrows, tree trunks, anthills, under rocks, in and near logs, holes in the ground, even cracks in the sidewalk.
3. If you have a camera, take a photograph of each *habitat*, or place where an animal lives, or draw a picture of it.
4. Later, name the animals and match their pictures with the pictures of their "houses."
5. An older brother or sister, parent, or high school student might enjoy helping you learn the scientific names of the animals to add to your journal or field trip report.

Description:

You will be amazed to discover the wide variety of animals living in homes in and near your own house. You will probably discover that you've found many more than you thought possible.

Animals are everywhere—from high in the trees (hawks) to far under the ground (earthworms). The homes that animals live in are designed to protect their young, shelter the animals from the weather, and help them defend against their enemies, and they are located where they can find the food they need.

From *MORE Science Adventures with Children's Literature: Reading Comprehension and Inquiry-Based Science* by Anthony D. Fredericks. Westport, CT: Teacher Ideas Press. Copyright © 2008.

LET'S PRETEND

Just for a moment, pretend that you are an animal. You could be an insect, a fish, a reptile, an amphibian, a bird, or a mammal. Now imagine that you have the ability to write (very much like the hero in the book *Diary of a Worm*). Think about some of the adventures (or misadventures) you would get into during the course of a week (let your imagination run wild). Now create a series of diary entries about those adventures for one week:

Sunday:

Monday:

Tuesday:

Wednesday:

Thursday:

Friday:

Saturday:

From *MORE Science Adventures with Children's Literature: Reading Comprehension and Inquiry-Based Science* by Anthony D. Fredericks. Westport, CT: Teacher Ideas Press. Copyright © 2008.

NO BONES ABOUT IT

Worms are members of a group of animals known as *invertebrates*. An invertebrate is any animal that does not have an internal skeleton—no bones whatsoever.

Investigate several different types of invertebrates using library or Internet resources. In the chart below, list seven different invertebrates and three features or characteristics of each one. The first one has been done for you.

Invertebrate	Feature 1	Feature 2	Feature 3
worm	lives underground	helps aerate the soil	eats dead fragments of plants

From *MORE Science Adventures with Children's Literature: Reading Comprehension and Inquiry-Based Science* by Anthony D. Fredericks. Westport, CT: Teacher Ideas Press. Copyright © 2008.

Around One Cactus:
Owls, Bats, and Leaping Rats

Anthony D. Fredericks

Nevada City, CA: Dawn Publications, 2003

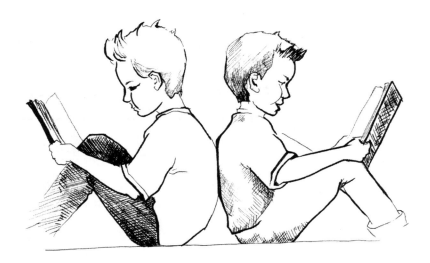

SELECTED CITATIONS

- **2004 Teacher's Choice Award**—International Reading Association

- "Combining an elegant text with dramatic artwork, this book is an attention-grabbing read-aloud and a winner for any collection."—*School Library Journal*

SUMMARY

This dynamically illustrated book takes readers into the heart of the Sonoran Desert to watch the "happenings" that take place in and around a single saguaro cactus. The young boy in the story doesn't think there is much going on at the cactus and so, near the end of the day, he leaves. But that's when all the activity begins. Rattlesnakes, elf owls, kangaroo rats, scorpions, and other denizens of the desert come out to "play and prey." This is an active community—one not often seen by visitors—that has lots of excitement and lots to discover.

SUGGESTED GRADE LEVELS: 1–4

LESSON OBJECTIVES

Science Standards

- Content Standard A: Science as Inquiry

    Abilities necessary to do science inquiry (K–4, 5–8)

    Understandings about science inquiry (K–4, 5–8)

• Content Standard C: Life Science

> The characteristics of organisms (K–4)
>
> Life cycles of organisms (K–4)
>
> Organisms and environments (K–4)
>
> Populations and ecosystems (5–8)
>
> Diversity and adaptations of organisms (5–8)

• Content Standard F: Science in Personal and Social Perspectives

> Populations, resources, and environments (5–8)

• Content Standard G: History and Nature of Science

> Science as a human endeavor (K–4, 5–8)

CRITICAL THINKING QUESTIONS

1. Which of the creatures did you enjoy the most?
2. Which animal would you like to learn more about?
3. How did the illustrations help you enjoy the story?
4. Are you similar to any of the creatures in this book?
5. What are some other animals that live in the desert?
6. If you could ask the author one question, what would it be?

COMPREHENSION LESSON (CLOZE)

Setting the Stage

Before distributing copies of the book to students, share the title with them. Invite students to make predictions about the story. What will it be about? What will they learn? Where will it take place?

Before Reading

Duplicate and distribute the Cloze project page. Tell students to read through the story on the sheet and think about words that might possibly fit into the blank spaces. After allowing sufficient time, ask students to set these sheets aside.

During Reading

Students may wish to read the book silently on their own, or you may decide to share the book as a read-aloud.

After Reading

When students have finished reading the story, invite them to return to their Cloze sheets and work at filling in the blank spaces. Students may wish to work individually or in small teams. After a sufficient amount of time, invite students to discuss the choices they placed in each of the blank spaces. Note that some words have synonyms that are appropriate (and meaningful) substitutions.

After a discussion period, invite students to turn to the "Field Notes" section in the back of the book. The selection used for the Cloze sheet is provided as the initial field note ("Saguaro Cactus") . Invite students to note the words the author used. Do their words make as much sense as the author's words? Are there any other words that could be used in the blank spaces? What were some of the most difficult words to fill in?

LITERATURE EXTENSIONS

Invite students to select one or more of the following

1. Invite students to write to one or more of the following national parks and request information about the flora and fauna that inhabit those special regions. When the brochures, flyers, leaflets, and descriptive information arrive, invite students to assemble them into an attractive display in the classroom or a school display case.

    Death Valley National Park
    P.O. Box 579
    Death Valley, CA 92328

    Great Basin National Park
    Baker, NV 89311

    Joshua Tree National Park
    74485 National Park Drive
    Twentynine Palms, CA 92277

    Big Bend National Park
    Big Bend, TX 79834

2. Students may enjoy creating a large wall mural about the four major desert areas in the United States. Assign each of four groups one of those desert areas (Sonoran, Mojave, Chihuahuan, Great Basin) and invite them to do the necessary research. Completed murals may be posted in the classroom or the school library. Interested students may also wish to do some comparative murals on U.S. deserts versus deserts in other locations around the world (e.g., Atacama, Sahara, etc.).

3. Using Styrofoam®, create a large replica of a saguaro cactus. Invite students to break 100 toothpicks in half and stick each of the broken pieces into the model cactus. You may wish to spray paint the creation and let it dry before placing it in a prominent position in the classroom. Students can arrange models around the cactus. Models can include creatures mentioned in the story as well as others students learn about during outside reading assignments.

4. Talk with students about some of the "Fantastic Facts" included in the back of the book. Which ones did they find most amazing? Invite students to assemble their own collection of "Desert Fantastic Facts" or "Cactus Fantastic Facts."

5. Invite students to log onto www.desertusa.com and select one of the animals profiled on this site. Encourage students to work in teams of two or three to assemble and collect information about their designated animals for presentation to the class.

6. Divide students into two groups. Assign one group the task of writing a prequel to the story and the other group the task of writing a sequel. Encourage students to discuss the various types of actions and creatures they could include in their additions.

7. Ask students to obtain different types of cactus plants from a nearby nursery or garden center. Ask them to arrange the cacti in an attractive display—a single cactus garden or several smaller groupings of cacti arranged around the classroom. Encourage students to research and assemble a guidebook on how to take care of cacti. Students may also wish to prepare a PowerPoint© presentation for other students on the various types of cacti found in the United States or throughout the world.

8. Invite students to read other desert books, such as the following:

    a. *Saguaro Moon: A Desert Journal* by Kristin Joy Pratt-Serafini
    b. *Desert Song* by Tony Johnson
    c. *Cactus Hotel* by Brenda Z. Guiberson
    d. *Desert Giant: The World of the Saguaro Cactus* by Barbara Bash
    e. *America's Deserts* by Marianne Wallace
    f. *One Small Square: Cactus Desert* by Donald M. Silver

9. Provide students, working individually or in small groups, with a small sponge saturated with water. Explain to them that this represents a desert animal with a limited amount of available water. Over a 24-hour period, students should take care of their "animal" in a manner that will best conserve the water it contains, using only natural materials. Their "animal" must be in the open for at least four hours during that time to "feed." To measure the beginning moisture content, each student or group should use the balance to determine the mass of its sponge. A control sponge should be left unprotected for the experiment's duration. Students should then plan a strategy and write it down along with predictions of what will happen. During the 24-hour period, students should make and record observations. At the end of the allotted time, students again record the mass of their sponges. Students should compare it with the previous mass and make inferences about the results in relation to real organisms with limited or temporary water supplies, such as lizards, pack rats, and coyotes. Have individuals or groups share their experiments and results with the entire class. Afterward, conduct a class discussion of methods, results, and how this experiment relates to adaptations for survival in real organisms.

10. Invite an employee of a local garden center or nursery to visit the classroom and discuss various types of cacti sold there. What are some planting techniques? How should cacti be cared for? Why are some cacti easier to grow than others? Ask students to gather the responses to those questions as well as their own into an informative brochure or PowerPoint presentation that could be shared with other classes.

CLOZE

The saguaro _____ lives exclusively in the Sonoran desert. The saguaro provides food, _____, and moisture for a wide variety of desert animals. It thrives in rocky areas from sea level to 4,500 _____ in elevation. It requires very little water and can go for two _____ without rain. It has a root system that is shallow and wide-reaching. This allows for quick absorption of _____ when it rains. Surprisingly, about 75 to 95 percent of the cactus's weight is water. The saguaro doesn't begin to _____ "arms" until it is at least 70 years old. From May to June, many large, white, waxy _____ blossom on the saguaro. The saguaro flower is the Arizona _____ flower.

Saguaros can grow as _____ as 56 feet, weigh as much as an African _____, and live to be over 200 years old.

From *MORE Science Adventures with Children's Literature: Reading Comprehension and Inquiry-Based Science* by Anthony D. Fredericks. Westport, CT: Teacher Ideas Press. Copyright © 2008.

HOME SWEET HOME

A terrarium is a miniature controlled environment containing plants in an artificial situation that can closely imitate the natural living conditions of desert organisms. Carefully set up, a desert terrarium can endure for long periods of time and provide you with a close-up look at this "sample" of nature.

Materials:

- glass container (a 10-gallon aquarium purchased at a pet store or garage sale or a large pickle jar can be used)
- small pebbles, gravel, and coarse sand
- potting soil
- plants, rocks, pieces of wood

Directions:

1. Be sure the container is thoroughly cleaned (be sure there is no soap or detergent residue left behind).

2. Spread a one-inch layer of gravel over the bottom of the aquarium. Combine three parts fine sand with one part potting soil. Spread this mixture over the base layer of gravel. Set the soil mixture about three inches deep toward the back of the terrarium and slightly shallower in front.

3. Decorate with rocks and small branches.

4. Sprinkle this mixture lightly with water. It's better to under- than over-water—too much water is deadly for most desert plants. Stick your finger into the soil;if it's damp, don't add water

5. Place several varieties of cactus into the terrarium (it might be a good idea to wear gloves). Most nurseries carry cacti, or they can be ordered through the mail from selected seed companies and mail-order nursery houses. The following varieties are suggested:

Gasteria	Aloe	Sedum	Astrophytum
Crassula	Adromischus	Lithops	Rebutia senilis
Pincushion cactus	Opunita	Fishhook cactus	Night-blooming cereus

6. When planting the cacti, be sure that the roots are covered completely by the sandy mixture.

From *MORE Science Adventures with Children's Literature: Reading Comprehension and Inquiry-Based Science* by Anthony D. Fredericks. Westport, CT: Teacher Ideas Press. Copyright © 2008.

HOME SWEET HOME (CONTINUED)

7. The desert terrarium can be left in the sun and does not need a glass cover. If you cannot leave it in the sun, rig a lamp over the terrarium. Put a 60 watt light bulb in the lamp and leave it on for about 10 hours every day.

Description:

Your miniature desert environment, when properly maintained, will survive for a long time. You will be able to observe your cactus plants regularly and see any growth patterns (they grow very slowly).

From *MORE Science Adventures with Children's Literature: Reading Comprehension and Inquiry-Based Science* by Anthony D. Fredericks. Westport, CT: Teacher Ideas Press. Copyright © 2008.

A LITTLE RAINFALL

Deserts get less than 10 inches of rain a year. Below is a chart of selected desert towns in the United States. Conduct some library or Internet research and fill in the amount of rain each town gets on an annual basis. Afterward, arrange the list of towns from low (least amount of rainfall annually) to high (most amount of rainfall annually).

Town	Rainfall
Mojave, CA	
Salt Lake City, UT	
Phoenix, AZ	6.5 inches
Kingman, AZ	
Needles, CA	
Ely, NV	
Tucson, AZ	
Death Valley, CA	
Cedar City, UT	
Palm Springs, CA	
Nogales, AZ	
Las Vegas, NV	4 inches
Barstow, CA	
El Centro, CA	
Yuma, AZ	
(your home town)	

From *MORE Science Adventures with Children's Literature: Reading Comprehension and Inquiry-Based Science* by Anthony D. Fredericks. Westport, CT: Teacher Ideas Press. Copyright © 2008.

CACTUS OLYMPICS

Cacti (the plural of cactus) come in all shapes and sizes. (Did you know that there are between 2,000 and 3,000 different species of cactus in the world?) You may be interested in learning about some of the most distinctive and unusual types of cactus plants.

The chart below has several different categories related to cacti. Consult resources in the school library as well as those on the Internet for the necessary information. You may wish to put together a booklet or notebook entitled *Cactus Olympics*—a compendium of the world records held by individual cactus species or single cacti throughout the world. Try to fill in every category—but don't get stuck!

Category	Information
World's tallest cactus	
World's oldest cactus	
World's smallest cactus	
Cactus with the longest roots	
Cactus with the biggest seeds	
Cactus with the smallest seeds	
Heaviest cactus	
Most common cactus	
Rarest cactus	

From *MORE Science Adventures with Children's Literature: Reading Comprehension and Inquiry-Based Science* by Anthony D. Fredericks. Westport, CT: Teacher Ideas Press. Copyright © 2008.

What Do You Do with a Tail Like This?

Steve Jenkins and Robin Page

Boston: Houghton Mifflin, 2003

SELECTED CITATIONS

- **2004 Caldecott Honor Book**—American Library Association

- "Steve Jenkins contributes another artistically wrought, imaginatively conceived look at the natural world."—*Publishers Weekly*

SUMMARY

With his distinctive torn and cut paper collages, Steve Jenkins once again presents students with an intriguing and exciting book that will have them involved from the cover all the way through to the illustration on the back. Punctuated with fascinating questions, this book asks readers to think about the various ways in which animals use their eyes, ears, noses, mouths, feet, and tails. Brief descriptions in the text are punctuated with more detailed explanations at the end of the book. This is one book that should be part of every animal unit—a wonderful "bridge" between science and art.

SUGGESTED GRADE LEVELS: 1–4

LESSON OBJECTIVES

Science Standards

- Content Standard A: Science as Inquiry

     Abilities necessary to do science inquiry (K–4)

     Understanding about science inquiry (K–4)

• Content Standard C: Life Science

The characteristics of organisms (K–4)

CRITICAL THINKING QUESTIONS

1. What was the most interesting animal in the book? Why?

2. What is something you can do that is similar to a specific animal in the book?

3. What would you like to do that an animal can do (but you can't)?

4. Which of the animals would you most like to have as a pet?

5. How many of these animals have you ever seen in person?

COMPREHENSION LESSON (SEMANTIC WEBBING)

Setting the Stage

Provide copies of the book, one for each student. Invite students to thumb through the book and look at all the illustrations (or look at the illustrations in your copy). What do they know about the eyes, ears, tails, noses, and feet? What can they share about different body features of animals? What are some of the most unusual or distinctive animal features?

Before Reading

Provide students with the Semantic Webbing project page. Let them know that there is a whale's tail in the center of the page, and that the tail represents several animal parts (noses, ears, eyes, feet, etc.). Around the "tail" are several spikes. Invite them to write words, phrases, or concepts related to "animal parts" or "animal features" on each of the spokes of the web. Note any misperceptions or biases students may have.

During Reading

Invite students to read the book silently (or listen to it being read aloud).

After Reading

Invite students to return to their original semantic web. Ask students to add words or terms from the book to the original web, using a different color of ink. Allow time for students to discuss any differences in their pre-reading and post-reading knowledge about animal parts. How have their perceptions changed as a result of reading the book?

LITERATURE EXTENSIONS

Invite students to select one or more of the following activities:

1. Invite students to write the names of each of the animals in *What Do You Do with a Tail Like This?* on individual 3-by-5-inch index cards. Then ask them to work in pairs

(additional research may also be necessary) to sort all the cards into the following categories:

    a. Diurnal vs. nocturnal

    b. Birds vs. mammals vs. reptiles

    c. Herbivores vs. carnivores vs. omnivores

    d. Vertebrates vs. invertebrates

2. Students may correspond with a zoologist or biologist at a local college or university. They may wish to obtain some firsthand information about selected creatures from the book. You may be able to make arrangements for the expert to visit your classroom and bring along several creatures from the book.

3. Invite students to rewrite part of the story from the perspective of one of the animals. For example, how would a giraffe view the actions of the other animals? How would the blue-footed booby view the other creatures?

4. Discuss the differences between venomous and nonvenomous snakes. Ask students to determine whether there are venomous snakes in the area where you live. Identify the venomous snakes in your area and where they can be found on a classroom map. Invite local emergency medical personnel to discuss caring for a snakebite wound.

5. Encourage students to write an "extension" for this book. What animals would they like to include in an "extension" of *What Do You Do with a Tail Like This?* Invite students to create and post their creations throughout the classroom.

6. Ask students to research the animals in this book according to the place to which each is indigenous. In which country would you find the largest concentration of giraffes? Scorpions? Mountain goats? Spider monkeys? Ask students to post a world map on a wall of the classroom. Have them write one animal on each of several index cards and post those cards around the map. Students may tape a piece of colorful yarn from each card to a representative country on the map. Is one country (or continent) represented more by these animals than another is?

7. Invite students to assemble a collage of animal tails, noses, ears, eyes, feet, or mouths. You may wish to divide the class into six separate groups, with each group responsible for creating a collage (from old magazines) of its representative body part. Which collage was the easiest to assemble? Which collage was the most challenging?

8. Discuss the illustrations in this book (which is a Caldecott Honor Book). How is this style of illustration similar to or different from other styles with which students are familiar? Invite students to research books in the library with other examples of torn or cut paper collages. Ask students to create a classroom or library display of this spectacular art form.

9. Assign each student one of the 30 animals in this book. Inform students that they are now each the class expert for their assigned animal. They are responsible for gathering important information regarding the animal's habitat, lifestyle, life span, diet, ecosystem, and other significant factors. Provide appropriate opportunities for students to share their collective information with each other and with another class.

10. For an exceptional collection of animal videos appropriate for classroom use, check out the National Geographic Web site (www.nationalgeographic.com). This collection is one of the most extensive and unarguably one of the most scientifically accurate assemblies of any commercial enterprise. Plan to showcase several of the animals in this book via one or more of these videos.

11. Invite students to examine other books by Steve Jenkins. What themes does he emphasize? How are his books different from other "animal books"? What is so distinctive about his artwork? How do his illustrations complement the text of his books?

SEMANTIC WEBBING

This whale's tail represents one of several animal parts (noses, ears, eyes, feet, etc.). Write words, phrases, or concepts related to "animal parts" or "animal features" on each of the spokes surrounding the picture.

From *MORE Science Adventures with Children's Literature: Reading Comprehension and Inquiry-Based Science* by Anthony D. Fredericks. Westport, CT: Teacher Ideas Press. Copyright © 2008.

WHAT DO YOU DO?

Just like the animals in the book *What Do You Do with a Tail Like This?*, humans have several different body parts—each used for one or more reasons. See if you can discover at least three different ways human use each of the following body parts. Some examples have been provided for you.

What do you do with:

Your Nose:

1. Smell_____
2. Hold up your glasses_____
3. _____

Your Mouth:

1. _____
2. _____
3. _____

Your Ears:

1. _____
2. _____
3. _____

Your Head:

1. _____
2. _____
3. _____

Your Feet:

1. A place to keep your shoes_____
2. _____
3. _____

Your Hands:

1. _____
2. _____
3. _____

Your Eyes:

1. _____
2. _____
3. _____

Your Arms:

1. _____
2. _____
3. _____

From *MORE Science Adventures with Children's Literature: Reading Comprehension and Inquiry-Based Science* by Anthony D. Fredericks. Westport, CT: Teacher Ideas Press. Copyright © 2008.

A SPECIAL CLASS

The animals in the book *What Do You Do with a Tail Like This?* each belong in a particular class of animals. Use library resources as well as Internet sites to list all the animals in the book according to which of the classes below they belong to. Which class has the most members?

Mammals:

Birds:

Fish:

Amphibians:

Reptiles:

Insects:

From *MORE Science Adventures with Children's Literature: Reading Comprehension and Inquiry-Based Science* by Anthony D. Fredericks. Westport, CT: Teacher Ideas Press. Copyright © 2008.

NO BONES ABOUT IT

A *vertebrate* is an animal with an internal skeleton—it has bones inside its body. An *invertebrate* is an animal with no internal skeleton—it has no bones inside its body. You are a *vertebrate* because you have an internal skeleton. An earthworm, on the other hand, is an *invertebrate* because it has no bones whatsoever.

Classify each of the animals in the book *What Do You Do with a Tail Like This?* according to whether it is a *vertebrate* or *invertebrate*. You may need to check some library resources or Web sites for information.

Vertebrates	Invertebrates

From *MORE Science Adventures with Children's Literature: Reading Comprehension and Inquiry-Based Science* by Anthony D. Fredericks. Westport, CT: Teacher Ideas Press. Copyright © 2008.

Part III
Extending the Possibilities: Readers Theatre

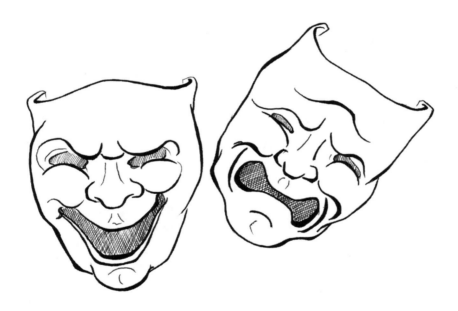

Readers theatre is a storytelling device that stimulates the imagination and promotes *all* of the language arts. Simply stated, it is an oral interpretation of a piece of literature read in a dramatic style. Readers theatre is an act of involvement, an opportunity to share, and a time to creatively interact with others. Readers theatre provides numerous opportunities for youngsters to make stories and literature come alive and pulsate with their own unique brand of perception and vision. Literature becomes personal and reflective—children have a breadth of opportunities to be authentic users of language.

Of no less importance is the significance of readers theatre as a method to enhance an appreciation of science. Too many youngsters envision science as a collection of facts and figures to be committed to memory and regurgitated on standardized tests or workbook pages. As you have probably gathered from the intent and focus of this book, science is an active engagement with the dynamics of children's literature. That focus can also be promoted with readers theatre. In fact, when teachers and librarians incorporate readers theatre into their respective programs, youngsters are offered multiple opportunities to, as one third-grade teacher put it, "become actively and personally involved in all that literature has to offer."

When children are provided with regular opportunities to use readers theatre, they develop a personal stake in the literature shared. They also begin to cultivate personal interpretations of that literature, which lead to higher levels of appreciation and comprehension. Practicing and performing stories is an involvement endeavor, one that demonstrates and utilizes numerous languaging activities. So too, do youngsters learn to listen to their classmates and appreciate a variety of presentations.

WHAT IS THE VALUE OF READERS THEATRE?

I like to think of readers theatre as a way to interpret science without the constraints of skills, rote memorization, or assignments. Readers theatre allows children to breathe life and substance into science concepts, an interpretation that is colored by kids' unique perspectives, experiences, and vision. It is, in fact, the readers' interpretation of an event that is intrinsically more valuable than some predetermined or preordained "translation" (something that might be found in a teacher's manual or curriculum guide, for example).

With that in mind, I'd like to share with you some of the many values I see in readers theatre, —particularly as it applies to elementary science:

- Readers theatre is a participatory event. The characters as well as the audience are all intimately involved in the design, structure, and delivery of the story. As a result, children begin to realize that learning science is not a solitary activity, but one that can be shared and discussed with others.

- Readers theatre stimulates curiosity and enthusiasm for learning. It allows children to experience learning in a supportive and nonthreatening format that underscores their active involvement.

- Since it is the performance that drives readers theatre, children are given more opportunities to invest themselves and their personalities in the production of a readers theatre. The same story may be subject to several different presentations depending on the group or the individual youngsters involved. Children learn that readers theatre can be explored in a host of ways and through a host of possibilities.

- Children are given numerous opportunities to learn about the major features of selected science concepts.

- Readers theatre is informal and relaxed. It does not require elaborate props, scenery, or costumes. It can be set up in any classroom or library. It does not require large sums of money to "make it happen." And, it can be "put on" in any kind of environment, formal or informal.

- Readers theatre enhances the development of cooperative learning strategies. It requires youngsters to work together toward a common goal and supports their efforts in doing so.

Readers theatre is not a competitive activity, but rather a cooperative one in which children share, discuss, and band together for the good of the production.

- Teachers and librarians have also discovered that readers theatre is an excellent way to enhance the development of communication skills. Voice projection, intonation, inflection, and pronunciation skills are all promoted within and throughout any readers theatre production.

- The development and enhancement of self-concepts is facilitated through readers theatre. Since children are working in concert with other children in a supportive atmosphere, their self-esteem mushrooms accordingly. Again, the emphasis is on the presentation, not necessarily the performers. Youngsters have opportunities to develop levels of self-confidence and self-assurance that would not normally be available in more traditional class productions.

- Creative and critical thinking are enhanced through the utilization of readers theatre. Children are active participants in the interpretation and delivery of a story; they develop thinking skills that are divergent rather than convergent, and interpretive skills that are supported rather than directed.

- Readers theatre provides wonderful opportunities for classroom teachers and school librarians to work together in a shared activity. Language arts and literature can be shared out and beyond the usual constraints of walls, textbooks, and curriculum guides. Teachers and librarians can plan cooperative ventures that expand the science program in a host of new dimensions.

- Readers theatre is fun! Children of all ages have delighted in using readers theatre for many years. It is delightful and stimulating, encouraging and fascinating, relevant and personal. Indeed, try as I might, I have not been able to locate a single instance (or group of children) in which (or for whom) readers theatre would not be an appropriate learning activity. It is a strategy filled with a cornucopia of possibilities and promises.

USING READERS THEATRE

Consider some of the following ideas for using readers theatre in your classroom or library:

- Use a readers theatre script in conjunction with a specific book or group of books.

- Use a readers theatre script as a "stand-alone"—that is, as a complete a total event.

- Use a readers theatre script as part of a larger unit. The unit may focus on a discipline of science (e.g., earth science, life science) or be part of a thematic unit (e.g., "Inventions and Inventors," "Ecosystems Near and Far").

- Use a readers theatre script to lead off a unit, in the middle of a unit, or as a final activity for a unit.

- Use a readers theatre script as a classroom activity, with follow-up in the library studying related children's literature.

- Use a readers theatre script in the library, with follow-up in the classroom via an entire unit or relevant materials in the science textbook.

- After completing a unit, invite students to create their own original readers theatre script for presentation to another class or group.

As you can see, the possibilities for using readers theatre in the classroom or the library are limitless. A coordinated effort between teachers and librarians can result in a plethora of learning opportunities throughout the science program.

PRESENTATION SUGGESTIONS

Here are some ideas for the presentation of readers theatre that you and the students with whom you work may wish to keep in mind, whether in a classroom setting or the school library:

- After a script has been selected for presentation, make sufficient copies for all the actors, as well as two or three extra copies (one for you and "replacement" copies for scripts that are accidentally damaged or lost). Place the copies between paper covers. Copies for the audience are unnecessary and are not suggested.

- Emphasize that a readers theatre performance does not require any memorization of the script. It's the interpretation and performance that count.

- Readers should have an opportunity to practice their script before presenting it to an audience. Take some time to discuss voice intonation, facial gestures, body movements, and other features that could be used to enhance the presentation.

- For most presentations, readers will stand or sit on stools or chairs. The physical location of each reader has been indicated for each of the scripts in this book.

- Usually all of the characters will be on stage throughout the duration of the presentation. For most presentations, it is not necessary to have characters enter and exit the staging area. If you place the characters on stools, they can face the audience when they are involved in a particular scene and then turn around whenever they are not involved in a scene.

- You may wish to make simple hand-lettered signs with the name of each character. Loop a piece of string or yarn through each sign and hang it around the neck of each respective character. That way, the audience will know the identity of each character throughout the presentation.

- Each reader will have her or his own copy of the script in a paper cover (see above). If possible, use a music stand for each reader's script (this allows readers to use their hands for dramatic interpretation as necessary).

- Several presentations have a narrator to set up the story. The narrator serves to establish the place and time of the story for the audience so that the characters can "jump into" their parts from the beginning. Typically, the narrator is separated from the other "actors" and can be identified by a simple sign.

- Much of the setting for a story should take place in the audience's mind. Elaborate scenery is not necessary; simple props are often the best. For example:

  – A branch or potted plant can serve as a tree.

  – A drawing on the chalkboard can illustrate a building.

  – A hand-lettered sign can designate one part of the staging area as a particular scene (e.g., swamp, castle, field, forest).

  – Children's toys can be used for uncomplicated props (e.g., a telephone, vehicles).

  – A sheet of aluminum foil or a remnant of blue cloth can be used to simulate a lake or pond.

- Costumes for the actors are unnecessary. A few simple items may be suggested by students. For example:

  – Hats, scarves, or aprons can be used by major characters.

  – A paper cutout can serve as a tie, button, or badge.

  – Old clothing (borrowed from parents) can be used as warranted.

Readers theatre holds the promise of "energizing" your classroom science curriculum, stimulating your library program, and fostering an active and deeper engagement of students in all dynamics of books and literature. For both classroom teachers and librarians, its benefits are enormous and its implications endless.

REFERENCES

Fredericks, Anthony D. *African Legends, Myths, and Folktales for Readers Theatre.* Westport, CT: Teacher Ideas Press, 2008.

———. *Frantic Frogs and Other Frankly Fractured Folktales for Readers Theatre.* Westport, CT: Teacher Ideas Press, 1993.

———. *Mother Goose Readers Theatre for Beginning Readers.* Westport, CT: Teacher Ideas Press, 2007.

———. *Nonfiction Readers Theatre for Beginning Readers.* Westport, CT: Teacher Ideas Press, 2007.

———. *Readers Theatre for American History.* Westport, CT: Teacher Ideas Press, 2001.

———. *Science Fiction Readers Theatre.* Westport, CT: Teacher Ideas Press, 2002.

———. *Silly Salamanders and Other Slightly Stupid Stories for Readers Theatre.* Westport, CT: Teacher Ideas Press, 2000.

———. *Songs and Rhymes Readers Theatre for Beginning Readers.* Westport, CT: Teacher Ideas Press, 2008.

———. *Tadpole Tales and Other Totally Terrific Treats for Readers Theatre.* Westport, CT: Teacher Ideas Press, 1997.

A Machine World
(Simple Machines)

SUMMARY

Simple machines are sometimes difficult for youngsters to understand. Constant and continual exposure to the principles and practices of simple machines in everyday life will help students appreciate their role as invaluable tools.

SUGGESTED GRADE LEVELS: 2–4

LESSON OBJECTIVES

Science Standards

- Content Standard B: Physical Science
  - Position and motion of objects (K–4)
- Content Standard E: Science and Technology
  - Abilities of technological design (K–4)

CRITICAL THINKING QUESTIONS

1. Why do you think simple machines are called "simple machines"?

2. In what ways do you think a simple machine is different from a complex machine?

3. How have you used simple machines in the past week or so?

4. Why do you think simple machines are important?

PROPS

Props are not necessary for this script. However, you may wish to provide each of the actors with an example of a simple machine to hold in her or his hands during the performance. As each character speaks, she or he can hold up the tool.

PRESENTATION SUGGESTIONS

Place a large sign around each of the six "simple machines" so that the audience is clear about each person's role. You may wish to draw a picture paste cut-out illustrations of a machine on each placard to help the audience identify each character.

A Machine World

STAGING: The two narrators can stand in front and to the side of the other characters. The six major characters should be on stools or can be standing.

The Lever	The Pulley	The Wheel & Axle
X	X	X
The Inclined Plane	The Screw	The Wedge
X	X	X

Narrator 1   Narrator 2
X   X

NARRATOR 1: Today we are going to introduce you to some machines.

NARRATOR 2: These are really some special machines.

NARRATOR 1: [points] They may not look like machines, but they are.

NARRATOR 2: Maybe we should tell them what a machine does.

NARRATOR 1: OK. A machine is something that makes work easier for people.

NARRATOR 2: That seems pretty simple.

NARRATOR 1: Well, we are going to meet some simple machines.

NARRATOR 2: So let me get this straight. A machine makes our work easier?

NARRATOR 1: Right.

NARRATOR 2: But I thought that a machine was something that was big and had a lot of parts.

From *MORE Science Adventures with Children's Literature: Reading Comprehension and Inquiry-Based Science* by Anthony D. Fredericks. Westport, CT: Teacher Ideas Press. Copyright © 2008.

NARRATOR 1: Well, those are machines, too. But something doesn't have to be big and noisy to be a machine.

NARRATOR 2: But I thought that a machine was something you had to plug into the wall. I thought that a machine was something that used electricity.

NARRATOR 1: Well, some machines use electricity. But other machines use running water. Some use wind. Others use energy from the sun to make them work.

NARRATOR 2: OK, now I understand. But what about those simple machines?

NARRATOR 1: I'm glad you asked. I brought along some simple machines. [points to the other characters] I'd like to introduce them to you.

NARRATOR 2: OK, sounds good.

NARRATOR 1: Would each of you [points again] tell us about yourself?

THE LEVER: I'm a lever. I help to lift things up. I can be a bar that is used to lift a rock.

NARRATOR 2: My father lifts large rocks in the garden with a bar.

THE LEVER: Then he is using me. But here's something else. A wheelbarrow is also a lever.

NARRATOR 1: I didn't know that.

THE LEVER: It's true. People use wheelbarrows to lift large loads. They carry them to a new place. Wheelbarrows are levers.

NARRATOR 2: What about you? [points to The Pulley]

THE PULLEY: I'm a pulley. I help move things, too. I have a rope and one or more wheels. A person can pull down on the rope and lift a load.

NARRATOR 1: I've seen you being used on big ships.

THE PULLEY:	You're right. People use me to lift big loads off big ships. They can raise them into the air. Then they can move them onto the docks.
THE WHEEL & AXLE:	Like my friend here [points to The Pulley], I have a wheel.
NARRATOR 2:	But isn't your wheel different?
THE WHEEL & AXLE:	Yes, it is. I have a bar or a rod that goes through the middle of my wheel. My wheel goes around that bar. The wheels on your car use me. Each wheel is on an axle. Each wheel can turn around on each axle.
NARRATOR 1:	That's cool. And what about you? [points to The Inclined Plane] Why are you special?
THE INCLINED PLANE:	I'm a simple machine, too. I sometimes have another name. Some people call me a ramp.
NARRATOR 2:	Well, what do you do?
THE INCLINED PLANE:	People use me to move things to a new level. You could use me to move something from a low level to a high level. Cars use freeway ramps to get from a low street level to a high level.
NARRATOR 1:	That's neat! And what about you? [points to The Screw]
THE SCREW:	I'm a simple machine, too. I'm a cousin to my friend The Inclined Plane.
NARRATOR 2:	Why is that?
THE SCREW:	Because I'm an inclined plane that has been wrapped around something else. Look at a screw and you will see threads going round and round. They are in a spiral pattern.
NARRATOR 1:	I know what you're going to say.
THE SCREW:	Yes, a screw is an example of an inclined plane.

NARRATOR 2: How about our last simple machine? [points to The Wedge]

THE WEDGE: I'm a cousin to my friend The Inclined Plane.

NARRATOR 1: It sounds like The Inclined Plane has lots of relatives.

THE WEDGE: That's correct. I'm actually two inclined planes put back to back.

NARRATOR 2: Didn't I see you somewhere before?

THE WEDGE: Yes, you did. A knife is an example of a wedge. You use a knife to cut into something. If you look closely at a knife, it's really an upside down triangle. It's really two inclined planes put back to back. A knife is really a wedge.

NARRATOR 1: Well, there you have it. Here are [points to all six characters] the six simple machines.

NARRATOR 2: And you can find these six simple machines in all the tools we use. They're everywhere!

NARRATOR 1: They're our friends. And now they can be your friends, too.

ALL: Hip, Hip, Hooray!

Hip, Hip, Hooray!

Hip, Hip, Hooray!

Adapted from Anthony D. Fredericks, *Nonfiction Readers Theatre for Beginning Readers* (Westport, CT: Teacher Ideas Press, 2007).

Day of the Wave
(Natural Hazards)

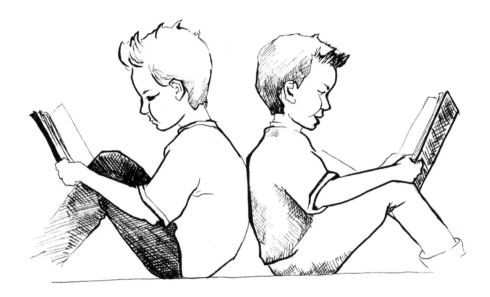

NOTE: This script is based on the book *The Tsunami Quilt: Grandfather's Story,* which is profiled on page 171 of this resource book. It illustrates how a single book can be used to develop an accompanying readers theatre script. Both teachers and librarians will find numerous opportunities to develop readers theatre scripts from other examples of children's literature profiled throughout *More Science Adventures with Children's Literature.*

SUMMARY

On April 1, 1946, shortly after sunrise, a series of giant waves devastated the northern coast of the island of Hawaii. Traveling 2,300 miles from the Aleutian Islands in less than five hours, the waves struck without warning and claimed 159 lives. Of all the states in the country, Hawaii is most prone to natural disasters. Hurricanes, tsunamis, volcanic eruptions, earthquakes, and oceanic storms have long been a part of Hawaiian history. There is also a human impact as well.

SUGGESTED GRADE LEVELS: 3–6

LESSON OBJECTIVES

Science Standards

- Content Standard D: Earth and Space Science

    – Changes in Earth and sky (K–4)

• Content Standard F: Science in Personal and Social Perspectives

– Science and technology in local challenges (K–4)

– Natural hazards (5–8)

CRITICAL THINKING QUESTIONS

1. What did you enjoy most about this story?

2. Have you ever been in a situation in which you were really scared?

3. What else would you like to learn about tsunamis?

4. What question would you like to ask Kimo?

5. Is this story similar to any other story you have heard?

PROPS

No props are necessary for this script. However, if students have access to Hawaiian shirts (from parents or relatives), they may elect to wear them for this production.

PRESENTATION SUGGESTIONS

The characters should all be having a friendly, casual conversation, much like they might do on the playground or during recess.

Day of the Wave

STAGING: The narrator should be placed off to the side and in front of the other actors. The actors should be seated on stools or chairs.

Pua	Ulani		
X	X		
		Noa	Kimo
		X	X
Narrator			
X			

NARRATOR: One of the ancient traditions of native Hawaiians is "talking story." It is one way Hawaiians preserve and share their history. More than just a factual history, it is often personal recollections of the members of a specific family; the funny anecdotes, humorous stories, and fond reminiscences about relatives that are shared during family gatherings. Because Hawaii is such a cultural melting pot, "talking story" is also a way of preserving qualities from each culture while blending them into a composite story. "Talking story" is similar to the conversations friends might have at a party.

NOA: So, Kimo, I understand that your grandfather was a very special person. You say that he was a big influence in your life.

KIMO: Yes, my grandfather was my all-time best friend. He always took me fishing down at the ocean.

From *MORE Science Adventures with Children's Literature: Reading Comprehension and Inquiry-Based Science* by Anthony D. Fredericks. Westport, CT: Teacher Ideas Press. Copyright © 2008.

We would sometimes take long walks along the shore. But maybe the best times we had were when he told me stories.

PUA: What kind of stories did he tell you?

KIMO: He liked telling fishing stories the best. He had been a fisherman all his life, and he used to tell fish tales whenever he could. Of course, as a fisherman, he was known to stretch the truth now and again. But, that was OK; I still liked to hear him tell stories,—especially the stories of long ago.

ULANI: Your grandfather sounds like a real neat guy. He must have had a lot of stories.

KIMO: Yes, but I think it was when he and I went down to Laupāhoehoe every spring that I remember the most.

NARRATOR: Laupāhoehoe [LAH-pah-hoy-hoy] is a small peninsula that juts out from the northern coast of the big island of Hawaii. It was formed by an eruption of Mauna Loa many thousands of years ago.

KIMO: Each spring my grandfather and I would walk along the shore. We never said much on those special visits. But each time my grandfather would walk over to a marble monument, lay his hands on the top, and look out over the sea.

NOA: Did he say anything to you?

KIMO: No, this was the only time in his life that I ever saw him so quiet.

PUA: Then, what?

KIMO: He said that one day he would tell me a story about this special place. He said the place was one of remembrance and also one of tragedy.

ULANI: What did he mean by that?

KIMO: I didn't know at the time. It wasn't until after my grandfather died that I learned what he meant.

NOA: What did he mean? What did he mean by a place of remembrance?

KIMO: Well, it was actually my father who told me the story. He said that many, many years ago there was a school at Laupāhoehoe. One day, all the kids were getting off the bus when they saw something happening to the ocean water.

PUA: What was happening?

KIMO: The water was moving away from the shore. There were lots of fish flapping on the sand.

ULANI: I think I know what's going to happen.

KIMO: Yes, there was a tsunami coming. Before anyone knew what was happening, the waves of the tsunami rolled onto the land. They were big. They were fierce. They swept everything around like in a giant washing machine.

NARRATOR: A tsunami can race across an open ocean at 500 miles per hour. When a tsunami nears shore, it slows down very quickly, and the water beneath the wave piles up. In a brief moment, a 2-foot-high wave at sea may be transformed into a 30-foot-high wave on the shore. Typically, there are several waves in a row: a tsunami wave train.

NOA: Was your grandfather there?

KIMO: Yes, he was. And so was his little brother. But he didn't know where his little brother was. My grandfather was on some high ground, and as soon as he saw the tsunami hit he ran uphill as

	fast as he could go. But he didn't know where his brother was.
PUA:	And then what happened, Kimo?
KIMO:	My grandfather kept running and running uphill. All he could hear were people crying. Children and adults were screaming and crying. It was awful, he said.
ULANI:	Did a lot of people die?
KIMO:	Yes, when it was over 24 people had died. Students and teachers had all been caught in the power of the tsunami. It was terrible.
NOA:	Don't tell me! Don't tell me!
KIMO:	Yes, one of the people who was killed that day was my grandfather's little brother. He felt helpless, because there was nothing he could do to save him. He was gone forever.
PUA:	So, is that why he went to Laupāhoehoe every year?
KIMO:	Yes, he wanted to honor the memory of his little brother. He wanted to remember his little brother in a special way.
ULANI:	That is a sad story . . . a very sad story.
KIMO:	Yes, and it is a story we should never forget. Because as my grandfather used to say, "The ocean gives, but it also takes."
NOA:	What else, Kimo?
KIMO:	Well, there is something else. But I cannot tell you. It is something you must see for yourself.
PUA:	What is it?
KIMO:	You must go to The Pacific Tsunami Museum in Hilo to see it for yourself. When you see it you will never be the same. It is something very

special. It is something you will always remember. It will touch you in a very magical way.

ULANI: What is it?

NARRATOR: It is "The Tsunami Quilt." But that is something for another story and another time. In the meantime, perhaps you will read the children's book about that story and about that time. The book is called *The Tsunami Quilt: Grandfather's Story*. It, too, is a story to remember.

Adapted from Anthony D. Fredericks, *Much More Social Studies Through Children's Literature* (Westport, CT: Teacher Ideas Press, 2007)

Fantastic Plants
(How Plants Grow)

SUMMARY

Students are always fascinated by growing things,—especially plants. This script introduces them to seed plants. The germination process is highlighted along with the three essential parts of a new plant:—roots, leaves, and stem.

SUGGESTED GRADE LEVELS: 2–4

LESSON OBJECTIVES

Science Standards

- Content Standard C: Life Science

  – The characteristics of organisms (K–4)

  – Life cycles of organisms (K–4)

CRITICAL THINKING QUESTIONS

1. Why are seeds important?

2. How are plants similar to animals?

3. What is the most important part of a plant? Why?

4. What can plants do that animals cannot?

5. What is the most interesting plant you know?

PROPS

No props are necessary for this script. You may wish to provide the "Seed" with paper "leaves" to hold during the presentation.

PRESENTATION SUGGESTIONS

The "Seed" will begin the presentation in a crouching position and eventually work her or his way into a fully extended standing position. The narrator and three characters can all be standing or could be sitting on stools.

Fantastic Plants

STAGING: There are four speaking parts and one non-speaking part ("Seed") for this script. The narrator can stand on the back and to the side of the three speaking characters. The "Seed" should be placed in the front and center of the staging area.

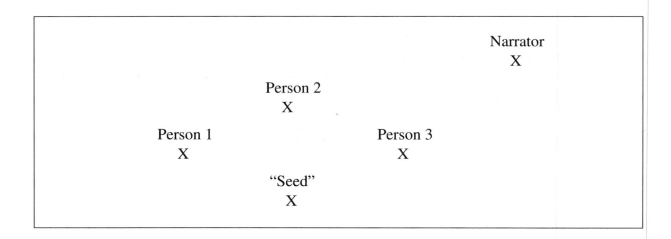

Narrator
X

Person 2
X

Person 1
X

Person 3
X

"Seed"
X

NARRATOR: Good morning. We are standing in a beautiful garden filled with all kinds of plants. In the middle of the garden are three people. This group of individuals is talking about a seed. You may think that's strange, but they actually want to plant the seed. I think that they want something to grow. The seed is waiting to be planted.

[The "Seed" should crouch down into a tight ball. She or he should have her or his arms wrapped around her or his knees.]

PERSON 1: You know, we've talked long enough. It's probably time that we plant our seed.

PERSON 2: Hey, I remember something I learned in school last year. We did this experiment with seeds. And

From *MORE Science Adventures with Children's Literature: Reading Comprehension and Inquiry-Based Science* by Anthony D. Fredericks. Westport, CT: Teacher Ideas Press. Copyright © 2008.

I remember that we can always get a plant to grow from a seed.

PERSON 3: Hey, I guess that a seed is very special.

PERSON 1: You bet it is. That's simply because a seed has a tiny plant in it. That's right: there's a little tiny plant inside each and every seed.

PERSON 2: But, I remember something else. A seed also has something besides just a tiny plant.

PERSON 3: Yeah, now I remember. I remember reading that a seed also has some food for the new plant.

[The "Seed" should move one hand in a slow, upward motion above her or his head.]

PERSON 1: Look. [points to "seed"] The tiny plant is beginning to grow.

PERSON 2: Hey, I wonder what is making it grow.

PERSON 3: Don't you remember? It is using the food inside to help it grow!

PERSON 1: That's right. As I remember, there is just enough food to get the new plant on its way.

[The "Seed" moves her or his other hand up and out. She or he lifts her or his head in an upward motion. She or he rises up to a semi-crouching position, hands above her or his head.]

PERSON 2: Hey, look guys. Now the tiny plant is growing some more. I guess it's starting to use up all that food that it had inside. That food is sorta like stored energy inside the seed.

PERSON 3: You're right. We also need to remember that this seed is underground.

PERSON 1: That's right. The seed is doing all this growing while it is under the soil.

[The "Seed" spreads her or his legs apart and slowly rises some more.]

PERSON 2:   Wow, look at that. The seed is breaking open. Roots are going down into the soil. Wow, I guess there's lots of thing happening all at the same time.

PERSON 3:   You bet. But did you know that the roots are important for the new plant?

PERSON 1:   Yeah. They're important because they help the new plant take up water from the soil. A new plant, any plant, needs water in order to grow.

PERSON 2:   But the roots also do something else. The roots help the plant get food from the soil, too.

[The "Seed" begins to "unfold" some more. Rising from a semi-crouching position, she or he spreads her or his legs apart a little more. She or he raises her or his hands high above her or his head. The body is still not fully extended.]

PERSON 3:   Wow, now look! Now there are leaves beginning to form on the new plant.

PERSON 1:   You're right. The leaves are now moving up and out of the soil.

PERSON 2:   I remember reading somewhere that the leaves are important, too. I think they help the new plant get sunlight. Without sunlight the new plant—any plant—wouldn't be able to develop and grow.

PERSON 3:   Hey, let's not forget the stem. The stem is important, too.

PERSON 1:   You're right. The stem helps supports the new plant. That keeps the plant upright so that it gathers in the necessary sunlight.

[The "Seed" is now fully extended. Arms are raised high into the air. The body is erect. The legs are straight and spread apart.]

PERSON 2:   Look. It's a new plant!

PERSON 3: Yeah, this new plant has roots that go into the soil. Those roots get water for the plant. They take up nutrients from the soil, too.

PERSON 1: And the new plant has leaves that help it get sunlight. Without sunlight, the new plant wouldn't be able to grow at all.

PERSON 2: And let's not forget that the new plant has a stem. The stem supports the plant and is also a way for water and nutrient to get up into the top parts of the plant.

PERSON 3: Wow! What an amazing act! From that tiny little seed grew a large plant that is able to get everything it needs. It has all the parts necessary to thrive and survive. All that from a tiny little seed!

A Healthy Life
(Keeping Healthy)

SUMMARY

Students need to understand that good health doesn't just happen. It is part of a concentrated effort by the individual and her or his family members. When students understand the four essential ingredients of good health, they can begin making lifestyle decisions that will help ensure a lifetime of good health.

SUGGESTED GRADE LEVELS: 2–5

LESSON OBJECTIVES

Science Standards

• Content Standard F: Science in Personal and Social Perspectives

– Personal health (K–4, 5–8)

CRITICAL THINKING QUESTIONS

1. Why should people take care of their bodies?

2. What are some healthy things you do every day?

3. What happens when people don't do healthy things?

4. What are some dangerous activities or practices people do?

5. What do you like most about your body?

PROPS

There are no specific props for this script. It would be advantageous to provide each character with a prominent sign indicating her or his name (e.g., Miss Sleep).

PRESENTATION SUGGESTIONS

Each of the characters should be seated on a stool or chair. The narrator (Mr. Body) talks to each of the characters individually. After a character has spoken, it is not necessary for her or him to exit the staging area.

A Healthy Life

STAGING: In this script the characters are the elements necessary for a healthy life-style. The narrator is a human body (male or female) who is seeking information about maintaining good health. The characters can all be standing at individual music stands or seated on stools.

	Mr. Food	Miss Exercise
	X	X
Narrator (Mr. Body)		
X		
	Miss Sleep	Mr. Water
	X	X

NARRATOR (MR. BODY): Hi, my name is Mr. Body and I'm the narrator for this story. I'm also a student; you know, someone who is always asking questions, someone who always wants to learn something new. Specifically, I want to learn more about myself. I want to learn how to stay healthy, not just now, but throughout my entire life. I don't like getting sick; in fact, I really hate being sick. So I want to grow up healthy, I want to grow up strong, and I want to live a very long time.

MR. FOOD: Well, hey, Mr. Body, we're here to help you.

MR. BODY: So, tell me, what should I do?

MR. FOOD: Well, to begin with, you need lots of me. That is, you need lots of good food in order to maintain a healthy lifestyle.

MR. BODY: Why is that?

 From *MORE Science Adventures with Children's Literature: Reading Comprehension and Inquiry-Based Science* by Anthony D. Fredericks. Westport, CT: Teacher Ideas Press. Copyright © 2008.

MR. FOOD: That's simply because good food—eaten regularly—helps you stay healthy.

MR. BODY: Really? Hmmmm, that's pretty interesting. What else does all that food do?

MR. FOOD: Well, to begin with, good food helps you play. It also supplies you with the energy you need to work—you know, like mow the lawn, do the dishes, and clean your room. And it helps you learn. That's because good food helps your brain work the way it should. And good brains mean good learning!

MR. BODY: Wow! That's really cool.

MR. FOOD: But, you have to eat the right kind of me. You might think that it's OK to eat lots of popcorn or lots of candy or lots of flavored drinks, but it's not. Those kinds of foods are not very good for you. If you want to stay healthy, you have to eat the right kinds of food.

MR. BODY: What do you mean by "right kinds of food"?

MR. FOOD: You have to eat dairy products like milk and cheese. You have to eat vegetables like carrots and beans. You have to eat meat, poultry, and fish. You have to eat fruit like apples and peaches. And you have to eat breads and cereals.

MR. BODY: Wow, that's a lot to eat. I just had my lunch so I'm really not very hungry right now.

MR. FOOD: You don't have to eat all that at the same time. You have to eat some of those each day. Eating a balanced diet and eating foods in moderation will help you get healthy and will help you stay healthy. Good food means a good life!

MISS EXERCISE: Hey, don't forget about me.

MR. BODY: Oh, hello there. Say, what can you do for me?

MISS EXERCISE:	Well, to be perfectly honest, you really need lots of me. That is, you need lots of exercise every day.
MR. BODY:	Why is that?
MISS EXERCISE:	Well, to begin with, good exercise helps you stay healthy. When you exercise on a regular basis you help make your muscles strong.
MR. BODY:	Hey, I'm pretty strong already!
MISS EXERCISE:	Yeah, I guess you are. But in order to stay strong and help keep diseases away, you need to exercise every day. Regular exercise keeps your body in tip-top shape, ready to meet any challenges. That's REGULAR EXERCISE, every day!
MR. BODY:	Every day?
MISS EXERCISE:	Yes, every day! You need that exercise to keep your heart healthy. Regular exercise will help keep your lungs healthy, too. In fact, regular exercise helps keep your whole body healthy.
MR. BODY:	OK, sounds pretty good! What else do I need to do?
MISS SLEEP:	You need lots of me.
MR. BODY:	[surprised] Oh, really?!
MISS SLEEP:	Yes, really. You need lots of rest and lots of sleep to stay healthy. Sleep gives your body time to refresh itself after a long day of running, climbing, jumping, and playing. In other words, your body needs some time off to "recharge its batteries." In short, sleep helps your body work better. Sleep also helps your body feel better.
MR. BODY:	Well, all that sounds good. Anything else?

MISS SLEEP: Yes, since you are still growing, you will need about 10 or 11 hours of sleep every day.

MR. BODY: Wow, that's sure a lot of sleep. I'm getting tired just thinking about all that sleep.

MISS SLEEP: You're right, 10 to 11 hours a day is a lot. But you could get sick if you don't sleep enough. Sleep is when your body can repair itself and build up energy for the next day's activities. Also, a good night's sleep helps you think better and learn better, too.

MR. BODY: [pointing to Mr. Water] I guess I need you, too.

MR. WATER: You are so right, my friend.

MR. BODY: OK, why do I need you?

MR. WATER: Well, water helps your body work. Water is necessary for a healthy body. In fact, most of your body is made up of water. Here's some really interesting facts about water in the human body:

- Approximately 66 percent of the human body consists of water.

- Water exists within all our organs.

- Human brains are 75 percent water.

- Human bones are 25 percent water.

- Human blood is 83 percent water.

MR. BODY: WOW!! OK, so I guess water is pretty important for me . . . and for everyone else, too. So, how much do I need?

MR. WATER: You need about 8 glasses of water every day.

MR. BODY: Eight glasses! Are you kidding me? That's a lot of water to drink every day!

MR. WATER: Yes, it is. But it will help you work better, it will help you think better, and it will help you play better. And . . .

MR. BODY: . . . and, it will help me stay healthy.

MR. WATER: Right!

MR. BODY: So, let me see if I have this right. In order to stay healthy I need four friends.

MR. FOOD: That's right! You need me!

MISS EXERCISE: And, you need me!

MISS SLEEP: AND, you need me!

MR. WATER: AND, you need me!

MR. BODY: I think I've got it! To stay healthy, now and throughout my whole life, I need all four of my friends. OK, let's get healthy!

Amazing Animals
(Learning about Animals)

SUMMARY

Students are always amazed at the incredible variety of animal species in the world. They are equally interested in some of the amazing features, characteristics, and habits of the world's animals. Not surprisingly, the study of animals continues to be one of the most exciting areas of discovery for any elementary classroom.

SUGGESTED GRADE LEVELS: 3–6

LESSON OBJECTIVES

Science Standards

• Content Standard C: Life Science

– The characteristics of organisms (K–4)

– Organisms and environments (K–4)

CRITICAL THINKING QUESTIONS

1. What is the most amazing animal you know?

2. Why do kids like animals so much?

3. What are some things animals can do that people cannot?

4. If you could have any animal as a pet, what would you choose?

5. What is your least favorite animal? Why?

PROPS

No props are necessary for this presentation.

PRESENTATION SUGGESTIONS

You may wish to have selected photos of various types of animals posted on the wall behind the characters in this script. Although not necessary, you may wish to display photos of the specific creatures mentioned in the script.

Amazing Animals

STAGING: This script has five speaking parts and no narrator. The characters can stand around in a loose formation as though they are talking things over on the playground.

```
Charlie
   X
            Bruce
              X
                        Taylor
                          X
            Hernando
              X
                        Rocky
                          X
```

CHARLIE: Hey, guess what?

BRUCE: What?

CHARLIE: Did you know that all frogs must close their eyes in order to swallow?

TAYLOR: Are you kidding?

CHARLIE: No. In fact, frogs use their eyeballs to help push food down their throats.

HERNANDO: Wow, that's cool! Here's something else I bet you guys didn't know. Did you know that a flying gecko is able to lick and clean its eyes with its tongue?

CHARLIE: Gee, I couldn't do that!

ROCKY: Here's something amazing that I learned while reading a book. The famous giant squid of the Atlantic Ocean reaches a length of 50 feet and a weight of two tons. Its eyes are the size of basketballs.

From *MORE Science Adventures with Children's Literature: Reading Comprehension and Inquiry-Based Science* by Anthony D. Fredericks. Westport, CT: Teacher Ideas Press. Copyright © 2008.

CHARLIE: That's unbelievable! Simply unbelievable!!

BRUCE: Here's something cool that I learned. A sea snake has only one lung. But with that single lung it can stay underwater for up to three and a half hours. Can you believe that—3½ hours?!

CHARLIE: Wow, that's neat. How about this—ccallops are marine animals with two shells, just like clams. But did you know that these creatures have between 30 and 100 well-developed eyes?

TAYLOR: Yes, he's right. And a scallop can lose all of its eyes and regrow them in two months.

HERNANDO: Hey, learning about animals is pretty cool. What else do we know?

ROCKY: Well, I heard that an ostrich's egg is the largest egg in the whole world. In fact, 5,000 hummingbird eggs (the world's smallest eggs) can fit inside a single ostrich egg!

CHARLIE: That's pretty cool stuff!

BRUCE: Hey, how 'bout this. Did you know that frogs don't drink water—they absorb it through their skin?

TAYLOR: Those frogs are sure some neat creatures!

HERNANDO: Here's one for you. There's a species of starfish called the Linckia starfish, which is able to pull itself in separate directions until it breaks into two parts. Each of the two parts can grow into a new animal.

ROCKY: Oh, boy! That's cool!

CHARLIE: Here's a new one for you. There is a lizard that lives in Central and South America called the basilisk lizard. When it is scared, it is able to run across the surface of a lake without falling in.

BRUCE: Cool!

TAYLOR: How about this one? Did you know that snails can have up to 20,000 little teeth, all on their tongues?

HERNANDO: Just imagine what I could do if I had 20,000 teeth. I could really do some serious damage to all that candy at Halloween!

ROCKY: Yeah, you bet!

CHARLIE: Here's a fact for you. The sloth is an animal that lives deep in the rain forests of Central and South America. It spends almost its entire life upside down. It walks upside down, sleeps upside down, and mates and gives birth to its babies while it hangs upside down.

BRUCE: He's right. And sloths happen to be some of the slowest moving animals in the world. The average "speed" for a sloth is about four feet a minute.

TAYLOR: Yeah, we could probably beat any sloth with both our hands and feet tied together!

HERNANDO: Hey, you know, learning about animals is pretty cool!

ROCKY: You're right. There's lots of really neat information to learn about animals.

CHARLIE: Some of that information we can learn in science books.

BRUCE: Some of that information we can learn at the library.

TAYLOR: And some of that information we can learn in magazines and other stuff.

HERNANDO: Yeah, there's a lot to learn about animals.

ROCKY: You bet there is.

CHARLIE:	So what do you guys say?
BRUCE:	I say, let's get reading!
TAYLOR:	I'm with Bruce!
HERNANDO:	OK., guys, let's read!
ALL:	We can't wait!

Far, Far Away
(Sun, Moon, and Planets)

SUMMARY

This script is a very brief introduction to the sun, moon, and four inner planets. Students' will be stimulated to learn more about these celestial bodies in additional lessons and resources.

SUGGESTED GRADE LEVELS: 2–4

LESSON OBJECTIVES

Science Standards

• Content Standard D: Earth and Space Science

– Objects in the sky (K–4)

CRITICAL THINKING QUESTIONS

1. What do you like about the moon?

2. What is the most unusual object in space?

3. If you could travel anyplace in space, where would you go? Why?

4. Why do you think the sun is so important?

PROPS

No props are necessary for this production other than hand-lettered signs looped around each player's neck.

PRESENTATION SUGGESTIONS

Students should be standing throughout the production. In the beginning, they remain in one place. Toward the end, several of the characters begin moving (revolving) around the "sun."

Far, Far Away

STAGING: The narrator stands in front and to the side of the staging area. Most of the dialogue belongs to the narrator (the other characters have minor speaking roles). Each character should have a hand-lettered sign around her or his neck indicating what celestial body she or he is. The narrator remains stationary; the other characters will move around (as directed in the script).

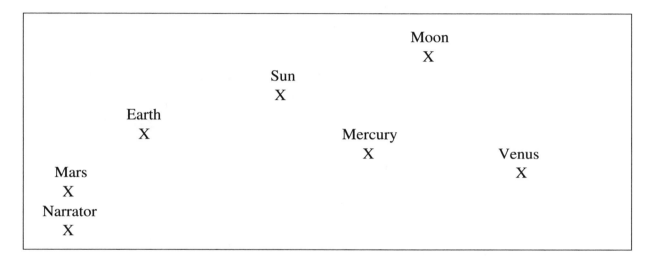

NARRATOR: Welcome to the universe. My friends [points] and I will tell you a little about ourselves. First, I'd like you to meet the sun.

SUN: Hi! [waves]

NARRATOR: The sun is shaped like a giant beach ball. Just like a beach ball, the sun is not solid. It is filled with lots of very hot gases. These gases give off lots of heat. All the heat on Earth is produced by the sun. The surface temperature of the sun is over 11,000 degrees. The sun is also a star. It is the most important star we know. It is the source of all life on Earth. Green plants need sunlight to grow, and animals eat plants for food. And humans need plants and animals to live, too.

SUN: That's right! I'm important to all you guys. [points]

NARRATOR: The weather we have is made by the sun. The sun affects the temperature of the air. It also affects the amount of rainfall we have. It affects the clouds overhead. Everything on Earth needs the sun.

MOON: Hey, what about me? [moves to the front of the staging area]

NARRATOR: Now, here's our friend the moon. The moon is the closest body in space to our planet. Humans have always been interested in the moon. Here's something interesting. The moon doesn't make its own light. The light we see is actually reflected sunlight.

MOON: I'm really very bright. Get it? I'm really very BRIGHT!

NARRATOR: Anyway, the moon orbits or goes around Earth. As it does, its position in the sky changes. The direction of the sun's light on it also changes. This means that part of the moon has light and part of the moon is dark. These are known as the phases of the moon. The phases are different throughout the month.

MERCURY, VENUS, EARTH, MARS: [together] Hey, what about us?

NARRATOR: Besides the sun and the moon, there are planets, too. One of the planets is Mercury, the closest planet to the sun. Venus is the next planet. Next comes our own planet, Earth. Then comes Mars. There are several other planets besides these.

They aren't here today. I think they're all out spinning around somewhere else.

Anyway, all these planets are going around the sun. [The "planets" begin to walk around the "sun" in a clockwise rotation.] Each planet is different, and each one is special.

MERCURY: It takes me only 88 days to go around the sun. The earth takes 365 days.

VENUS: I'm the second planet. I was named for the Roman goddess of love.

EARTH: I'm really old, more than four and a half billion years old. Maybe I need a rocking chair, I'm so old.

MARS: I have the largest volcano in the whole solar system. It's more than 17 miles high!

NARRATOR: Well, as you can see, there are lots of interesting things in the solar system. I hope you have a chance to learn more about all my friends here. It's a lot of fun!

Adapted from Anthony D. Fredericks, *Nonfiction Readers Theatre for Beginning Readers* (Westport, CT: Teacher Ideas Press, 2007).

An Annotated Bibliography of Children's Literature

The number of books available in science is limitless. My own investigations led me to thousands of literature possibilities—many of which could be easily integrated into all aspects of the science curriculum. Obviously, no resource book this size could do justice to the scores of literature selections you can choose for your classroom or library program. I have therefore tried to provide you with a variety of possibilities—with an emphasis on the new and fascinating books available for every aspect of a science curriculum.

This appendix contains two annotated bibliographies. The first is a collection of trade books appropriate for students in grades K–4. These books have been organized according to the *Science Content Standards* described earlier in this book. The second part of this appendix is a similar collection of trade books appropriate for students in grades 5–8 (also organized according to the *Science Content Standards*). Any one book may, of course, encompass more than one standard as well as more than one topic. In other words, the organization of books within the various standards may be arbitrary and certainly arguable. Nevertheless, I hope these selections offer a plethora of potential literature selections for all areas of your science curriculum—no matter what its scope, sequence, or instructional emphasis. Both classroom teachers and school librarians will find much to savor here—and much to explore!

GRADES K–4

Content Standard B: Physical Science

Greenberg, Dan. *Amusement Park Science.* Philadelphia: Chelsea Clubhouse Books, 2003.
Explore the different forces at work in an amusement park.

Hammond, Richard. *Can You Feel the Force?* New York: DK Publishing, 2006.
Each page in this book explodes with color and creativity about physical science of the past, present, and future.

Murphy, Stuart. *Mighty Maddie.* New York: HarperCollins, 2004.
This book portrays a girl cleaning her room and discovering how various objects are different.

Riley, Gail. *Benjamin Franklin and Electricity.* New York: Children's Press, 2004.
This is a biography of Ben Franklin and his exploration of electricity.

Rosinsky, Natalie. *Light.* Minneapolis, MN: Picture Window Books, 2003.
How do Mirrors work? What makes shadows? These are some of the interesting questions that you will explore in this book.

———. *Magnets.* Minneapolis, MN: Picture Window Books, 2003.
Learn how magnets help humans in our everyday lives.

———. *Sound.* Minneapolis, MN: Picture Window Books, 2003.
Experience different tones such as loud, soft, high, low, and echo. These are just a few of the terms covered in this book.

Stille, Darlene. *Electricity.* Minneapolis, MN: Picture Window Books, 2004.
Learn about an amazing force of nature that we can use to benefit humans.

———. *Energy.* Minneapolis, MN: Picture Window Books, 2004
What is energy? Follow a group of friends through various activities that describe what energy is.

Yamamoto, Lani. *Albert.* Chelsea, MI: Sleeping Bear Press, 2004.
The imagination of a small boy runs wild with the wonders of science.

———. *Albert 2.* Chelsea, MI: Sleeping Bear Press, 2005.
After learning valuable information in his first book, this small boy continues to wonder about the oddities of science.

Content Standard C: Life Science:

Arlon, Penelope. *Eye Know.* New York: DK Publishing, 2006.
A creative layout will grab beginner scientists and engulf them in the wonder of nature.

Base, Graeme. *The Waterhole.* New York: Penguin, 2001.
>   In this counting book, readers have an opportunity to see the variety of animals that come together for water.

Behrens, Janice. *Let's Find Rain Forest Animals: Up, Down, Around.* New York: Children's Press/Scholastic, 2007.
>   In a beginning readers book discover some of the different animals in the rainforest.

Blackstone, Stella. *I Dreamt I Was a Dinosaur.* Cambridge: Barefoot Books, 2005.
>   This book delivers basic information about dinosaurs through innovative, hand-sewn illustrations.

Breen, Steve. *Stick.* New York: Penguin, 2007.
>   Follow a frog named Stick through his natural habitat and other strange environments, with the help of a dragonfly.

Browne, Michael. *Give Her the River.* New York: Simon & Schuster, 2004.
>   In this book a father shares his dreams for his daughter while watching her in the river habitat around her.

Cannon, Janell. *Pinduli.* New York: Harcourt, 2004.
>   A young hyena learns about his place in the vast East African lands.

Carryl, Charles. *The Camel's Lament.* New York: Random House, 2004.
>   This story is a poem about a camel's life and habitat in the desert.

Davies, Nicola. *Surprising Sharks.* Cambridge: Candlewick Press, 2003.
>   Visualize sharks of all shapes and sizes and learn how they are some of the most incredible creatures on Earth.

Ehlert, Lois. *Leaf Man.* New York: Harcourt, 2005.
>   Follow different leaves on a trip to various parts of the country, in a unique way.

————. *Pie in the Sky.* New York: Harcourt, 2004.
>   In this story nature changes and grows with each passing season.

————. *Waiting for Wings.* New York: Harcourt, 2001.
>   Dazzling color and pop-off-the-page illustrations show the wonders of butterflies and growing.

Greenberg, David. *Skunks!* New York: Little, Brown, 2001.
>   Imagine the worst smelling animal you can think of! Now learn why skunks are actually a wonder of nature.

Halfmann, Janet. *Life in a Tide Pool.* Minneapolis, MN: Creative Education, 2001.
>   This book is a story of one of the smallest habitats on Earth, the tide pool.

Herkert, Barbra. *Birds in your Backyard.* Nevada City, CA: Dawn Publications, 2001.
   In this book you will peer through binoculars and watch the wonderful birds in your backyard environment.

Jacobs, Francine. *Lonesome George the Giant Tortoise.* New York: Walker, 2003.
   This story is an adventure of one of the oldest creatures on Earth.

Jenkins, Steve. *Actual Size.* Boston: Houghton Mifflin, 2004.
   Twelve inches, seven pounds, and thirty-six inches. How do these measurements relate? Explore real creatures living in today's world and their unusual sizes.

———. *Almost Gone.* New York: HarperCollins, 2006.
   Amazing species of animals are disappearing from Earth! Learn about the coelacanth, moa, and iriomote, among various other endangered/extinct animals.

———. *Prehistoric Actual Size.* Boston: Houghton Mifflin, 2005.
   What is a diplocaulus? It is a meat-eating amphibian! Explore other interesting facts about the unusual creatures of our past.

———. *What Do You Do with a Tail Like This?* Boston: Houghton Mifflin, 2003.
   Animals all have ears, eyes, and mouths. One major difference, the tail, can help us identify them.

Jeunesse, Gallimard. *Flowers.* New York: Scholastic, 2005.
   This book introduces young children to plants and other life around them in nature.

Kudlinski, Kathleen. *Boy, Were We Wrong about Dinosaurs!* New York: Penguin, 2005.
   Oops! Discover the mistakes scientists thought were true about the great dinosaurs of our past.

Lerner, Carol. *Butterflies in the Garden.* New York: HarperCollins, 2002.
   There are many different varieties of butterflies, and even more types of plants in the gardens where they live.

McGinty, Alice. *The Jumping Spider.* New York: Rosen Publishing, 2002.
   This book is a collection of photographs and interesting information about one of nature's essential critters.

McLimans, David. *Gone Wild.* New York: Walker, 2006.
   In this book learn about habitat, range, and threats to valuable endangered animals.

O'Brien, Patrick. *Megatooth.* New York: Henry Holt, 2001.
   Ten million years ago, giants ruled the planet. However, one creature, the megalodon, ruled the oceans.

O'Donnell, Kerri. *Ugly Sea Creatures.* New York: Rosen Publishing, 2007.
   Discover some of the world's ugliest and scariest creatures.

Patent, Dorothy. *Colorful Captivating Coral Reefs.* New York: Walker, 2003.
Explore coral reefs in Hawaii, the Indian Ocean, the Atlantic Ocean, and the Pacific Ocean. Be exposed to exotic fish and their colorful habitats.

Pearson, Tracey. *Bob.* New York: Farrar Straus Giroux, 2002.
Every animal has a sound . . . but what happens when one forgets what to do?

Pfeffer, Wendy. *Wiggling Worms at Work.* New York: HarperCollins, 2004.
Digging though dirt isn't the only thing that earth worms are good at. Explore their fascinating lives and how they help the earth and humans.

Prelutsky, Jack. *Behold the Bold Umbrellaphant and Other Poems.* New York: Greenwillow Books, 2006.
This story is a collection of poems that share the characteristics of many animals in the world.

Pringle, Laurence. *Whales! Strange and Wonderful.* Honesdale, PA: Boyds Mills Press, 2003.
This story provides a vivid description of different whales and their habitats, as well as illustrations of these rare creatures.

Rockwell, Anne. *Becoming Butterflies.* New York: Walker, 2002.
Follow a class through the process of raising a butterfly.

Sidman, Joyce. *Butterfly Eyes.* Boston: Houghton Mifflin, 2006.
A mysterious creature lives in nature, always watching, and floating through the air.

Sill, Cathryn. *About Insects.* Atlanta, GA: Peachtree Publishers, 2000.
This book presents a look at insects from how a child would perceive them.

Content Standard D: Earth and Space Science

Amato, William. *The Space Shuttle.* New York: PowerKids Press, 2002.
Blast off into outer space in an amazing vehicle that allows you to fly through outer space and see all kinds of new things.

Banks, Kate. *The Great Blue House.* New York: Frances Foster Books, 2005.
Delve into an intriguing story of a house and its travels through the seasons.

Blackstone, Stella. *Jump into January.* Cambridge: Barefoot Books, 2004.
This story is an adventure using single words relating to all the seasons.

Dahl, Michael. *On the Launch Pad.* Minneapolis, MN: Picture Window Books, 2004.
In this counting book, a young reader can learn how a spaceship lifts off.

Goodman, Susan. *Ultimate Field Trip 5.* New York: Atheneum Books, 2001.
Blast off into outer space for the ultimate class field trip.

Harrison, David. *Earthquakes.* Honesdale, PA: Boyds Mills Press, 2004.
Earth is always shifting and changing. Travel through time, learning about different global effects of earthquakes.

McNulty, Faith. *If You Decide to Go to the Moon.* New York: Scholastic Press, 2005.
In this story a young boy imagines a trip into space.

Nardo, Don. *Space Travel.* San Diego: Kidhaven Press, 2003.
People of Earth have always been fascinated with space. In this book we explore whether we can we live in space. How can this be possible?

Rau, Dana. *Constellations.* Minneapolis, MN: Compass Point Books, 2005.
Looking up into the sky, explore the things created by our stars.

————. *The International Space Station.* Minneapolis, MN: Compass Point Books, 2005.
Through the use of the International Space Station, this book shows its readers what space is really like and how we can learn so many things from a man-made object.

Sayre, April. *Stars Beneath your Bed.* New York: Greenwillow Books, 2005.
Dust is everywhere. Explore how dust can influence our everyday lives.

Schaefer, Lola. *An Island Grows.* New York: Greenwillow Books, 2006.
What grows deep beneath the ocean? Volcanoes! Watch as one grows.

Simon, Seymour. *Destination Space.* New York: HarperCollins, 2002.
How is it possible to see the things that we do in space? In this book the Hubble telescope opens our eyes to a vast new place.

Solway, Andrew. *Can we Travel to the Stars?* Chicago: Heinemann Library, 2006.
This story ponders the idea of space travel. Are we able to travel to different planets and beyond?

Tanaka, Shelley. *A Day That Changed America: Earthquake!* New York: Hyperion Books, 2004.
This is a story of a defining moment of the American people caused by Earth.

Tomecek, Steve. *Moon.* Washington, DC: National Geographic Society, 2005.
Unexplored no more! Take a ride to a place that most kids dream of discovering.

Whitman, Walt. *When I Heard the Learn'd Astronomer.* New York: Simon & Schuster, 2004.
In this fantastic book, a young boy fantasizes about space and beyond.

Content Standard E: Science and Technology

Boskey, Madeline. *Natural Disasters.* New York: Children's Press, 2003.
Natural Disasters happen all the time. Over the centuries humans have developed ways to predict when these disasters could hit.

Bruce, Linda, Jack Bruce, and John Hilvert. *Space Technology*. Minneapolis, MN: Smart Apple Media, 2006.
> This book describes how technology and space are used together.

Carruthers, Maragret. *The Hubble Space Telescope*. New York: Franklin Watts, 2003.
> Investigate how the Hubble telescope works. Learn about its amazing capabilities and how it has helped advance scientific learning.

Castaldo, Nancy. *Pizza for the Queen*. New York: Holiday House, 2005.
> An inventive look at how baking has become an essential development in human history.

Graham, Ian. *Space Vehicles*. Chicago: Raintree, 2006.
> Explore vehicles in space that are operated by humans through the use of remote controls.

Harrison, Ian. *The Book of Inventions*. Washington, DC: National Geographic Society, 2004.
> This book is the ultimate reference to describe great things created by scientists.

MacLeod, Jilly. *How Nearly Everything Was Invented*. New York: DK Publishing, 2006.
> This book offers terrific time lines and detailed explanations to showcase some great scientific discoveries.

O'Brien, Patrick. *The* Hindenburg. New York: Henry Holt, 2000.
> Discover one of science's greatest inventions and its greatest disasters.

Oxlade, Chris. *Canals*. Chicago: Heinemann Library, 2000, 2006.
> A look at some of humanity's greatest developments in man-made objects.

———. *Dams*. Chicago: Heinemann Library, 2006.
> Dams are one of the largest man-made devices in the world. Explore how they can be helpful and harmful at the same time.

Rossi, Ann. *Bright Ideas*. Washington, DC: National Geographic School Publishing, 2005.
> This book is an overview of various inventions in America from 1870 to 1910.

Schwartz, David. *Millions to Measure*. New York: HarperCollins, 2003.
> Science and the metric system are intertwined. How do we measure? What do we measure? Explore how people have made devices to help us learn.

St. George, Judith. *So You Want to Be an Inventor?* New York: Scholastic, 2002.
> Examine what it takes to be a great science inventor by exploring the path of others.

Content Standard F: Science in Personal and Social Perspectives

Arnold, Tedd. *Even More Parts*. New York: Putnam, 2004.
> The sequel to *More Parts* takes us on an even crazier adventure through the human body.

———. *More Parts*. New York: Putnam, 2001.
> Watch Out! Crazy things can happen to the human body.

Branzei, Sylvia. *Grossology and You*. New York: Penguin, 2002.
> A divine description of all the gross and disgusting things our bodies can do and already have done.

French, Vivian. *Oliver's Milkshake*. New York: Orchard Books, 2001.
> Milk, orange soda, fruit, and other yummy bits are what Oliver likes. However, what happens to Oliver's body when he likes something too much?

Henderson, Kathy. *Look at You! A Baby Body Book*. Cambridge: Candlewick Press, 2006.
> Investigate a perfect book for beginning readers to explore their own bodies.

Lears, Laurie. *Becky the Brave*. Morton Grove, IL: Albert Whitman, 2002.
> Becky has epilepsy. Her younger sister deals with this on a daily basis. She learns why Becky's body is different and how she can be helped.

Miller, Edward. *The Monster Health Book*. New York: Holiday House, 2006.
> What do we need to survive? Food! Explore all the different ways to keep healthy and happy.

Pearson, Susan. *Hooray for Feet*. Maplewood, NJ: Blue Apple Books, 2005.
> Kids use them for everything. Feet come in all sizes, and we can do all sorts of things with them.

Schaefer, Lola. *Body Pairs*. Chicago: Heinemann Library, 2003.
> This story takes a look at the different thing on our bodies that come in pairs.

Schuh, Mari. *Drinking Water*. Minneapolis, MN: Capstone Press, 2006.
> This book has real-life photos and describes why water is vital to the health of growing bodies.

Seuling, Barbra. *From Head to Toe*. New York: Holiday House, 2002.
> Take a journey through the human body from head to toe and all the "stuff" in between.

Simon, Seymour. *Eyes and Ears*. New York: HarperCollins, 2003.
> This book examines how our eyes and ears function and help us.

———. *Guts: Our Digestive System*. New York: HarperCollins, 2005.
> This story is an interesting look at an important part of the human body.

Wheeler, Lisa. *Mammoths on the Move.* New York: Harcourt, 2006.
>During the Ice Age, woolly mammoths ruled the planet. Discover how and why it all came to an end.

Content Standard G: History and Nature of Science

Altman, Linda. *Singing with Momma Lou.* New York: Lee and Low Books, 2002.
>This is a story, from a child's point of view, of having a family member with Alzheimer's and learning how to overcome her fears about the disease.

Brown, Don. *Odd Boy Out: Young Albert Einstein.* Boston: Houghton Mifflin, 2004.
>Ponder the thoughts of one of the greatest mathematicians and physicists who ever existed, from when he was a young boy.

Busby, Peter. *First to Fly.* New York: Crown Publishers, 2002.
>An intriguing look at how the Wright brothers created one of the greatest inventions of our time.

Camp, Carole. *American Women Inventors.* Berkeley Heights, NJ: Enslow, 2004.
>This story takes a look at several women who made tremendous impacts on science.

Gianopoulos, Andrea. *Isaac Newton and the Laws of Motion.* Minneapolis, MN: Capstone Press, 2007.
>Discover the person who developed the idea of universal gravitation.

Goodall, Jane. *The Chimpanzees I Love.* New York: Byron Preiss Book, 2001.
>Discover the challenge of communicating and forming bonds with a species so close to being human.

Lassieur, Allison. *Marie Curie.* New York: Franklin Watts, 2003.
>Learn about the first woman to receive the Nobel Prize for works in science.

Macdonald, Fiona. *Edwin Hubble.* Chicago: Heinemann Library, 2001.
>Explore a life filled with many ups and downs leading up to a great creation.

McNeese, Tim. *The* Challenger *Disaster.* New York: Children's Press, 2003.
>This is a story of sadness and a nation learning from its mistakes and how to improve in the future.

Ray, Deborah. *The Flower Hunter.* New York: Frances Foster Books, 2004.
>A biography of America's first naturalist and his journey to identify new things.

Robbins, Trina. *Elizabeth Blackwell.* Minneapolis, MN: Capstone Press, 2007.
>In this book you will learn about America's first woman doctor.

Steele, Phillip. *Marie Curie: The Woman Who Changed the Course of Science*. Washington, DC: National Geographic, 2006.
> This book takes you along a time line about one extraordinary woman.

Williams, Marcia. *Hooray for Inventors*. Cambridge: Candlewick, 2005.
> Delve into old and new inventions at an easy to read level.

GRADES 5–8

Content Standard B: Physical Science

Bodanis, David. *Electric Universe*. New York: Crown Publishers, 2005.
> An in-depth look at electricity and all things it is used for.

Burnett, Betty. *The Laws of Motion:* Understanding Uniform and Accelerated Motion. New York: Rosen Pub. Group, 2005.
> Addresses Newton's law of motion and describes motion with excellent charts.

Hawking, Stephen. *The Universe in a Nutshell*. New York: Bantam Books, 2001.
> This book explains the secrets we have always wanted to know about our universe.

Hunter, William. *Solving Crimes with Physics*. Philadelphia: Mason Crest Publishers, 2006.
> This is a turn of the century book displaying physics in a new and interesting manner.

Isaacs, April. *Characteristics and Behaviors of Waves*. New York: Rosen Publishing, 2005.
> This book presents an in-depth look at various types of waves that we encounter in life.

McCarthy, Rose. *The Laws of Thermodynamics: Understanding Heat and Energy Transfers*. New York: Rosen Pub. Group, 2005.
> Entertain your brain with the scientific topic of energy transference.

Michels, Dia. and Nathan Levy. *101 Things Everyone Should Know about Science*. Washington, DC: Science Naturally, 2006.
> This book offers a variety of different facts about several different areas of science.

Parker, Barry. *Physics 101*. New York: Hydra Publishers, 2007.
> This book which is for an upper level reader, discusses the 101 most important things to know about physics.

Suplee, Curt. *The New Everyday Science Explained*. Washington, DC: National Geographic Society, 2004.
> This book brings life to the things we use everyday in our lives that relate to science.

Content Standard C: Life Science

Davies, Nicola. *Extreme Animals.* Cambridge: Candlewick Press, 2006
>This book provides an in-depth look at various animals from all over the globe and their habitats.

Dipper, Frances. *Secrets of the Deep Revealed.* New York: DK Publishing, 2003.
>This book examines all the various life-forms, technology, and treasures at the bottom of the ocean.

Fridell, Ron. *Decoding Life.* Minneapolis, MN: Lerner Publications, 2005.
>In this book you will investigate what a genome is and why it is so important.

Llewellyn, Claire. *Great Discoveries and Amazing Adventures.* Boston: Kingfisher, 2004.
>This book is a collection of various human discoveries and adventures throughout time on Earth.

Montgomery, Sy. *Quest for the Tree Kangaroo.* Boston: Houghton Mifflin, 2006.
>Explore the great cloud forest of New Guinea and discover the world around you while searching for a rare tree kangaroo.

Stille, Darlene. *Genetics: A Living Blueprint.* Minneapolis, MN: Compass Point Books, 2006.
>Delve into the meaning of heredity and how it can determine what so many things look like.

Walker, Richard. *Microscopic Life.* Boston: Kingfisher, 2004.
>An in-depth look at what makes our bodies function and what makes the world around us work.

Content Standard D: Earth and Space Science

Barnett, Alex. *Space Revealed.* New York: DK Publishing, 2004.
>Explore all the wonders of space through captivating photography.

Chaikin, Andrew. *Space: A History of Space Exploration in Photographs.* Richmond Hill, ON: Firefly Books, 2004.
>Blast into marvelous pictures taken from various areas in space and see the unique creations people have been able to develop as well as beautiful photos of Earth.

Graham, Ian. *e.guides: Space Travel.* New York: DK Publishing, 2004.
>Walk on the moon through exquisite photographs and picturesque spacescapes. Then delve into the written word about the universe and what makes it all work.

Hannah, Julie, and Joan Holub. *The Man Who Named the Clouds.* Morton Grove, IL: Albert Whitman, 2006.
>Luke Howard loved clouds and the sky. He enjoyed them so much he eventually developed names for many varieties.

Jenkins, Alvin. *Next Stop Neptune*. New York: Houghton Mifflin, 2004.
Imagine floating through space, and then your feet touch down. You've landed in a strange place . . . Neptune!

Jerreris, David. *Future Space: Robot Explorers*. New York: Tangerine Press, 2003.
Explore outer space with the technology of robots.

Lynch, John. *The Weather*. New York: Firefly Books, 2002.
Indulge yourself in the nature of weather, from the harshest storms to dancing clouds.

O'Meara, Donna. *Into the Volcano*. New York: Kids Can Press, 2005.
Bright skies, loud booms, and ground-shattering movements are just a few effects you will learn about in this book.

Paulsen, Gary. *The Time Hackers*. New York: Wendy Lamb Books, 2005.
Two best friends set off on an impossible journey through space and explore various things up close and personal.

Ride, Sally, and Tam O'Shaughnessy. *Exploring Our Solar System*. New York: Crown Publishers, 2003.
This book presents a broad overview of many things in space through wonderful text and excellent pictures.

Skurzynski, Gloria. *Are We Alone?* Washington, DC: National Geographic Society, 2004.
This book showcases space from its individual planets and asks, "Could there be life other than humans?"

Sohn, Emily, and Science News for Kids. *Space and Astronomy*. New York: Infobase Publishing, 2006.
This book examines many different parts of the solar system and beyond.

Content Standard E: Science and Technology

Langley, Andrew. *Da Vinci and His Times*. New York: DK Publishing, 1999, 2006.
This book showcases one of the greatest thinkers and his many advances in the scientific world.

Langone, John. *How Things Work: Everyday Technology Explained*. Washington, DC: National Geographic Society, 1999, 2004.
This is an eclectic book, covering technology from the simple and everyday to those devices that make us wonder, "How does it work?"

Levy, John. *Really Useful: The Origins of Everyday Things*. Richmond Hill, ON: Firefly Books, 2002.
Enjoy inventions categorized by which rooms of your house they go in.

Parramon's Editorial Team. *Essential Atlas of Technology.* New York: Barron's Educational Series, 2006.
> A straightforward look at the progression of humankind through time.

Rodriguez, Louis. *From Elephants to Swimming Pools.* Easton, PA: Canal History and Technology Press, 2006.
> Discover how one of the most used devices today was developed.

Thimmesh, Catherine. *Team Moon: How 400,000 People Landed Apollo 11 on the Moon.* New York: Houghton Mifflin, 2006.
> Discover how technology made it possible to land a spacecraft on the moon.

Thomas, Peggy. *Artificial Intelligence.* Farmington Hills, MI: Lucent Books, 2005.
> Engulf yourself in the abilities of technological design and go through the different steps to see the final product that researches are working with today.

Tomecek, Stephen. *What a Great Idea!* New York: Scholastic, 2003.
> The essential inventions that helped advance humans.

Content Standard F: Science in Personal and Social Perspectives

Batigne, Stephanie, Nathalie Fredette, and Josee Bourbonniere. *Major Systems of the Body.* Milwaukee, WI: World Almanac Library, 2002.
> This book explores all the major systems in the body.

Dash, Joan. *The World at Her Fingertips.* New York: Scholastic, 2001.
> A biography of being physically handicapped in many ways, but still teaching others the things the human body can overcome.

Davidson, Sue, and Ben Morgan. *Human Body Revealed.* New York: DK Publishing, 2002.
> This book examines several different parts of the human body.

Fine, Jil. *Hurricanes.* New York: Children's Press, 2007.
> Jump into the eye of the storm with this book. Take the ride of a lifetime as you explore what makes a hurricane tick.

George, Linda. *Gene Therapy.* San Diego: Blackbirch Press, 2003.
> A look at how gene therapy has come to be practiced today.

Millier, Mara. *Hurricane Katrina Strikes the Gulf Coast: Disaster & Survival.* Berkeley Heights, NJ: Enslow Publishers, 2006.
> See Earth at its most volatile. After reading this book you will understand more about natural hazards and personal struggles resulting from such a massive event.

Payment, Simone. *Nuclear, Biological, and Chemical Disasters: A Practical Survival Guide.* New York: Rosen Publishing, 2006.
> This is a good book to read about what human technologies can do to harm others. It will also prepare you for what to do in case such an event occurs.

Routh, Kristina. *Medicine*. North Mankato, MN: Smart Apple Media, 2006.
Explore how scientists are using all resources to develop new ways to extend human life.

Torres, John. *Hurricane Katrina*. Hockessin, DE: Mitchell Lane Publishers, 2007.
Take a sad walk through devastated resources, populations, and habitats and see all the natural hazards created by a force of nature.

Walker, Richard. *e.guides: Human Body*. New York: DK Publishing, 2005.
Explore the human body through a fantastic visual journey of photographs and detailed descriptions.

Watts, Claire. *Natural Disasters*. New York: DK Publishing, 2006.
Amazing photographs show the devastation to habitats, animals, and humans when a natural disaster strikes.

Wilson, Patrick. *Surviving Natural Disasters*. Broomall, PA: Mason Crest Publishers, 2003.
What do you do what a natural disaster strikes? Panicking is not a good answer! This book will guide you through valuable steps to take if nature ever unleashes its fury near your home.

Content Standard G: History and Nature of Science

Balchin, Jon. *Science: 100 Essential Scientists*. New York: Enchanted Lion Books, 2003.
Introduce yourself to 100 of the greatest scientists.

Fradin, Dennis. *Who Was Ben Franklin?* New York: Grosset & Dunlap, 2002.
Discover a man who had success in many fields but triumphed in the field of science.

Frith, Margaret. *Who Was Thomas Alva Edison?* New York: Grosset & Dunlap, 2005.
Meet the person who changed the way we all get ready for school and work in the morning, the inventor of the lightbulb!

Hakim, Joy. *Aristotle Leads the Way*. Washington, DC: Smithsonian Books, 2004.
Indulge in some of Aristotle's great "almost" discoveries and some of the mind boggling theories of his time.

Lightman, Alan. *The Discoveries: Great Breakthroughs in 20th Century Science*. New York: Pantheon Books, 2005.
This is an advanced read for a typical eighth grader. When broken into sections, this book showcases some of the modern wonders in science development and how they came to be.

McClafferty, Carla. *Something out of Nothing*. New York: Farrar Straus Giroux, 2006.
A biography of Marie Curie and the discovery that made her famous.

Steele, Phillip. *Galileo: The Genius Who Faced the Inquisition.* Washington, DC: National Geographic, 2005.
> Discover one of the world's greatest physicists and astronomers and the obstacles he overcame.

Strickland, Sidney. *The Illustrated Timeline of Science.* New York: Sterling Publishing, 2006.
> Striking photographs represent science over the years.

Whitfield, Peter. *The History of Science.* Danbury, CT: Grolier Educational, 2003.
> Explore everything about science, from its beginnings until the present, from all around the world.

Reading Aloud in Science Class

Stimulating imaginations, enhancing listening skills, and introducing students to a variety of literature can all be facilitated when you read aloud to them, particularly when this sharing activity is made a regular and featured part of every science lesson. Children of all ages enjoy listening to someone read aloud from a new or familiar book. Reading aloud makes language active. It stimulates creativity, develops an appreciation for the wide variety of literature that children can begin reading on their own, assists children in the development of vivid mental pictures, and promotes an easy and natural enjoyment of stories.

As you might suspect, there are many benefits associated with the read-aloud experience —particularly in the area of science instruction, including the following:

- Reading aloud stimulates children's interest in books and literature. Old "classics" as well as new tales broaden students' exposure to a variety of literature.

- Students' reading and science interests are broadened and enlarged when teachers and librarians utilize read-aloud literature from several areas.

- Students are introduced to the patterns of language, including sentence structure and sequence, as well as to the development of story themes.

- Children are provided access to books that may be beyond their independent reading level.

- Reading aloud fosters positive attitudes about science and about books.

- Reading aloud helps develop a community of learners (and scientists) within the classroom or library.

- Reading books from many different sources helps children expand their backgrounds of experience, an important element in comprehension development.

- When teachers and librarians read books to their students, they are serving as positive reading models. Students see the enjoyment and excitement of reading demonstrated by an accomplished reader.

- Reading aloud enhances the development of appreciative, comprehensive, and critical listening skills in a variety of informal contexts.

- Reading aloud stimulates children's imaginations—a necessary element of science exploration.

- Reading aloud provides a host of pleasurable sharing experiences and facilitates teacher–student communication.

- Reading aloud helps promote reading and science as lifelong activities.

Following are some guidelines you should consider to make the read-aloud experience enjoyable and gratifying for both you and your students.

Making a Read-Aloud Successful

1. Take the time to read the book before reading it to your students. This will give you a sense of the story necessary for an effective reading.

2. Select a book you enjoy as well as a book your students will enjoy!

3. Occasionally provide opportunities for students to select the literature to be read.

4. Make reading aloud a daily part of your science program. When possible, include more than one read-aloud session each day. Consider the beginning of the school day, immediately after a recess or gym period, after lunch, or just before students are dismissed at the end of the day.

5. Sit so that you are positioned in front of the children. This allows for appropriate voice projection and permits all youngsters an opportunity to listen. Also, if you wish to show illustrations in the book, everyone will be able to see them.

6. Emphasize that read-aloud time is solely for the purpose of listening to a book being read aloud. It should not be an opportunity to talk, interrupt, or fidget. Establish a set of "read-aloud rules" and adhere to them.

7. Practice reading with expression. Give different voices to each of the characters, highlight dramatic points in the plot through voice inflection, and speed up or slow down the reading depending on the action. Dramatic readings (when appropriate) draw listeners in to the "action" of a book.

8. Be cognizant of the pace of your reading. Provide opportunities for youngsters to create "pictures" in their minds (e.g., mental imagery). It may be necessary to "slow down" your reading to allow children to develop appropriate images.

9. Provide frequent opportunities for youngsters to engage in directed comprehension strategies. It is not necessary to do this for every read-aloud book, but reading aloud can easily and naturally segue into appropriate comprehension opportunities.

10. Begin your read-aloud sessions with short stories and books and gradually progress to longer readings. Be mindful of your students' attention spans and adjust the reading time accordingly.

11. Be sure to expose youngsters to a wide variety of books. Throughout the year, select books from all the genres of children's literature.

Reading aloud can and should be a natural element in your classroom science program. With regular exposure to the best in children's literature, students quickly get a sense that science is much more than a simple collection of dry facts—it is filled with an abundance of intriguing concepts and fascinating perspectives on the world around them. Science read-alouds provide learning opportunities that can magically expand and extend the science curriculum in a hundred different ways. In short, reading aloud brings life to science and science to life!

Teacher Resources

by
Anthony D. Fredericks

The following books are available from Teacher Ideas Press (88 Post Road West, Westport, CT 06881); 1-800-225-5800; http://www.teacherideaspress.com.

African Legends, Myths, and Folktales for Readers Theatre. ISBN 978-1-59158-633-3. (140pp.; $25.00).

> Explore folktales and stories from a wide variety of African countries in this engaging collection of adapted scripts. Students will gain a newfound appreciation of the power of storytelling with this bountiful book.

Frantic Frogs and Other Frankly Fractured Folktales for Readers Theatre. ISBN 1-56308-174-1. (124pp.; $19.50).

> Have you heard "Don't Kiss Sleeping Beauty, She's Got Really Bad Breath" or "The Brussels Sprouts Man (The Gingerbread Man's Unbelievably Strange Cousin)"? This resource (grades 4–8) offers 30 reproducible satirical scripts for rip-roaring dramatics in any classroom or library.

The Integrated Curriculum: Books for Reluctant Readers, Grades 2–5. 2nd ed. ISBN 0-87287-994-1. (220pp.; $22.50).

> This book presents guidelines for motivating and using literature with reluctant readers. It contains more than 40 book units on titles carefully selected to motivate the most reluctant readers.

Investigating Natural Disasters Through Children's Literature: An Integrated Approach. ISBN 1-56308-861-4. (194pp.; $28.00).

Tap into students' inherent awe of storms, volcanic eruptions, hurricanes, earthquakes, tornadoes, floods, avalanches, landslides, and tsunamis to open their minds to the wonders and power of the natural world. .

Involving Parents Through Children's Literature: P–K. ISBN 1-56308-022-2. (86pp.; $15.00).

Involving Parents Through Children's Literature: Grades 1–2. ISBN 1-56308-012-5. (96pp.; $14.50).

Involving Parents Through Children's Literature: Grades 3–4. ISBN 1-56308-013-3. (96pp.; $15.50).

Involving Parents Through Children's Literature: Grades 5–6. ISBN 1-56308-014-1. (108pp.; $16.00)

This series of four books offers engaging activities for adults and children that stimulate comprehension and promote reading enjoyment. Reproducible activity sheets based on high-quality children's books are designed in a convenient format so that children can take them home.

The Librarian's Complete Guide to Involving Parents Through Children's Literature: Grades K–6. ISBN 1-56308-538-0. (138pp.; $24.50).

Activities for 101 children's books are presented in a reproducible format, so librarians can distribute them to students to take home and share with parents.

MORE Frantic Frogs and Other Frankly Fractured Folktales for Readers Theatre. ISBN 978-1-59158-628-9 (166pp.; $25.00).

Remember all the fun you had with the original *Frantic Frogs*? Well, they're back!! Here's another laugh-fest overflowing with scripts that will leave students (and teachers) rolling in the aisles (Don't miss "The Original Hip-Hop (by Busta Frog)").

More Social Studies Through Children's Literature: An Integrated Approach. ISBN 1-56308-761-8. (226pp.; $27.50).

Energize your social studies curriculum with dynamic, hands-on, minds-on projects based on such great children's books as *Amazing Grace*, *Fly Away Home*, and *Lon Po Po*. This book is filled with an array of activities and projects sure to "energize" any social studies curriculum.

Mother Goose Readers Theatre for Beginning Readers. ISBN 978-1-59158-500-8. (168pp.; $25.00).

Designed especially for educators in the primary grades, this resource provides engaging opportunities that capitalize on children's enjoyment of Mother Goose rhymes. There is lots to share and lots to enjoy in the pages of this resource.

Much More Social Studies Through Children's Literature: A Collaborative Approach. ISBN 978-1-59158-445-2. (278pp.; $35.00).

This collection of dynamic, literature-based activities will help any teacher or librarian energize the entire social studies curriculum and implement national (and state) standards. This resource is filled with hundreds of hands-on, minds-on projects.

Nonfiction Readers Theatre for Beginning Readers ISBN 978-1-59158-499-5. (220pp.; $25.00).

This collection of science and social studies nonfiction scripts for beginning readers is sure to "jazz up" any language arts program in grades 1–3. Teachers and librarians will discover a wealth of creative opportunities to enhance fluency, comprehension, and appreciation of nonfiction literature.

Readers Theatre for American History. ISBN 1-56308-860-6. (174pp.; $30.00).

This book offers a participatory approach to American history in which students become active in several historical events. These 24 scripts give students a "you are there" perspective on critical milestones and colorful moments that have shaped the American experience.

Science Adventures with Children's Literature: A Thematic Approach. ISBN 1-56308-417-1. (190pp.; $24.50).

Focusing on the *National Science Education Standards,* this activity-centered resource uses a wide variety of children's literature to integrate science across the elementary curriculum. With a thematic approach, it features the best in science trade books along with stimulating hands-on, minds-on activities in all the sciences.

Science Discoveries on the Net: An Integrated Approach. ISBN 1-56308-823-1. (316pp.; $27.50).

This book is designed to help teachers integrate the Internet into their science programs and enhance the scientific discoveries of students. The 88 units emphasize key concepts—based on national and state standards—throughout the science curriculum.

Silly Salamanders and Other Slightly Stupid Stuff for Readers Theatre. ISBN 1-56308-825-8. (162pp.; $23.50).

The third entry in the "wild and wacky" readers theatre trilogy is just as crazy and weird as the first two. This unbelievable resource offers students in grades 3–6 dozens of silly send-ups of well-known fairy tales, legends, and original stories.

Social Studies Discoveries on the Net: An Integrated Approach. ISBN 1-56308-824-X. (276pp.; $26.00).

This book is designed to help teachers integrate the Internet into their social studies programs and enhance the classroom discoveries of students. The 75 units emphasize key concepts—based on national and state standards—throughout the social studies curriculum.

Social Studies Through Children's Literature: An Integrated Approach. ISBN 1-87287-970-4. (192pp.; $24.00).

Each of the 32 instructional units contained in this resource utilizes an activity-centered approach to elementary social studies, featuring children's picture books such as *Ox-Cart Man, In Coal Country,* and *Jambo Means Hello.*

Songs and Rhymes Readers Theatre for Beginning Readers. ISBN 978-1-59158-627-2. (178pp.; $25.00).

Bring music, song, and dance into your classroom language arts curriculum with this delightful collection of popular rhymes and ditties. Beginning readers will enjoy learning about familiar characters through this engaging collection of scripts.

Tadpole Tales and Other Totally Terrific Titles for Readers Theatre. ISBN 1-56308-547-X. (116pp.; $18.50).

A follow-up volume to the best-selling *Frantic Frogs and Other Frankly Fractured Folktales for Readers Theatre,* this book provides primary level readers (grades 1–4) with a humorous assortment of wacky tales based on well-known Mother Goose rhymes. More than 30 scripts and dozens of extensions will keep students rolling in the aisles.

Index

About the Author

Anthony (Tony) D. Fredericks (afredericks60@comcast.net) is a nationally recognized children's literature expert, well known for his energetic, humorous, and highly informative author visits throughout North America. His dynamic presentations have captivated thousands of students, teachers, and librarians in Canada, Mexico, and across the United States—all with rave reviews!

Tony is a former elementary teacher and reading specialist. He is the author of more than 100 books, including over 65 teacher resource books and more than three dozen award-winning children's books. His education titles include the best-selling *Frantic Frogs and Other Frankly Fractured Folktales for Readers Theatre* (Teacher Ideas Press), the hugely popular *Much More Social Studies Through Children's Literature* (Teacher Ideas Press), the highly praised *Guided Reading in Grades 3–6* (Harcourt Achieve), and the celebrated *African Folktales, Myths and Legends for Readers Theatre* (Teacher Ideas Press).

His award-winning children's titles include *Under One Rock: Bugs, Slugs and Other Ughs* (2002 Teacher's Choice Award), *Slugs* (2000 Outstanding Science Trade Book), *Around One Cactus: Owls, Bats and Leaping Rats* (2004 Teacher's Choice Award), *Near One Cattail: Turtles, Logs and Leaping Frogs* (2006 Green Earth Book Award), and *The Tsunami Quilt: Grandfather's Story*, among others.

Tony currently teaches elementary methods courses in science, social studies, language arts, reading, and children's literature at York College in York, Pennsylvania.